Were the Jews a Mediterranean Society?

Were the Jews a Mediterranean Society?

Reciprocity and Solidarity in Ancient Judaism

SETH SCHWARTZ

PRINCETON UNIVERSITY PRESS

Princeton and Oxford

Published by Princeton University Press, 41 William Street, Princeton, New Jersey 08540

In the United Kingdom: Princeton University Press, 6 Oxford Street, Woodstock, Oxfordshire OX20 1TW

Library of Congress Cataloging-in-Publication Data

Schwartz, Seth.
Were the Jews a Mediterranean society? : reciprocity and solidarity in ancient Judaism / Seth Schwartz.
    p. cm.
Includes bibliographical reference and index.
ISBN 978-0-691-14054-4 (hardcover)
1. Jews—Social life and customs—To 70 A.D. 2. Jews—Identity—History—To 1500.
3. Jews—History—168 B.C.–135 A.D. 4. Judaism—History—Post-exilic period, 586 B.C.–210
A.D. 5. Reciprocity (Psychology)—Religious aspects—Judaism. 6. Social interaction
—Palestine—History—To 1500. 7. Jews—Palestine—Politics and government. 8. Mediterranean
Region—Intellectual life. 9. Bible. O.T. Apocrypha. Ecclesiasticus—Criticism, interpretation,
etc. 10. Talmud Yerushalmi—Criticism, interpretation, etc. I. Title.
DS112.S425 2010
933—dc22

                                                                              2008053720

British Library Cataloging-in-Publication Data is available

This book has been composed in Minion.
Printed on acid-free paper. ∞
press.princeton.edu
Printed in the United States of America
10 9 8 7 6 5 4 3 2 1

To the memory of Keith Hopkins, 1934–2004

CONTENTS

ACKNOWLEDGMENTS

I am grateful to Simon Goldhill, Amy Kalmanofsky, Renate Schlesier, and Dina Stein, who read and helpfully commented on drafts of this book. Beth Berkowitz read early versions of chapters 1, 2, and 5 with unsettling critical acuity, Richard Kalmin helped me turn chapter 5 into something resembling competent Talmudic scholarship, and Martin Goodman—yet again serving as the press's anonymous reader no. 1—made many important suggestions about the entire manuscript, which this time I had the good sense to take seriously. They bear no responsibility for the defects of the resulting book.

I am also grateful to Hannah Cotton and Jonathan Price for including me in the Roman epigraphy project at the Institute for Advanced Studies of the Hebrew University of Jerusalem (2002–3), where I wrote very early versions of chapters 3 and 4 in a delightful institutional environment in a city then enduring an exceptionally difficult time. In 2006–7 I had the further good luck of being a member of the School of Historical Studies at the Institute for Advanced Study, Princeton, where I wrote chapters 1, 2, and 5. I am grateful, too, to the National Endowment for the Humanities, which provided me with a fellowship that enabled me to take unpaid leave for the full academic year of 2006–7. In the fall of 2007 I was a fellow of the Center for Advanced Judaic Studies at the University of Pennsylvania, to whose director, David Ruderman, I am grateful as well, as also to Arnie Eisen, chancellor of the Jewish Theological Seminary, for allowing me to bend the rules (in other words, blatantly violate them) by taking part of a second consecutive year off.

It would be fair to say that my dearest Judy Margolin was mildly surprised by the neurotic energy unleashed by the process of writing an academic book, at least for me, but she did much more than take it in stride: she reacted with immense and totally undeserved kindness, solicitude, affection, and even pride (which I hope will survive the reviews). How can I ever reciprocate?

Finally, my beloved friend Keith Hopkins *z'l* died before any part of this book was in good enough shape for me to send it to him for a reading, but I had a palpable sense of his presence every minute I spent writing it. Keith once told me that he never got over Sir Moses Finley's death in 1986, because he felt he had lost his reader. Now I understand what he meant. But Keith was not only my reader, he was the most intellectually exciting and personally vivid man I have ever met. William Harris was right when he said that Keith made everyone he spoke to feel smarter and more interesting than they actually were. I should have dedicated my last book to him because it was only due to his personal influence that I had the confidence to attempt so large a project, apart from his intellectual influence on its substance, but I was too abashed to offer him what I regarded as an unworthy gift. Now, unfortunately, instead of a gift I offer this book as a memorial to Keith, who, to paraphrase Rabban Shimon ben Gamliel, needs none.

Were the Jews a Mediterranean Society?

CHAPTER ONE

Reciprocity and Solidarity

Can a Social History of the Ancient Jews Be Written?

How should we picture an average Jewish man in antiquity?[1] What sort of person was he? How did he express feelings of love, affection, anger, jealousy, pity, and fear? What was his life like? To whom did he feel connected, why, and how? How did he stand when he talked to you, and what language or languages could he talk to you in? Could he read, and if he could, did he bother? Was he free in using his fists, or was he proud of his restraint? Given that he was in all likelihood a small farmer, perhaps on land owned by someone else, did he regard the landlord—or his wealthy neighbor—with fear, react to him with deference, with cheerful bonhomie or chutzpah, with veiled hatred and resentment? Should we imagine him—to set out two extreme stereotypes, neither meant to be taken absolutely literally—as the kind of southern Italian or Greek villager that modern ethnographers, among others, have acquainted us with, shrewd, irascible, zealous for his honor, concerned about his family above all, hostile to or suspicious of authority, prone to think the worst of outsiders and to act on such thoughts—in sum, as a "typical Mediterranean"?[2] Or should

---

[1] I say "man" intentionally, not to foreshadow any neglect of issues of gender in the book that follows but to make the questions posed in this introductory chapter even remotely answerable. Let me add here a note on terminology and coverage: my focus is on Palestine but does not exclude the major diasporic communities in the Roman Empire (Parthian and Sasanian Mesopotamia are excluded); my chronological range is 200 BCE to some time in late antiquity (a term I use in its ancient historical sense to mean roughly 284–700 CE, and not in its history of religions sense, according to which it begins in the Iron Age). The country roughly corresponding to the contemporary state of Israel, plus the West Bank, Gaza Strip and Golan Heights, plus the strip of land on the east bank of the River Jordan called in antiquity Peraea I refer to as Palestine. Judaea designates the district of Jerusalem, whose northern border was approximately the modern city of Ramallah and whose southern border was near Beth Zur, just southwest of Bethlehem. To the north lies Samaria and to the south, Idumaea. When I wish to write of the Roman province of Judaea (which existed from 70 to 135 CE and was subsequently renamed Syria Palaestina), I will call it Provincia Judaea.

[2] The scare quotes are meant seriously here. For a critique of the idea of Mediterranean culture, see the next chapter.

1

we think of him as a sort of religious kibbutznik, or someone like Tevye the dairyman in Sholem Aleikhem's stories, something of a *naïf*, pious and mild, engaged in contemplation of God's laws, hardworking and scrupulously respectful of others, obedient to authority, provided it minimized its interference in his religious life, having a powerful sense of responsibility to other Jews, but as a result of these things ready to give his life—and to take those of others—if his carefully ordered world was threatened?

We might, of course, look to the Hebrew Bible to answer these questions. The Pentateuch seems to provide rules for just about every facet of life, and if one makes the assumption—an assumption that is probably roughly correct for many periods—that by the later Second Temple period (starting, say, around 150 BCE), most Jews tried to lead their lives according to these rules, then it is easy to conclude that we can after all produce a kind of ethnography of the ancient Jews, or at any rate of the pious majority of them. Indeed, the New Testament scholar and ancient Judaist Ed Sanders did something of the sort in his great phenomenology of what he called "common Judaism."[3] Impressive as this account indubitably is, Sanders did not in fact set out to write an ethnography of the Jews in first-century Palestine. It would be best to take the title of the book seriously; it concerns Judaism, a religious system.

I do not know if Sanders assumed that an account of Judaism as practiced is tantamount to an account of the culture or sociology of the Jews, but I would argue that any such assumption is perforce incorrect. A conventional social history or ethnography would begin logically not with an investigation of the ideological center and its mediators (the Torah, the temple, and the priesthood) or with the political leadership (the Roman state, Herod and his descendants, the provincial governors). It would begin with dirt, with what and how much was grown on the land, and by whom; what land tenure arrangements looked like, and as a corollary, how families, village communities, and networks of social dependency operated, if such things existed, and if they did not, what sorts of institutions or practices (warfare, brigandage, or commerce, for example) performed comparable redistributive functions. In other words, the social historian or ethnographer would wonder how or whether people protected themselves from the consequences of drought, crop failure, disease, invasion, or other disasters, or how they coped with the simple fact that they could not always grow enough to sustain themselves. At this point

---

[3] *Judaism, Practice and Belief: 63 BCE–66 CE* (Philadelphia: Trinity Press International, 1992).

social history and ethnography might part company, with social historians tracing redistributive systems and institutions farther up the political
ladder and ethnographers pausing to consider what sort of culture went
along with the rural socioeconomic regime just investigated. In either
case, though, the result would be very different from the center-out
method used by Sanders and other students of Jewish religious institutions, however rich their accounts may be.

Easier said than done, though: the Torah makes many assumptions
and gives some laws about land tenure and family relations but provides
no truly systematic prescription, and even if it did, laws are sometimes
made to be evaded. No one has ever seriously suggested that the most far-
reaching piece of Pentateuchal legislation about land—that all fields must
be returned to their original owners every fifty years (Lev 25.8–12)—was
ever, or could ever have been, put into practice. There is other evidence
about such issues—late biblical, postbiblical, and rabbinic literature, occasionally helpful or suggestive archaeological remains, and a precious
handful of documentary papyri about the business deals and legal activities of a Jewish family resident in the Roman province of Arabia (south
and east of the Dead Sea) in the decades before the Bar Kokhba revolt.
But with the exception of these documents and the richly detailed if not
impeccably reliable writings of Josephus in the later first century CE, this
literature provides little more than hints.[4]

Our core problem is that ancient Jewish literature was preserved almost entirely by later religious communities little interested in the sorts
of questions that concern modern historians or social scientists. Indeed,
the surviving texts were preserved because of their single-minded con-
centration on religious issues. They are almost all products of what the
anthropologist Robert Redfield famously called the "great tradition"—the
rationalized and systematized high culture of emerging urban civilizations—and had little concern, and less sympathy, for any rural and supposedly unself-conscious "little tradition" (notwithstanding Sanders's truly
heroic and by no means entirely futile efforts to recover it)[5] still less did

---

[4] No polemics except to point out that even the more restrained attempts at writing the social and economic history of Persian, Hellenistic, and later Roman Palestine have relied heavily
on unacceptable generalization from scraps of evidence, often based on simplistic application of
deterministic economic or sociological models. In the case of the latest period just listed an exception is the sophisticated, cautious, and self-conscious (and therefore to some extent aporetic)
work of Hayim Lapin (especially *Economy, Geography, and Provincial History in Later Roman
Palestine* [Tübingen: Mohr Siebeck, 2001]). The period from Herod to the destruction of the
Second Temple in 70 CE has to be considered separately, for reasons to be specified.

[5] See M. P. Redfield, ed., *Human Nature and the Study of Society: The Papers of Robert Redfield*, 2 vols. (Chicago: University of Chicago Press, 1962), 1.342–50. Redfield himself adduced

they provide perspicuous and realistic descriptions of the agrarian life—
again, not surprising, given their urban orientation—or for that matter of
the urban life, or of the social and political institutions that made rural
and urban life possible. By contrast, classical literature was preserved by
people interested in literary or rhetorical style, or sometimes practical
knowledge (such as medicine and architecture), or by people who even in
the Middle Ages found at least elements of ancient intellectual traditions
compelling. There was thus reason to preserve not only the writings of
such decidedly secular historians as Thucydides and Tacitus but also the
richly informative orations of Demosthenes and Isocrates, great corpora
of the personal letters of Cicero, the younger Pliny, and Libanius, color-
fully evocative novels, such as *Daphnis and Chloe* or the *Golden Ass*, and
so on, and this apart from the rich documentary evidence surviving from
Hellenistic and Roman Egypt and the several hundred thousands of inscriptions from all over the Roman Empire (though Roman Palestinian
epigraphy is unusually poor). And despite all this, much remains unrecoverable about the lives of the inhabitants of the Hellenistic world or the
Roman Empire, especially the poorer ones.

To generalize broadly but not, I think, too irresponsibly, the extant
parts of ancient Jewish literary tradition conceal the social and cultural
conditions that produced them behind a shimmering (to offer a brief
homage to Peter Brown) veil of biblicism, archaism, classicism. While this
in itself is a highly significant cultural fact about the ancient Jewish "clerisy" that wrote the books, it is hard to avoid the feeling that it does not tell
us all we need to know even about that clerisy, let alone anyone else.[6] It

---

the Torah as a characteristic product of the "great tradition." Of course, the point of any functioning great tradition is that it has interpreters whose job it is to mediate it for the practitioners
of the "little tradition" (for the Torah's functioning in this way, see S. Schwartz, *Imperialism and
Jewish Society, 200 BCE to 640 CE* [Princeton, NJ: Princeton University Press, 2001; hereafter
IJS], 49–99); indeed, the relationship between Redfield's great and little traditions is bound to be
reciprocal. Arguably, tension between great and little traditions is thematized more explicitly in
rabbinic literature than in Jewish literature written before the destruction.

The exceptional books here, those that may tell us a bit more about the little traditions, may be
some of the highly problematic (because their text history is so complicated and poorly under-
stood) magical texts of perhaps late antique origin, such as Sefer Harazim, Harba De-Moshe,
Sefer Yetzirah, and the Hekhalot texts. For surveys, see P. Schäfer, *The Hidden and Manifest God:
Themes in Early Jewish Mysticism* (Albany, NY: SUNY Press, 1992); M. Swartz, *Scholastic Magic:
Ritual and Revelation in Early Jewish Mysticism* (Princeton, NJ: Princeton University Press, 1996);
Y. Harari, *Harba De-Moshe: Mahadurah Hadashah U-Mehqar* (Jerusalem: Akademon, 1997).

[6] I borrow the term "clerisy," the literate elite and subelite components of the "agroliterate"
society, the formulators and mediators of the great tradition, from E. Gellner, *Nations and Nationalism* (Ithaca, NY: Cornell University Press, 1983), 8–18; according to the *OED* the term was
introduced as early as 1818 by S. T. Coleridge to refer more narrowly to a nonreligious intellectual
elite.

would be wonderful if we could lift the veil to get a better look at how ancient Jewish society and culture really worked, outside the center, and outside the minds of the priestly and scribal authors. But the fact that, we cannot does not mean we are completely helpless.

In the chapters that follow I explore, through the close reading of three textual corpora, two closely related questions that have both social historical and social anthropological aspects. To what extent were Jews, in their social relations, discourse, imagination, and even cultural practice, "normal" inhabitants of the ancient Mediterranean world? Why was the Jews' integration in the Roman Empire so much more difficult than that of other provincial populations, and in what ways did it eventually succeed? In this chapter I begin by outlining what I think may have been entailed in "normal" behavior and attitudes. I first discuss institutionalized reciprocity—as exemplified in exchange-based relationships such as friendship, vassalage and clientele—and explain why I think it was an important issue for the ancient Jews, why they had problems with it, and how they coped with those problems. Reciprocity was not the only aspect of the ambient social world the Jews had to confront. They lived in the quite specific environment of the Mediterranean basin. Just how specific this environment was, however, and whether it is really productive to think of the Mediterranean as a single cultural zone is the subject of an enduring debate among historians and anthropologists. We can scarcely afford to ignore this debate, given the Torah's item-by-item rejection of what appears to be ethnographic mediterraneanism, which is conceptually related to its rejection of reciprocity. Therefore, chapter 2 begins with the question of Mediterranean culture. I argue that the concept retains some heuristic utility if we think of it as a Weberian "ideal type," not as an actual cultural system widespread transhistorically in the Mediterranean basin and only there. Finally, the Jews lived in the still more specific environment of the Roman Empire, a state commonly thought to have relied for its effective functioning on the mobilization of local networks of social dependency (more reciprocity, then), and of crucial mediterraneanist praxes such as honor. Roman-Jewish relations remain a matter of great interest to historians of either group, and within the constraints of my basic concern in this book, in the second part of chapter 2 I address briefly but systematically the question of the Jews' integration, initially abortive, into the Roman Empire.

In doing all this I am trying not only to recover lost or concealed components of the Jews' social relations and cultural practices but also to change the way we think about relations between the Jews and their neighbors and rulers. In my view it is no longer adequate to draw up inventories

of cultural items the Jews are likely to have borrowed from their neighbors and use these to argue about the extent of the Jews' hellenization or
acculturation or assimilation. In its most extreme form, this method utterly deprives the Jews of agency: they were acted on by outside influences,
playing no role in the formation of their own culture. But even more sophisticated versions of the cultural inventory approach often overlook the
fact that the processes of hellenization or assimilation did not occur in a
social or political vacuum. It follows that the individual items in the inventory had very varied cultural and political valences: imported table-
ware meant something different from images on coins or statues or books
or political institutions, and these meanings were not stable over time. To
make matters worse, many scholars slip all too easily from cultural inventory to politically charged historical judgment: to put it in an extreme
way, one can draw up a list of Greek phrases and loanwords in the Talmud, conclude that the rabbis—a fortiori the Jews in general—were helle-
nized, and move easily from there to a celebration of post-Bar Kokhba
Roman-Jewish coexistence. It is characteristic of post-Second World War
American Jewish scholarship that the political-historical aspects of this
account were rarely explored or spelled out, but they were obvious enough.
Indeed, this particular type of argument was probably more common a
generation ago than it is today, and there is now no shortage of highly sophisticated analyses of cultural borrowings produced by theoretically
aware and politically conscious updaters of Saul Lieberman.[7] Nevertheless,

---

[7] For Joshua Levinson's work, among others', see chapter 5; for an earlier period, see the
flawed but still suggestive work of S. Weitzman, *Surviving Sacrilege: Cultural Persistence in Jewish
Antiquity* (Cambridge, MA: Harvard University Press, 2005).

  Beyond the two seminal volumes written by Saul Lieberman, *Greek in Jewish Palestine*
(New York: JTS, 1942) and *Hellenism in Jewish Palestine* (New York: JTS, 1950), some important
examples of the older scholarship were collected in H. A. Fischel, ed., *Essays in Greco-Roman
and Related Talmudic Literature* (New York: Ktav, 1977; with bibliography, pp. xxxi–lxxii).
Fischel himself was an ardent advocate of the inventory (xxvii–xxviii) but paid little attention
to the political or social implications of the results. Lieberman himself, whose immense learning and prestige helped legitimize the search for "Hellenistic" content especially in rabbinic literature, did not sentimentalize Roman-Jewish relations. Among the many factors in addition to
Lieberman's prestige that contributed to the receptivity of mid to late-twentieth-century American Jewish scholars to this project we may also mention Salo Baron's rejection of the "lachry-
mose" view of Jewish history, especially of the medieval and early modern periods. Since lach-
rymose history tended to focus on the Jews' allegedly disastrous relations with the state—in
other words, with politics—the rejection of lachrymosity sometimes entailed the embrace of a
somewhat depoliticized social and cultural history. This tendency is evident even in David Biale's introduction to *The Cultures of the Jews: A New History* (New York: Schocken, 2002), where
one might have expected the mildly postmodern orientation (not to mention Biale's own well-
known interests—see *Power and Powerlessness in Jewish History* [New York: Schocken, 1986])
to have encouraged a renewed interest in politics. See S. Schwartz, "Historiography on the Jews

the inventory lives on, especially among empiricist historians. Certainly it is a method shared by scholars as different as Louis Feldman (*Jew and Gentile in the Ancient World*) and Martin Goodman (*Rome and Jerusalem: The Clash of Ancient Civilizations*).

Shifting the focus from "assimilation" or hellenization to integration allows what in my view is a correct emphasis on power, politics, and social relations, and those hitherto largely overlooked aspects of the culture of the Jews that bear most directly on them. Though some of my argument is pitched at what many historians will undoubtedly regard as an uncomfortably high level of abstraction, I am aiming at the production of a precise and specific account of what I think were politically and socially the most important elements of ancient Jewish culture. I am suggesting that the deep probe is better suited to the construction of such an account than the flattening list.

Reciprocity

In a seminal sociological discussion, Alvin Gouldner declared that reciprocity as a moral norm ("one good turn deserves another") is, like the incest taboo, likely to be universal.[8] Such statements are of course very difficult to evaluate, but it must be said that in its most elementary forms, reciprocity is probably very widespread. There is certainly no reason to think that the Israelites or after them the Jews especially resisted reciprocity in this sense, and one of the central theological tendencies of the Hebrew Bible, the so-called deuteronomic theology, is based on the conceptualization of the relations between God and Israel in reciprocal terms: God benefits Israel when Israel treats him properly. And yet it is remarkably difficult to find any positive valuation of human-human reciprocity in biblical texts, except sporadically in wisdom literature. What the Torah offers instead are generalized exhortations to fairness, just treatment of one's fellows, and so on. Perhaps the closest we can get to reciprocity-based rules are injunctions like that not to loathe the Egyptian, "for strangers [more correctly: resident aliens] were ye in his land" (Dt 23.8), in whose

in the Talmudic Period," in *The Oxford Handbook of Jewish Studies*, ed. M. Goodman (Oxford: Oxford University Press, 2002), 79–114.

[8] A. Gouldner, "The Norm of Reciprocity: A Preliminary Statement," *American Sociological Review* 25 (1960): 161–78. On the question of the universality of the incest taboo, see K. Hopkins, "Brother-Sister Marriage in Roman Egypt," *CSSH* 22 (1980): 303–54, especially 304–12 (but see now S. Huebner, "Brother-Sister Marriage in Roman Egypt: A Curiosity of Humankind or a Widespread Family Strategy?" *JRS* 97 [2007]: 21–49).

conceptual background are rules about the mutual obligations that bind guests and hosts.[9] In fact, it is largely on this metaphorical or subterranean level that we can detect important traces and more of reciprocity in biblical literature. Strikingly, when Jesus, in the Sermon on the Mount, declares his rejection of reciprocity as an ethical norm and commands his followers to love their enemies as well as their friends, he achieves the necessary adversative effect ("You have heard it said that. . . . But verily I say to you. . . .") by misquoting a Pentateuchal verse that itself already constituted a rejection of reciprocity (Lev 19.18: "Thou shalt love thy neighbor as thyself").

I would like to introduce a distinction between reciprocity in Gouldner's sense, as an ethical norm that requires that we return favors or at least refrain from harming those who have helped us, and what I am calling institutionalized reciprocity. In the latter, mutual exchange is thought to create and sustain enduring relationships of dependency, whether between individuals or between groups. The relationships in question may be legal institutions, such as ancient Near Eastern vassalage or debt bondage, or they may constitute social institutions, more or less governed by widely understood norms but not regulated by laws; an example is Roman patronage. Institutionalized reciprocity may be a powerful shaper of social relations.

Though ethical reciprocity is fundamental to institutionalized reciprocity, the opposite is not the case. We, for example, may happily teach our children to express gratitude for acts of kindness while regarding some institutional versions of this impulse, for example political patronage, as corrupt. This book concerns reciprocity in this latter sense. The modern study of institutionalized reciprocity begins with Marcel Mauss's and Bronislaw Malinowski's seminal ethnographic and theoretical reflections on gift exchange and has ever since been a major topic of social theoretical and anthropological investigation.[10] Like many such concepts it

---

[9] The law prohibiting association with Ammonites and Moabites because of their ancestors' mistreatment of the Israelites may in this case serve as an example of "negative reciprocity" in Gouldner's, not Sahlins's, sense of the term. (See M. Sahlins, *Stone Age Economics* [New York: Aldine, 1972, 195-96]. In Sahlins's conception, which has not been widely accepted, "negative reciprocity" means "trying to get something for nothing.") Given that the Egyptians had enslaved and oppressed the Israelites, according to the biblical narrative, the law's goodwill is rather mysterious.

[10] M. Mauss, "Essai sur le don: Forme et raison de l'échange dans les sociétés archaïques," *L'Année sociologique*, new series, 1 (1925) (*The Gift: The Form and Reason for Exchange in Archaic Societies*, trans. W. D. Halls [New York-London: Norton, 1990]; B. Malinowski, *Argonauts of the Western Pacific* (London: Routledge, 1922). The subsequent history of the question has been frequently surveyed, in, for example, J. Davis, *Exchange* (Minneapolis: University of Minnesota Press, 1992), 9–27; M. Bloch and J. Parry, Introduction, in *Money and the Morality of Exchange*, ed. M. Bloch and J. Parry (Cambridge: Cambridge University Press, 1989), 1–32; and H. van Wees,

has come to seem rather unwieldy, and some preliminary pruning is necessary to restore its utility as an analytical tool.[11]

Exchange of some sort, not necessarily material, is a feature of all human relationships by definition. What is distinctive about the sorts of relationships I am concerned with here—formal friendship, patronage, vassalage, euergetism (in a Roman context, private donation for public benefit reciprocated by honor and loyalty)—is that the exchange involved is ongoing; in theoretical terms this requires that each individual set of reciprocal exchanges be unequal and delayed, because an immediate and perfectly equal return is in danger of bringing the relationship to a close[12]; the inegalitarian potential inherent in all gift exchange, or its competitive quality (which amounts to roughly the same thing), is important for my purposes; I return to it below. In any case, a benefactor who ceases to support his city is no longer its benefactor; a patron might still regard someone he fails to help as his client, but it is obvious that such a relationship will be highly unstable, and the client may feel he has good reason to bolt.[13]

This proviso raises more questions than might be apparent at first glance. How often must exchange occur in order to sustain the relationship, without imposing an excessive burden on one or both parties? What is the status of the initial gift, which is by definition free, in that it is not given in response to anything? Does it create the inevitable obligation to reciprocate (as Mauss, not to mention Cicero [De Officiis 1.48], argued), or is it rather the first act of response that constitutes the crucial step toward the establishment of the relationship, not the first donation? The very questions suggest that where such exchange-based relationships exist as culturally validated social institutions, they are bound by norms: the successful patron knows how much to give to and demand of his client, even if, as the French social theorist Pierre Bourdieu insisted, such norms are constituted by, constantly refracted and renegotiated through, and

"The Law of Gratitude: Reciprocity in Anthropological Theory." in *Reciprocity in Ancient Greece*, ed. C. Gill, N. Postlethwaite, and R. Seaford (Oxford: Oxford University Press, 1998), 13–49.

[11] For a critique of reciprocity's analytic utility, see Davis, *Exchange*, 22–27.

[12] This was noted already by Seneca, *De Beneficiis* 6.35.3. "Balanced reciprocity," or reciprocity in which equality of exchange is required, is ethnographically attested, but for very limited and specific purposes. It tends not to establish the types of relationships with which I am concerned. Ethnographers often classify it as trade. See Sahlins, *Stone Age Economics*, 194–95; on the inegalitarian character of most reciprocity, see 206–10.

[13] Though there is ethnographic evidence that patrons and clients might retain the ceremonial aspects of the relationship even in the absence of meaningful exchange; see S. Silverman, "Patronage as Myth," in *Patrons and Clients in Mediterranean Societies*, ed. E. Gellner and J. Waterbury (London: Duckworth, 1977), 7–19. This warns us that such relationships, once institutionalized, might take on a life of their own, only loosely anchored in the material conditions that generated and were supposed to sustain them.

sometimes evaded or simply ignored in, actual practice.[14] In other words, Bourdieu's skepticism about observers' attempts to extract rules from practice—or indeed about actors' claims that there exist rules they always follow—should not be confused with the vulgar claim that "everyone was making it up as they went along." In a Bourdieuian scheme, structures may constantly crystallize and decay, or indeed may exist only infinitesimally, in the act, or in the purely notional moment of stasis between crystallization and decadence (and so not really be structures at all), but social life may still be shaped by the constant and productive tension between ostensible norms, objective material constraints, and practice.[15]

Institutionalized Reciprocity in Antiquity: Three Arguments

Such relationships, I argue, constituted an important part of the social, cultural, economic, and political landscape in the Mediterranean world in which the ancient Jews lived, but the Jews were heirs to a set of strongly antireciprocal cultural imperatives. The importance of such relationships can be argued on several different though interrelated levels of generality. In this chapter and the next I explore each of these in some detail, starting with the most abstract argument. First, though, I present each in brief.

On the lowest level of abstraction, it may be sufficient, especially for patronage and euergetism, to restate what anyone who has ever studied Roman history knows: they were important practices in the Roman Empire, and probably even—to adopt a structural-functionalist pose—played an important role in making the empire work.[16] An investigation of their reception by the Jews thus constitutes a good, solid historical project.

[14] P. Bourdieu, *Outline of a Theory of Practice* (Cambridge: Cambridge University Press, 1977 [first published 1972]), 1–32.

[15] Bourdieu, *Outline of a Theory of Practice*, 78: "The habitus, the durably installed generative principle of regulated improvisations, produces practices which tend to reproduce the regularities immanent in the objective conditions of the production of their generative principle, while adjusting to the demands inscribed as objective potentialities in the situation, as defined by the cognitive and motivating structures making up the habitus." Bourdieu's habitus is comparable, though not identical, to A. Giddens's notion of structuration. Both refer to the sense of practice—human social behavior—as a system of constrained contingencies. For a discussion of the relationship between Giddens's and Bourdieu's ideas, see L. Wacquant, "The Structure and Logic of Bourdieu's Sociology," in P. Bourdieu and L. Wacquant, *An Invitation to Reflexive Sociology* (Chicago: University of Chicago Press, 1992), 3–4.

[16] See R. Saller, *Personal Patronage under the Early Empire* (Cambridge: Cambridge University Press, 1982), and P. Veyne, *Bread and Circuses: Historical Sociology and Political Pluralism* (London: Penguin, 1990). Veyne would not accept the structural-functionalist argument, though.

At a higher level of abstraction, we may observe that such relationships have tended to be conspicuous in the Mediterranean societies studied by ethnographers, as well as in many of those of the region's pre-ethnographic past, not just Rome.[17] In such societies they have frequently been associated with ideas like honor and revenge. This entire cultural complex is demonstrably important in all the texts I study in this book, which in any case are not all products of the Roman imperial period, so it seems reasonable to consider our problem also as one of Mediterranean, not just Roman, culture, whatever that controversial term might mean. (I try to clarify this issue in chapter 2).

At the highest level of abstraction, we may consider the following. Mauss had argued that gift exchange was the primitive equivalent of trade. To be sure, Mauss was mainly concerned with the cultural aspects of the gift, with its relationship to competitive display, with the idea that the gift contained as it were a part of the giver and so was in some sense inalienable. Nevertheless, he also believed it functioned as a form of redistribution, the main form available in primitive or prerational societies, with the consequence that the development of trade marked an evolutionary step forward and reduced gift exchange from central social ritual to trivial ceremonial adjunct of an economy based on rational contractual exchange. After more than eighty years of criticism, this position is no longer tenable. Most critics have regarded the inalienability of the gift as an ethnographic peculiarity Mauss was incorrect to generalize. Furthermore, in most societies, gift exchange and trade have demonstrably coexisted; it will simply not do to speak of two types of society in polar opposition, though it may be possible to imagine a spectrum of options, with Mauss's Pacific islanders or Kwakiutl Indians, who supposedly lived in societies dominated by ceremonial gift exchange, at one end and contemporary bourgeois citizens of the First World at the other. Nor, as a corollary, should we think of an opposition between gift and contract (the latter rational, concerned with precise equivalency, and thought precisely not to establish an enduring relation between the parties). For our purposes it is important to observe that even today, even apart from the obvious fact that routine business deals often are fraught with wholly affective or emotional issues, such as a sense of loyalty, certain highly complex, partly reciprocity-based, personal relationships, such as that between husband and wife, may be established by contract. In the pre Hellenistic Near East,

---

[17] J. Davis, *People of the Mediterranean: An Essay in Comparative Social Anthropology* (London: Routledge and Kegan Paul, 1977), 132–50—a not wholly satisfactory survey.

even such fully reciprocal relationships as friendship and vassalage were established by contracts (which were not necessarily written).

Nevertheless, Mauss was surely right to perceive something fundamentally premodern ("primitive," in his terms) in institutionalized gift exchange, in the sense that it tends to be marginalized, or at any rate to play a very different role, in stable, relatively technologically advanced states.[18] Historians of ancient Greece have made fertile use of Mauss's opposition between gift exchange and trade as a way of explaining aspects of the politics and culture of the emerging city-state of the late archaic period.[19] This hypothesis has also made excellent sense of some difficult biblical episodes. For example, in Genesis 23, Abraham insists on paying Ephron the Hittite for the Cave of the Machpelah rather than receiving a burial cave as a gift, presumably because he is reluctant to become embroiled in a relationship of dependency with the Hittites.[20] This suggests that Mauss's view retains some heuristic utility. Later I apply aspects of this model where it is most appropriate, in the biblical book of Proverbs and the apocryphal Wisdom of Ben Sira. I show that it does not work; that is, Ben Sira does not oppose gift and trade but conflates them and is warily accepting of both. This suggests a limitation on the heuristic utility of Mauss's thesis and resonates instead with Bloch and Parry's demonstration that gift exchange and trade have in most societies been incompletely differentiated, and in any case are by no means in opposition.

Be this as it may, we may posit a reason for the association of the gift-based relationship with premodernity. The ideal premodern state was necessarily weaker than the ideal modern one: if states are defined by their monopolization of legitimate violence, as Weber observed, modern states, with higher population densities, better technology and communications, and enhanced ability to mobilize and organize manpower, have

[18] This is not to say that it has become wholly unimportant: one need only think of the impact on the U.S. economy of the institution of the Christmas gift. Of course, this does not imply that gifts are necessarily economically significant for the givers or the recipients. But there remain subcultures even in the most up-to-date corners of the United States in which gift exchange of a type that resonates strongly with many of the ethnographic varieties continues to play a very important (and highly fraught) social and cultural role, and a by no means negligible economic one. This is certainly true of the New York Jewish world in which I live. For general discussions of gift exchange in the contemporary world, see Davis, *Exchange*, and A. Komter, *Social Solidarity and the Gift* (Cambridge: Cambridge University Press, 2005).

[19] Earliest, of course, was M. I. Finley, *The World of Odysseus* (New York: Viking, 1954). More recently, see L. Kurke, *Coins, Bodies, Games, and Gold: The Politics of Meaning in Ancient Greece* (Princeton, NJ: Princeton University Press, 1999); and S. von Reden, *Exchange in Ancient Greece* (London: Duckworth, 1995).

[20] See C. Hinnant, "The Patriarchal Narratives of *Genesis* and the Ethos of Gift Exchange," in *The Question of the Gift: Essays Across Disciplines* ed. M. Osteen (London: Routledge, 2002), 105–17.

more violence to monopolize.[21] Premodern states had to work harder to
more limited effect. They were necessarily less centralized, less able to
control the lives of their constituents, had to cede power to local authorities, and aspired at best to co-opt them. The weakness of the state meant
the importance of the local grandee. He, for his part, had good reason
(survival, competition with his peers for power and prosperity) to try to
bind his neighbors to himself with ties of dependency based on unequal
reciprocal exchange, and to turn his equals into friends and allies. As for
the dependents, they were still more vulnerable, and so had reasons of
their own for submitting to the oppressive ministrations of a successful
neighbor. In weaker states such grandees might be something like warlords or feudal noblemen, or even brigand chiefs, their position quite directly dependent on their access to armed force and control of resources.[22]
Successful or more centralizing premodern states, though, co-opted such
grandees, made their positions quasi-official, and used them to mediate
the power of the state to its subjects. In the high Roman Empire such men
often became city councillors, responsible for raising taxes to be transmitted to the state. The role of the patron shifted slightly: while it continued
to include exploitation and protection of clients, intermediation between
client and state now became important, too (a similar shift occurred in
early modern Western Europe).[23] The patrons for their part were happy to
be co-opted because their association with a powerful state enhanced
their position at home and also opened new opportunities at the center: a
local grandee might hope to marry up, for example, or form other sorts of
partnerships or alliances that could propel him or, more likely, his children to higher positions.

Two Theories of the Integration of Society

Highly localized systems of exchange and dependency—based on ties such
as clientele, vassalage, and friendship, and probably most of all (though of
secondary importance in my account) family and clan—in a premodern
environment thus appear to have a certain inevitability. In principle, this
sense—which is implicit in the functionalism of the account—must be

[21] See M. Weber, *Economy and Society: An Outline of Interpretive Sociology*, G. Roth and C.
Wittich, eds. (Berkeley and Los Angeles: University of California Press, 1978), 54.
[22] See M. Sahlins, "Poor Man, Rich Man, Big-man, Chief: Political Types in Melanesia and
Polynesia," *CSSH* 5 (1963): 285–303.
[23] For patronage as mediation, see the fundamental article of S. N. Eisenstadt and L. Roniger,
"Patron-Client Relations as a Model of Structuring Social Exchange," *CSSH* 22 (1980): 42–77.

resisted. First of all, the local systems just described, and the states into which they were assembled, frequently failed. In fact, they were systems only from the reductively schematizing perspective of the distant observer; to the participants they must have seemed unstable mixtures of common sense ("we've always done things this way"), improvisation ("and yet new situations always arise"), and accidental contingency (drought or invasion leading to the dissolution of a patronage network, clan, or village).[24] Furthermore, there were other ways, not necessarily inherently more or less "functional" than the patronage network, of doing things. I do not know whether truly egalitarian rural communities (not actually controlled by a rich proprietor) have ever been common in any society, but they are not wholly unattested in the ethnographic past (how reliably I have no way of knowing).[25] In any case, it is certainly possible to imagine communities based in part on generalized reciprocity, what Sahlins called "pooling," in which individual exchange relationships matter less than the regular pullulation of goods and benefits through the group as a whole.[26] Also, in the Mediterranean, the Middle East, Europe, and India, for example, there have long existed religious communities that have at least partly avoided organization along patronal or feudal lines. Sometimes even entire premodern states—admittedly normally very small or otherwise unusual ones—have attempted to opt out of organization based on local clan or patronal structures: one thinks here of democratic Athens.

In fact, we may formulate this point more sharply. Let us posit that there exist two ways of imagining societies. In the first conception, societies are bound together by densely overlapping networks of relationships of personal dependency constituted and sustained by reciprocal exchange. This may sound like modern social theory, but in fact there is ample ancient attestation for it, especially in Greece (especially in more aristocratic circles) and Rome. Certainly it was shared by such diverse thinkers as Aristotle (*Eudemian Ethics* 7.1.2; 7.10.14ff.) and Seneca (*De Beneficiis* 1.4.2; cf. Cicero, *De Officiis* 1.22).[27] In this view, reciprocity

---

[24] Cf. Bourdieu, *Outline of a Theory of Practice*, 78–95.

[25] See discussion in Davis, *People of the Mediterranean*, 75–89.

[26] Such a conception of the Jewish town underlies the remarkable rabbinic rule that a man who forbids his wife to visit mourners is required to divorce her (that is, liberate her by paying the debt stipulated in their marriage contract as marking the conclusion of their marriage), "for when the time comes that her dead relation is stretched out before her, not a creature will come to care for her"; similarly, he is forced to divorce her if he forbids her to lend her sieve, "because he is thereby damaging her reputation among her neighbors" (Y. Ketubot 7.5, 31b). The rabbis sought to discourage "free riding," or, rather, assumed it could not be counted on to be rewarded.

[27] See M. Griffin, "*De Beneficiis* and Roman Society," *JRS* 93 (2003): 92–113, especially the survey of Aristotelian and Stoic thought at 92–93. B. Inwood, "Politics and Paradox in Seneca's *De*

generated primarily social cohesion, and though its tendency to inegalitarianism was acknowledged, the latter was thought theoretically subordinate to the exercise of individual self-control and wise government. In the second conception, societies are bound together not by personal relationships but by corporate solidarity based on shared ideals (piety, wisdom) or myths (for example, about common descent). This too resonates with modern social theory, for example, the influential work of Benedict Anderson, but is very amply attested for antiquity. The Torah is one proponent of such a theory; Plato was another. Both theories have emotional content: one is expected or even obligated to love, or at least have amicable or loyal feelings toward, those to whom one is connected. But this factor is responsible for a significant practical difference between the two, for the first theory requires you to love your patrons, clients, kinsmen, and friends, but not all members of your nation, though it may be expected that your connections will love their connections, and so on, so that everyone is ultimately bound together in an indirectly solidary, segmented society. It may alternatively be thought that your friendship, kinship, and patronage networks are in the aggregate coextensive with your state, a concept only slightly unrealistic for an Aristotle, writing about the relatively small-scale classical polis, but certainly a fantastic idea if applied to the Rome of Cicero or Seneca, with its population of one million.[28] By contrast, the second theory requires you to love all members of the group whether or not they are personally connected to you. The Torah commanded all Israelites to love their fellows, and Pericles urged his Athenian compatriots to be *erastai*, lovers, of their polis (so Thucydides wrote, 2.43.1, right after having Pericles claim that at Athens, unlike most other places, friendship was based on feelings of fellowship, not on reciprocal obligation). In this scheme, kinsmen, patrons, and friends enjoy no advantages.

Thus, although the two approaches are not irreconcilable, they are definitely in tension with each other. In fact, an Aristotle might assume a hierarchy of solidarities, and thereby reconcile loyalties to or affection toward household, patronage network, and polis. Furthermore, all theorists,

---

beneficiis," in *Justice and Generosity: Studies in Hellenistic Social and Political Philosophy,* ed. A. Laks and M. Schofield (Cambridge: Cambridge University Press, 1995), 241–42 (article: 241–65), discusses the Aristotelian background of the idea that certain things "hold together" (*sunekhein*) a state.

[28] In Stoic thought, one was expected to love and be prepared to be generous to all of humanity, in a way that in principle blunted or neutralized the political force of the sentiment entirely. But Seneca or Cicero could write about humanity but clearly intend Rome, and a small but privileged slice of Roman society at that.

ancient and modern, recognized that states need laws and a sense of order, the effect of which is necessarily to restrain the untrammeled operation of institutionalized reciprocity; the latter is thus understood to be on some fundamental level antithetical to the interests of the state, even as it is thought to constitute an advance over the primordial or presocial Hobbesian "warre of all against all" (see below on mediterraneanism as antithesis of order).[29] But adherents of the second social theory might find it more challenging to incorporate local loyalties in their system without subverting it completely. In some sense the whole point of the theory is to overcome the clan-group and patronage network[30]: it derives its emotional strength from its rejection of reciprocity-based loyalties and imagines that it is pursuing a "higher" set of ideals. If, as suggested above, gift exchange has an inescapable tendency to be inegalitarian, the relationships created by it will slip inexorably into exploitation and injustice. The point of the second theory thus may be precisely to pursue equality and justice, and pure love of one's fellow, by rejecting reciprocity a priori. The not insignificant corollary of this is that the solidarity-based theory tends to construct the reciprocity-based theory as normal, and itself as revolutionary or countercultural.

Notwithstanding the tension between them, neither theory is entirely self-sufficient; they need each other. This implies that in their real-life manifestations, and even in their most highly elaborated theoretical expositions, the two positions are not always far apart.[31] The reciprocity-based theory needs the solidarity-based theory in two ways. First, reciprocity works best for small, localized, "face-to-face" societies, since it leaves un-

---

[29] Contrast Gouldner, "The Norm of Reciprocity," 176. But he also characterizes reciprocity as a "starting mechanism" that logically and chronologically precedes the development of "a differentiated and customary set of status duties." In Gouldner's view, it is thus, I would infer, formative of society but prior to the state. More explicitly: Sahlins, *Stone Age Economics*, 168–71.

[30] See E. Leach, *The Political System of Highland Burma: A Study of Kachin Social Structure*, LSE Monographs on Social Anthropology 44 (London: Athlone Press, 1970 [first published 1954], 197–204, on the countercultural or revolutionary nature of the republican (*gumlao*) Burmese villagers, who, even according to their own corporate mythology, claimed to have rebelled against the hierarchical and exchange-oriented (the latter point noted by Leach in passing but not emphasized) norms of general Kachin society. The obvious comparison here is with Athenian and Roman stories of the establishment of democratic or republican regimes following the expulsion, respectively, of the tyrannical Peisistratids and the monarchical Tarquinii. The Jews had no such myth (the story of the Exodus is hardly comparable), since the Babylonians had ended their monarchy for them. But they had stories opposing monarchy (for example, 1 Sam 10.17–27) and laws restricting it (Dt 17.14–20).

[31] Cf. Leach, *The Political System of Highland Burma*, 197. In general, my argument here is structurally indebted to Leach's discussion (on pages 197–212) of the analytical antinomy between hierarchically organized (*gumsa*) and republican or egalitarian (*gumlao*) Kachin (Burmese hill country people) and its tension with the practical tendency of the two systems to merge into each other.

clear why anything larger than the local network should cohere. Or, to put it differently, a complex society that possesses no ideological foundation beyond gratitude and loyalty to benefactors and kinspeople will in short order dissolve into its segments.

Solidarity based on ideals rather than exchange was an important feature even of states that embraced reciprocity as a fundamental value. For example, though benefaction and gratitude were crucial components of the Roman system, the success of the Roman state lay precisely in its ability to organize this sense of personal loyalty pyramidally: modest subjects were expected to feel gratitude toward benefactors (governors, senators, emperors) who had given them nothing, whom they had never even seen. And this success was bolstered by a flow of propaganda from the center that presented the Roman state and the emperor as embodiments of ethical and cultural values. A state that allowed reciprocity free rein could never survive.

In addition to providing the ideological structure for the integration of local patronage and kinship systems into larger societies, nonreciprocal ideologies might perform a secondary function in reciprocity-based ideological systems; as I discuss in more detail in the next chapter, they might provide an escape valve. As already indicated, reciprocity-based systems tend toward inequality; they are often experienced—and not only by those in the position of client or vassal—as oppressive; furthermore, they consume resources mercilessly. Indeed, in Mauss's scheme destruction of wealth was one of the essential features of the gift exchange economy, and this appears to have been as true of Roman euergetism as of native American potlatch. Therefore, there are always people who wish to opt out. The French historian E. Leroy Ladurie provided a fine example in the form of the Duc de Saint-Simon, a noble beneficiary of the highly elaborate systems of patronage and precedence that prevailed at Louis XIV's court. Fearing that he was being crushed by a system even he had difficulty navigating, Saint-Simon dreamed of life in a Carmelite monastery, whose inhabitants "dwell in perpetual silence, in the poorest of cells . . . [and] take common meals in the refectory, which are very frugal, and exist in a state of almost perpetual fasting, strictly observing [liturgical] office, and sharing their time between manual work and contemplation." This was, in sum, the polar opposite of the toxic little society of Versailles, with its endless conspiratorial chatter, debt-inducingly competitive displays of luxury, and obsessive anxiety about honor and access.[32] For Roman-era examples

---

[32] E. Leroy Ladurie, "The Court Surrounds the King: Louis XIV, the Palatine Princess, and Saint-Simon," in *Honor and Grace in Anthropology*, ed. J. G. Peristiany and J. Pitt-Rivers (Cambridge: Cambridge University Press, 1992), 51–78. Saint-Simon's letter is quoted on page 71.

of antireciprocal solidarity-based organizations serving as escape hatches, we might consider the attractiveness, by no means especially to the poor, of philosophical sects, mystery cults, Christianity, and even diasporic Judaism itself.

Like the reciprocity-based theory, the solidarity-based theory in its purest form works best in small groups. Such groups can easily attain through self-selection a sense of solidarity derived from shared purpose and an equitable distribution of resources, without needing to rely on relationships of personal dependency. In larger entities, the only way at least partially to enable a more or less reciprocity-free society might be by assuring that the need rarely arise for people to rely on the personal generosity of their neighbors.[33] This is the purpose of much Pentateuchal legislation. All Israelites are required to support all their fellows by leaving behind parts of their harvest, by periodically handing over to the poor ten percent of their agricultural production, by the obligatory provision of interest-free loans to those who have become impoverished, and, most radical of all, by the septennial cancellation of debts and manumission of debt bondsmen and, twice a century, by the redistribution of landholding. The Bible's elaborate rules are meant to ensure that the charitable donation (and likewise the donations meant to form the livelihood of the priestly and levitical temple staff) never degenerates into the dependency-generating gift. The pauper, like the priest, is meant to feel no gratitude— at least not toward the donor. Rather, charity is a prime expression of Israelite corporate solidarity, of the obligation of all Israelites to love one another regardless of familial or other connection.

But here, too, there are problems. First, given the ostensible naturalness of ethical reciprocity, or at least the fact that even small, hyperegalitarian societies have trouble eradicating it, there is an inexorable tendency for charitable donation to turn into gift. In other words, the donors might expect the poor to show gratitude, and the poor might comply, because common sense tells them, or because they feel constrained, to do so. James Laidlaw's analysis of the priestly *dan* (a charitable gift loosely comparable to the biblical *terumah*—"heave offering"—given to priests) among the Jains is important for demonstrating how much work it takes to ensure that charitable donation retains its "purity."[34] Historically, among Jews and Christians, there has almost always been slippage between charity and gift. On the one hand, the sense persists in both communities that

---

[33] See Sahlins, *Stone Age Economics*, 188–91, on the distinction between reciprocity and "pooling," and for a fundamental account of the social and symbolic aspects of the latter. My discussion here is anticipated by Sahlins's account of the "sociology of primitive exchange" (185–275).

[34] "A Free Gift Makes No Friends," in Osteen, *The Question of the Gift*, 45–66.

the best and purest donation is one that cannot be reciprocated, and ideally is even anonymous. At the same time, Jewish and Christian charity
adopted features of Greco-Roman patronage and euergetism at a very
early date; since then (if not even before), Jewish communal life—to focus
more narrowly on our subject—has never lacked reciprocal elements.[35]

A second problem with ideologies of nonreciprocal solidarity is that in
large-scale societies, the only way to impose truly effective, as opposed to
mainly symbolic, nonreciprocal redistributive systems such as charity is
through the functioning of a powerful state, or something similar. The
Pentateuch's redistributive laws may or may not have been sufficient in
principle to reduce the roles of clans or patronage networks. But without
a strong state administering the rules, that is, with the rules being practiced on what amounted to a voluntary basis, reciprocity could not be
eliminated. (Important historical questions remain and are addressed
later: What form might reciprocal institutions take in such a case? What
sort of symbolic validation might they enjoy in a society that professes to
reject them in principle but remains in some measure reliant on them?)
Indeed, the Pentateuch itself makes allowances for institutions that it
clearly opposes, such as debt bondage, and it is not clear whether the biblical legislators meant periodic redistribution of land as anything other
than a utopian ideal.

Given, then, both the conflict between ideals of reciprocity and solidarity and their mutual dependence in practice, how did the Jews, as adherents of a strongly antireciprocal normative system, cope with life in a
world in which institutionalized reciprocity was very hard indeed to
escape?

In the core of this book I discuss three textual corpora that have turned
out to be profoundly concerned with both normative and descriptive aspects of the question of how Jews should cope with institutionalized reciprocity. Ben Sira wrote about gift exchange itself and about all sorts of social relationships generated by it, though with perhaps a slight emphasis
on friendship. Josephus had much to say about friendship and patronage[36]
but his comments on euergetism are in some ways of special interest, in

---

[35] On the relationship between Jewish charity and Greco-Roman euergetism, see S. Schwartz,
IJS, 275–89. For an account of a Christian society that convincingly treats charitable donation
under the rubric of gift exchange while noting the ways in which it does not fit, see N. Z. Davis,
The Gift in Sixteenth Century France (Madison: University of Wisconsin Press, 2000).

[36] I have written about these issues elsewhere: "Josephus in Galilee: Rural Patronage and Social Breakdown," in *Josephus and the History of the Greco-Roman Period: Essays in Memory of
Morton Smith*, ed. F. Parente and J. Sievers (Leiden: Brill, 1994), 290–308; "King Herod, Friend of
the Jews," in *Jerusalem and Eretz Israel: Arie Kindler Volume*, ed. J. Schwartz, Z. Amar, and I.
Ziffer (Tel Aviv: Rennert Center, Bar Ilan University / Eretz Israel Museum, 2000), *67–*76.

part because they have been so little noticed and are of peculiar historical importance. For its part, the Palestinian Talmud struggled to come to grips with all sorts of issues of social hierarchy but seems especially concerned with patronage in all its ceremonial trappings. I am not proposing that the texts reflect an evolutionary development in Jewish thought about these issues, only that they constitute successive attempts to adapt the Torah's utopian antireciprocity to altered political and social realities. None of these texts addresses reciprocity in a cultural vacuum. All of them, like the Hebrew Bible itself, understand the relationships they are concerned with as embedded in various complexes of cultural practice, and here is where mediterraneanism enters the picture, because the cultural complexes they write about bear a striking resemblance to the historical and ethnographic construct (as I think we must describe it). In particular the sense of honor or shame, a central concept in mediterraneanist ethnography, plays a peculiarly important but very varied role in each of these texts: Ben Sira, who associates it with domination, embraces honor but insists it is conferred by wisdom or piety above all; Josephus claims the Jews reject it; rabbinic texts (which also tend to associate it with domination) display great anxiety and confusion about it. This is all somehow connected to the fact that the Bible is reticent about ascribing honor to any humans. But there is more: the Bible often reads like an item-by-item rejection of the ethnographers' Mediterranean culture. Why?

CHAPTER TWO

The Problem with Mediterraneanism

In much historiography and social anthropology of the recent past, Mediterranean culture was regarded as a corollary of an agrarian economic regime characterized by slightly above-subsistence-level dry farming, especially of wheat and barley, olives, and grapes.[1] These goods, among others, were distributed to some extent by a constant small-scale "Brownian motion" of local trade,[2] piracy, brigandage, and war, the latter generated by the proliferation of small political entities sometimes vaguely controlled by weakly centralized empires. Furthermore, Mediterranean societies were characterized by the pervasive importance of highly formalized institutions of reciprocal exchange, whether in the form of legal institutions such as vassalage, debt bondage, and friendship in its ancient Near Eastern, contractual modulation or in the paralegal forms of patronage, clientele, and Greco-Roman-style friendship. Such institutions were important in this world as in other premodern economic regimes because the chronic shortage of resources and the weakness of states required people to rely on localized redistributive systems. Why institutionalized reciprocity took the specific forms it did in the Mediterranean world—why, for example, patronage loomed so large (if indeed it did)—is far less clear.

In this cultural system, honor and shame are supposed to have been pervasively important, and female sexuality was supposed to have been especially dangerous, as one of the chief threats to male honor.[3] There is thus said to have been a type of personal disposition or construction of

---

[1] For a summary, restrained, and nuanced account (though still one that assumes rather than demonstrates the integrity, however loose, of the Mediterranean basin as a *Kulturgebiet*) of mediterraneanism, see Davis, *People of the Mediterranean*.

[2] See P. Horden and N. Purcell, *The Corrupting Sea: A Study of Mediterranean History* (Oxford: Blackwell, 2000), who follow Braudel in making much of *cabotage*, or small-scale local maritime trade (such as a farmer loading a few items on a boat and trying to sell them to another farmer down the coast or on a neighboring island), which is obviously not a realistic option for anyone living even slightly inland.

[3] Davis, *People of the Mediterranean*, 89–100, denies to female sexuality any central role in threatening male honor.

the self—as, for men, touchily honor-obsessed, jealous, prone to violent revenge,[4] aggressively macho (the *eghoismos* of Michael Herzfeld's Cretan villagers; see below), all combined with what ethnographers called "amoral familism"[5]—broadly diffused in the Mediterranean world, allegedly in almost all historical periods, cutting across linguistic, ethnic, and religious boundaries.

There are serious problems with mediterraneanism, but I believe that it can be salvaged, if not as a meaningful ethnographic hypothesis, then at least for our purposes as a heuristic tool. Let me state matters more strongly: for anyone working on the social and cultural history of the ancient Jews, mediterraneanism cannot be ignored.[6] Here's why: mediterraneanism was an idea that enjoyed particular prominence between the 1960s and 1980s, owing partly to the influence of two important books. One of them was Fernand Braudel's *The Mediterranean and the Mediterranean World in the Age of Philip II*, and the other, also published in the 1960s, was a volume called *Honor and Shame: The Values of Mediterranean Society*, edited by the anthropologist J. G. Peristiany. The roots of the conception, though, can be traced back to nineteenth-century and earlier travel literature, among other things.[7]

In the course of the 1980s a reaction set in, led especially by Michael Herzfeld, by training and practice an ethnographer of rural Greece, whose experience led him to be suspicious of the utility of so broad and deterministic a construct, and led him also to observe—and subsequently to write an entire book, *Anthropology Through the Looking Glass: Critical Ethnography in the Margins of Europe*, on—the often problematical political uses to which mediterraneanism was put. As W. V. Harris observed, in Herzfeld's writing, mediterraneanism is a cousin of Edward

[4] But note J. E. Lendon, *Empire of Honor: The Art of Government in the Roman World* (Oxford: Clarendon, 1997), 41–42, on aristocratic Romans: honor-obsessed but largely duel- and vendetta-free, possibly because of the transcendent aristocratic value of gentlemanly restraint, *sophrosyne*; but was this value absent in eighteenth-century England or nineteenth-century Austria? Should the duel, vendetta, and blood feud be conflated, as Lendon does? For a different approach to the question as it applies to classical Athens, see G. Herman, *Morality and Behaviour in Classical Athens: A Social History* (Cambridge: Cambridge University Press, 2006).

[5] Originally: E. C. Banfield, *The Moral Basis of a Backward Society* (Glencoe, IL: Free Press, 1958).

[6] For arguments roughly similar to those that follow, though with perhaps excessive commitment to the empirical validity of a broad and diversified version of mediterraneanism (a commitment not necessarily misplaced, but unnecessary for his argument), see D. Cohen, *Law, Sexuality, and Society: The Enforcement of Morals in Classical Athens* (Cambridge: Cambridge University Press, 1991, 35–69).

[7] The history of the idea is discussed in W. V. Harris, "The Mediterranean and Ancient History," in *Rethinking the Mediterranean*, ed. W. V. Harris (Oxford: Oxford University Press, 2005, 1–42).

Said's orientalism. It would be misleading to say that as a result of Herzfeld's work—which was part of a growing discomfort among anthropologists and others with functionalism, large-scale reductive normative models, "*grands récits*," and everything that smacked of imperialism, both actual and metaphorical—mediterraneanism died, but it certainly seems to have faded in importance among anthropologists (if not among travel and food writers). We must not forget, though, one of the key achievements of mediterraneanism: it (in theory) allowed observers to trace cultural continuities across what otherwise appeared to be the unbridgeable chasm between Christianity and Islam.[8] This is important for my purposes, because I too will be seeking continuities—though also differences—across the ancient religious boundaries between Jews and pagans. Furthermore, I find it hard not to sense not far below the surface in the writing of some antimediterraneanist ethnographers a faint feeling of injury at grouping Iberians, say, with Arabs (for example, de Pina-Cabral, cited below; this is certainly not true of Herzfeld). Antimediterraneanists sometimes have unwholesome political agendas of their own.

Unsurprisingly, for those of us in Jewish studies and cognate fields, at the moment of its decline as an ethnographic hypothesis, mediterraneanism was embraced, in its crudest and most deterministic form, by scholars of the Hebrew Bible and the New Testament. Leaf through volumes of *Semeia, Journal for the Study of the Old Testament,* and other relatively progressive journals of biblical studies from the 1990s and early 2000s and you will find nearly the whole agenda of mediterraneanist ethnography applied to the Bible and the ancient Israelite and Jewish worlds in a way that strikes me in most cases as staggeringly vulgar. For example, *Semeia* dedicated an entire volume to articles trying very hard but with dismayingly little success to find traces of the honor-shame complex in the Bible, on the grounds, as one editor put it, that since the Israelites and their descendants were a Mediterranean people and honor and shame were centrally important in all Mediterranean lands, they must have been central for the Jews, too.[9] It hardly needs to be said that this deterministic

---

[8] This issue is emphasized by D. Abulafia, "What is the Mediterranean?" in *The Mediterranean in History*, ed. D. Abulafia (London: Thames and Hudson, 2003), 11–26. Abulafia also provides a somewhat friendlier response to Horden and Purcell than Harris does.

[9] See V. Matthews and D. Benjamin, "Social Sciences and Biblical Studies," *Semeia* 68 (1994/1996): 7–21. It is remarkable that the sensibly restrained comments of the anthropologist J. K. Chance at the end of the volume ("The Anthropology of Honor and Shame: Culture, Value, and Practice," 139–51) had no impact on the editors. Similarly, S. Olyan notes the ubiquity of the concepts in ancient Israel and its environment (read: in biblical and Akkadian texts) but succeeds in demonstrating only that in the former, possession of honor was restricted to God, parents or elders, and the dead; see "Honor, Shame, and Covenant Relations in Ancient Israel and

syllogism is very far from what Braudel and the great team of anthropologists assembled by Peristiany had in mind in tracing out subtle continuities in Mediterranean culture.[10] Such work may at least serve as a warning to us about the consequences of incautious use of reified social scientific hypotheses.

In the meantime, the controversy about mediterraneanism has returned to the agenda, thanks to *The Corrupting Sea*, published in 2000 by Peregrine Horden, a medievalist, and the Roman historian Nicholas Purcell. In a densely argued, detail-choked 800 pages (with a second volume soon to appear), they in effect promoted a partial revival of Mediterranean culture, especially in its Braudelian form, in a way that connects it intimately to the ecology of the region (this despite their self-conscious self-distancing from Braudel).

The Corrupting Sea is of special importance for our concerns because it illustrates the way premodern historians do not have the same issues at stake in the mediterraneanist debate as ethnographers, sociologists, and modern historians do. A competent ethnographer might well decide that, precisely because she has abundant empirical data, the mediterraneanist hypothesis has nothing valuable to contribute to her understanding of some set of highly localized conditions, that, just as Herzfeld argued, even if true, it is trivial, lacking in explanatory power, and at worst is an invitation to invidious misperception. Other models, functioning at a higher level of abstraction or having less of a sense of inadequately theorized regional distinctiveness, are likely to be more useful. But for premodernists it is not trivial, since we are not looking for analytical tools alone but tend to use our models as ways of filling in gaps, of providing ourselves with sets of social-historical assumptions (in the absence of real information) against which we can measure the exiguous fragments of information we do have. Whatever anthropologists may think, mediterraneanism is *potentially* important for us because, if it turns out to be not pure projection but at least a plausible if partial account of how some premodern society somewhere lived—if, in other words, it is tolerably coherent if only as a construct—and if it is then used with cautious skepticism, not as a determinist frame into which to force evidence, it could conceivably help us better understand biblical and rabbinic texts and the societies and cultures

---

Its Environment," *JBL* 115 (1996): 201–18. On 218, Olyan admits the rarity of honor in prescriptive texts.

[10] See, on this point, the balanced comments of J. de Pina-Cabral, "The Mediterranean as a Category of Regional Comparison: A Critical View," *Current Anthropology* 30 (1989): 399–406. In de Pina-Cabral's view much ethnographic mediterraneanism of the 1970s and 1980s lost moderation and subtlety, too.

that generated them. And for this reason many of the anthropological queries about mediterraneanism—how widespread was it? How early did it appear? Is it really Mediterranean at all, as opposed to being a cultural complex that can be found in all sorts of premodern, agrarian, weakly centralized societies, for example?—for my purposes matter much less than its heuristic utility: what does it matter if Mediterranean culture in real life was found only in southwestern China, as long as it helps us understand our own topic better by offering fuel for structural comparison?

The Torah as Mediterranean Counterculture

Given how fraught mediterraneanism is, why should we bother with it in the first place, if we can at all avoid it? Why not follow the implications of the last paragraph and W. V. Harris's advice and draw our ethnographic comparisons from "everywhere"?[11] We should do so, of course. But there remains a banal though not necessarily trivial reason—a shared ecology—for us to privilege Mediterranean ethnography: it makes good aprioristic sense to compare, say, hill country dry-farming communities specializing in grain and olives one with the other because geology and climate do, after all, impose significant constraints on some categories of human behavior, though these may rarely extend to details of culture, and they certainly do not *determine* kinship structures, religious beliefs and practices, and so forth.[12]

---

[11] Harris, "The Mediterranean and Ancient History," 38–42.

[12] See G. Woolf, "A Sea of Faith?" *Mediterranean Historical Review* 18 (2003): 126–43. And even so, comparative mediterraneanist material is most effective when used to generate caution and skepticism. To take one important example, historians usually compose their descriptions of land tenure practices in ancient Palestine on the basis of the very meager scraps of information provided by Josephus, the New Testament, and (mainly prescriptively) the Mishnah (the Babatha papyri might add complexity to the picture but unfortunately reflect the atypical ecology of the arid northern Aravah). Such accounts can be subtle and intelligent (M. Goodman, *The Ruling Class of Judaea*: The Origins of the Jewish Revolt Against Rome A.D. 66–70 [Cambridge: Cambridge University Press, 1987], 51–75) or crude (J. Pastor, *Land and Economy in Ancient Palestine* [London: Routledge, 1997]). But in either case, a survey of ethnographic material—which describes small dry-farming communities with bewilderingly complex land tenure arrangements, so that a single man may simultaneously own his own small plot, farm another plot as tenant of an absentee nobleman, and farm a third as sharecropper for an elderly relative, while also working part time as an agricultural laborer, craftsman, or shopkeeper (with the state, on top of all this, playing an obscure but pervasive role in the organization and taxation of land holding)—would have imposed restraint, especially in using simplistic terms like "landless peasants." This is not because ancient Judaeans necessarily divided up their land as south Italian peasants of the 1950s did, but because we do not know how they divided up their land, and the Italian case informs us of the range of options available in a roughly similar sort of environment.

More to the point, I would argue that the fact that the Torah's prescriptions constitute mediterraneanism's nearly perfect antithesis requires an explanation. There is no way to avoid engaging with the issue, the challenge is only to figure out *how* to engage. The rejection of Mediterranean norms is not restricted to the Torah (here we add some detail to the schematic account presented in the last chapter). To be sure, some biblical heroes, most prominently David (in his early life an "outlaw" pastoralist and brigand)[13] and the judges (who lived, the Bible repeatedly reminds us, at a time when "there was no king in Israel and each man did what was right in his eyes"), are the subjects of stories that portray them approximately as idealized Mediterranean men. Nevertheless, on the whole, the non-Pentateuchal biblical books have little good to say about Mediterranean culture either. Instead, the Torah, for its part, has a radically anti-Mediterranean vision of Israelite society: the only fully legitimate relationship of personal dependency for Israelites is that with their God, who is their father, master, friend, and lover; hence the importance of charity, a type of redistribution intentionally set up so as to hinder the proliferation of personal ties of dependency. The only individual who is to be regarded as unconditionally honorable is, once again, God, though parents and elders are to be at least respected (or in other passages feared). Consequently, the vendetta—revenge for wounded honor—has no place among the Israelites (Lev 19.18). Israelites are not to be bound together by ties of personal dependency, whether in the form of vassalage, clientele, or friendship: the Torah regards even the family, notwithstanding so much American Jewish mythology about the subject, with remarkable equivocality. "Amoral familism" was not to be an option. Stories were told about such behavior (for example, Gen 34), but it was strongly condemned (Gen 49.5–7). Rather, Israelites are united by shared devotion to God and his laws, and by a peculiar type of unconditional love (*ahavah*), or sense of group solidarity. The Israelites are thus meant to be more or less equal one to the other and slaves only to God, not to other (Israelite) men, with the accumulation of landholding expressly forbidden. There is to be no conventional aristocracy. To be sure, there is

---

Such comparative material enriches our account by destabilizing it. See Davis, *People of the Mediterranean*, 41–55. Of course, the ethnographic comparison could just as easily come from India.

[13] For example, 1 Sam 22.2: "And there gathered unto him [in the Cave of Adullam] every man in straits, and every man who had a creditor, and every man of bitter spirit, and he was their ruler." Indeed, the entire narrative cycle is built around David's doomed or failed formal Mediterranean-style reciprocal relationships, with Saul, Jonathan, Ahimelekh, son of Ahitub, priest of Nob, and his son Ebiathar, and with Absalom, among others. For proof that the biblical writers understood thoroughly how such relations worked, see the densely packed dialogue in the scene of David's reconciliation with Saul in the cave of En Geddi, 1 Sam 24.

a priesthood to mediate between God and Israel, but by denying it the right to own land and making it dependent on the contributions of the Israelites, the Torah tried to ensure that it would be not an aristocracy but a class of functionaries or enablers, suspended between privilege and pauperdom.

The Torah, and the biblical corpus in general, also rejected another element of Mediterranean culture given great prominence by Horden and Purcell, connectivity. What this rather portentous term means is the tendency of people all around the shore of the sea to engage in constant small-scale exchange with neighboring settlements, cities, and islands. This exchange could take the form of trade, gift exchange, even piracy and brigandage; the concept acquires its coherence from its economic role: whatever cultural form it took, connectivity made life sustainable in an environment where autarky—local self-sufficiency—was normally unattainable. Now, many groups have idealized autarky, but for the Jews such idealization had a special edge, since it was fuelled by a strong sense of group particularism. Dependence on other nations—which was not necessarily identical with political domination by them, since it could include indebtedness to resident aliens—was seen as a divine curse (Dt 21 passim). The God of the Torah was Israel's only God, and was jealous to boot. The Torah thus set obstacles in the way of Israelites' socialization with their neighbors, obstacles raised still higher in other biblical texts. As among the classical Athenians, among the ancient Jews a heightened sense of group solidarity, egalitarianism, and particularism went hand in hand. The Jews' texts express the pervasive fear that contact with non-Israelites would lead Israel to whore after alien gods (as the Bible puts it, imagining the relationship of God and Israel as that of husband and wife). Thus, no encouragement of interstate trade, even in the modest of form of Braudelian *cabotage*. To be sure, the book of Kings takes pride in Solomon's acquisition—through what the text describes as an act of gift exchange rather than of trade[14]—of large quantities of cedar and cypress from Hiram king of Tyre for use in constructing a temple in Jerusalem (1 Kgs 5.15–25). But it emphasizes that Hiram blessed Yahweh—not his own god, Ba'al King of the City (Melqart)—when he received Solomon's request: surely the biblical author's assurance that the friendship between the two kings (1 Kgs 5.26: "and there was an alliance between Hiram and Solomon, and the two of them made a covenant") and the exchange that it entailed had no problematic religious consequences. In general, the Bible so

---

[14] Hiram received twenty towns in Galilee, though not very good ones, the author admits, in return for his gift: 1 Kgs 9.11–13.

little associates Israelites and interstate trade that the biblical word for merchant is *kena'ani* ("Phoenician"). To some extent, the commercial aspects of connectivity—the periodic routine of loading a boat with one's excess crops and selling it down the coast or on the neighboring island—were less available to the Jews as inhabitants of the hill country than to Phoenicians or Greeks.[15]

But there is little question that another type of connectivity, the formal foreign friendships known to the Greeks as *xenia*, was important for the Israelites and the ancient Jews, and was an institution biblical texts regarded at best with strong ambivalence. The "deuteronomic historian" (the term of art for the author of the biblical histories, especially Judges–2 Kgs) could nod at Solomon's friendship with Hiram, because it enabled the construction of the temple and because the historian had convinced himself that the king of Tyre was a worshiper of Yahweh. The same resignation was not possible, though, in the case of the wives Solomon received from his friendships with Egyptian and other grandees, because these led to his construction of altars to his wives' gods, much to Yahweh's disapproval (1 Kgs 11.1–10).

Similarly, it is tempting to read Ruth and Ezra-Nehemiah as staking out oblique positions in a debate about *xenia* and its religious consequences: Ezra and Nehemiah simply oppose it, claim to have driven the Ammonite friends of the Judahite high priests out of Jerusalem (Neh 13.4–9) and ordered the well-to-do Jerusalemites to dismiss their foreign wives (Ezra 10; Neh 13.23–31), best understood as artifacts of foreign friendships. The Jews are a "holy seed" (Ezra 9.2) and must not pollute themselves through association with foreigners—even, the point appears to be, if the foreigners are pious, like Hiram of Tyre, and prepared to make important contributions to the religious life of their *xenoi*. The author of Ruth responds that such relationships are acceptable, even desirable: if the Bethlehemite Elimelekh had not had Moabite friends who married off their righteous daughter Ruth, who had left her gods in her father's house and accepted only the God of her new family, to his son, there would never have been a King David. In other words, as in the case of Hiram, friendship with the neighboring nations is permitted—indeed, it is recognized as essential to the well-being of the Israelites—provided (somewhat unrealistically) the foreigners are prepared to make all the religious concessions to their Israelite *xenoi*. This position is not far from that underlying the later practice of conversion to Judaism, which also functioned at

---

[15] For a remarkable and unusual mention of *cabotage* (necessarily on a very small scale, since it is situated in the shallow Jordan River) in a rabbinic text, see Y. Shabbat 4.2, 7a.

first as a way of allowing Jews to conduct untrammeled friendships with their non-Judaean neighbors.[16]

How can we explain the Bible's antimediterraneanism? There are several contradictory possibilities. We may, for example, argue that the precise antithesis between biblical prescription and ethnographic construct supports a skeptical, Herzfeldian approach by suggesting that the ethnographic construct is in effect a modern Christian, or Judaeo-Christian, projection of the barbarous "Other," one that reflects the Bible's own ideas; in this view, Mediterranean culture is basically a fantasy, imagined by people whose sense of civilization was shaped by scriptural religions. Think once again of the Bible's description of the lawless, "Mediterranean" era of the judges: "in those days there was no king in Israel and every man did what was right in his eyes."[17] Such a notion is nearly explicit also in the expression which Carlo Levi said he had heard from southern Campanian and Basilicatan peasants (*Cristo si è fermato a Eboli*; Christ stopped at Eboli) and used as the title of his great book: in many European languages, including Italian (or rather Neapolitan) as Levi observed, Christianity equals civilization, so barbarism is the absence of Christian or, more broadly, of biblical values. Thus, no really "Mediterranean" society ever existed, or at any rate the ethnographers' Mediterranean culture was never a significant and historically continuous component of life in the Mediterranean basin.

Positivists, though, might argue that the biblical legislators and storytellers were presumably reacting against *something* (and they do indeed constantly remind the Israelites that they are not like, or should not be like, their neighbors), and the resemblance of the cultural complex against which the Bible polemicizes and the ethnographic construct—based ostensibly, at least to some extent, on observation, however partial and flawed—actually provides important evidence for the construct's significance and historical continuity (no responsible anthropologist or historian today would go beyond this rather qualified presentation).

I prefer an intermediate position. It seems generally accepted that some ethnographers and historians, in their search for the authentic and

---

[16] This summarizes my argument in "Conversion to Judaism in the Second Temple Period: A Functionalist Approach," in *Studies in Josephus and the Varieties of Ancient Judaism: Louis H. Feldman Jubilee Volume*, ed. S. Cohen and J. Schwartz (Leiden: Brill, 2007), 223–36.

[17] Yet even as they distanced themselves from them, the biblical writers and editors embraced these "savage" tales, at least to the extent to which they could be subordinated to the deuteronomistic theology, just as Greek writers of the classical age with similar ambivalence embraced the blood-soaked stories of the Trojan War. Thus, not only did Mediterranean culture generate its own countercultures, these countercultures were meaningless without their antitheses.

the archaic, forgot or ignored the fact that even their wildest subjects usually lived in states, however weak and ineffective, and were always, at least
technically, adherents of one or another of the scriptural religions.[18] Thus,
while "pure" mediterraneanism may have had some sporadic peripheral
existence, it was probably in almost all periods rare. Rather than viewing
Mediterranean culture as the real, normative culture of the Mediterranean basin throughout history, we should perhaps understand and use it
as a Weberian ideal type, whose real-life manifestations were almost always diffuse, adulterated, partial: neither ubiquitous in the Mediterranean world, wherever its boundaries might be, nor necessarily exclusive
to it. In other words, the resemblance of the culture the Bible rejects to
that of the ethnographic Mediterranean may be essentially coincidental
or may be due to broad similarities in political regime and economic development, in addition to some ecological continuities, however cautiously we evaluate their cultural impact.

Above I argued that my two hypothetical theories of the integration of
societies, though in principle opposed to one another, in practice were in-
terdependent: the reciprocity-based theory needed the solidarity-based
theory both to provide a rationale for integration above the level of the
patronage or kinship network and to provide an escape hatch for those
oppressed by the demands of competitive reciprocity. The solidarity-
based theory, though constituted in some measure in opposition to the
reciprocity-based theory, needed it to perform the redistributive tasks it
could not for the most part perform itself. Furthermore, it could never
fully tame the widespread sense that there was something "natural" about
reciprocity, and so had to find ways of accommodating it. Here I would
like to expand the focus of this suggestion beyond the narrow limits of
reciprocity and suggest that wherever some version of Mediterranean culture existed, it coexisted with—was adulterated and modified by—its own
counterculture. Conversely, Mediterranean countercultures always have
to find ways of accommodating what they themselves tend to regard as
the cultural mainstream.

The Torah clearly imagines itself as countercultural, warning the Israelites not to engage in what it portrays as a large complex of normative
behavior. It would be a mistake simply to reify the Torah's constructed
other into a real-life cultural system, whether we call it Mediterranean or
something else. Nevertheless, some of the things the Torah rejects really
were widespread in the eastern Mediterranean of the Iron Age and later.
Very few premodern agrarian nations or other large groups could survive

---

[18] See, on these points, the sharp comments of Davis, *People of the Mediterranean*, 5–10.

for long without highly localized institutions regulating relationships of personal dependency. Honor and shame, though rejected as human characteristics in the Torah, were so deeply embedded in the language and consciousness of the biblical writers (see Olyan, "Honor and Shame") that we must suppose the concepts to have been important to them, however ambivalent they may have been about them.

This alone, whatever the validity of large-scale hypotheses about the existence of a continuous and widespread Mediterranean culture, makes it clear that the Torah did demand of its adherents that they reject many norms commonly accepted by their neighbors. Thus, the Torah constituted what I am calling here a Mediterranean counterculture. At the same time, it was, like the philosophical schools and to a far more limited extent Athenian democracy, utopian.[19] But the philosophical schools were tiny communities, often of wealthy youths, and so could afford to turn their backs on some of the social norms that made the general society work, and for its part Athenian democracy was funded, for its brief lifetime, by Athens's maritime empire: the Athenians could afford to break the power of the oligarchs and concentrate all redistribution of surplus in the hands of a notionally egalitarian citizen body because it was deriving a tremendous income from its enslaved (as Thucydides put it) neighbors. The Israelites were not a small, self-selecting sect but a state, and a poor one, with no overseas holdings to exploit, and so the Torah's utopianism was especially difficult to enact.

To put it differently, the Jews had a range of possible responses to the utopianism—or the dysfunctionality—of their normative ideology. At one extreme lay sectarian withdrawal. In antiquity there were small Jewish groups that attempted to enact the Torah's social vision without compromise, such as the Essenes or Dead Sea sectarians, who rejected not only patronage, friendship, and the trappings of honor but even, apparently, family and property—anything that would interfere with a life devoted to the service of God and his Torah.[20] The Essenes and similar groups, such

---

[19] For brilliant accounts of why and how Athenian democracy was less utopian than its congeners, see D. Cohen, *Law, Sexuality, and Society* and *Law, Violence, and Community in Classical Athens* (Cambridge: Cambridge University Press, 1995). It may be worth emphasizing again that what I am calling Mediterranean cultures and Mediterranean countercultures are in reality bound together: reciprocity-based societies normally validate a religious or political escape hatch, and antireciprocal societies at best can only try to subordinate reciprocity, not eliminate it (unless they are very small sectlike groups), so that both sets might in real life might be much closer than in my account, but this constant accommodation and how it plays out culturally is precisely my topic in this book.

[20] For a general discussion, see A. Baumgarten, *The Flourishing of Jewish Sects in the Maccabean Era: An Interpretation* (Leiden: Brill, 1997).

as the philosophical schools of Old Greece, relied on the existence in pre-destruction Judaea of unusually large numbers of well-to-do pious men from whom they could draw new adherents and new funds.[21] The one such Jewish extremist group known to us that was devoted not to self-enclosure but to expansion, the Christians, almost immediately was forced to compromise its highly egalitarian and communitarian ideals, which were in the event left to small groups of Christian extremists, such as monks.[22]

At the opposite extreme lay radical integration, the abandonment of all but the most symbolic adherence to the Jews' distinctive Torah-derived ideology, if that. This was an option taken in Hellenistic and Roman antiquity by many more Jews than the evidence shows, because Jews who became fully integrated in their environments are, ipso facto, nearly or totally invisible in the evidence.[23] A significant exception may be the situation in northern Palestine for a century and a half after the Bar Kokhba revolt. I have argued that archaeological and some literary evidence demonstrates that this was a society that remained loosely Jewish and in which the strongly Jewish rabbis coalesced as a group and began to acquire support, but whose public life was dominated by conventional eastern Roman urban cultural norms, including religious norms.[24] To be sure, not every critic has been convinced, but if I am right, the case of high imperial Galilee shows that even radical conformism was compatible with the retention of some sense, however attenuated, of Jewish identity.

Between these extremes, though, lay a range of accommodative techniques that, I argue, were in fact the norm for all Jewish groups that wished to retain some sort of devotion to the normativity of the Torah and also function effectively as social and economic agents.

The Wisdom of Ben Sira is one of the earliest attempts by a Jewish sage and author to lay out a rationale for one such type of accommodation. Scholars have long noticed Ben Sira's pervasive tendency to yoke together "wisdom" and "piety," to use the language of modern theological scholarship. What they mean by this is that Ben Sira seems, on the one hand, completely devoted to Torah-based deuteronomistic piety—that is, the idea that those Israelites who observe the terms of the Covenant prosper and those who do not, suffer. On the other hand, Ben Sira's view of human

[21] See Schwartz, IJS, 91–98.

[22] See, for example, J. Rives, "Christian Expansion and Christian Ideology", in The Spread of Christianity in the First Four Centuries: Essays in Explanation, ed. W. V. Harris (Leiden: Brill, 2005), 15–41.

[23] On this, see G. Bohak, "Ethnic Continuity in the Jewish Diaspora in Antiquity," in Jews in the Hellenistic and Roman Cities, ed. J. Bartlett (London: Routledge, 2002), 175–92.

[24] Schwartz, IJS, 103–76.

social behavior is very pessimistic: exploitation and betrayal are everywhere, and sinners most definitely do not suffer, at least in the short term. Indeed, a large proportion of Ben Sira's teaching consists of advice about how to conduct successful friendships, and how to avoid falling victim to oppressive patrons and jealous or resentful relatives (especially wives and daughters), slaves and clients; no ancient Jewish text, including other wisdom texts, is as obsessed with gift exchange and institutionalized reciprocity as Ben Sira, nor is any other ancient Jewish text as focused on honor. But Ben Sira repeatedly insists that, while reciprocity is dangerous, the wise = pious = Torah observant (the three are equivalent in Ben Sira's thought) will succeed in mastering it, will dominate without being dominated, and indeed, that true honor inheres not (or not only) in wealth and worldly power but primarily in the fear of God. I will argue that Ben Sira is trying here to Judaize reciprocity and honor, to find a place for them in Jewish praxis despite the Torah's opposition or obliviousness.

The Jews' Integration in the Roman Empire

One of the most familiar problems in Western history concerns the long-term success of Rome's imperial project. Rome was a tremendously aggressive conqueror and came to rule an imperial state that was much more centralized and culturally uniform than any previous Mediterranean or Near Eastern empire had been (though it was still drastically less centralized and uniform than successful modern states of comparable size). And yet, for at least three centuries, starting with the Principate of Augustus (27 BCE), it employed a tiny amateur bureaucracy—provincial governors had no qualifications beyond the fact that they were landowning aristocrats, and had minuscule administrative staffs—and an army that was small (about 300,000 troops), given the population (estimated at ca. 50 million) and geographic extent of the empire.[25] In any case, the army was disproportionately concentrated on the northwestern frontier, along the Rhine and Danube rivers, leaving broad swaths of the most populous regions with no legionary presence at all. Some towns and cities had something like police, or at least municipal officials entrusted with keeping the peace, but many did not, and there is good reason to doubt

[25] On the size and amateurishness of the Roman imperial bureaucracy, often compared with that of imperial China, see K. Hopkins, *Death and Renewal: Sociological Studies in Roman History 2* (Cambridge: Cambridge University Press, 1983), 186–88; Saller, *Personal Patronage*, 111–16; and P. Garnsey and R. Saller, *The Roman Empire: Economy, Society and Culture* (Cambridge: Cambridge University Press, 1987), 21–26.

the efficacy of such officials as did exist in an environment where many people were routinely armed.[26] How, then, did Rome rule its empire so successfully?

There is no single solution to this problem. Terror, generated by Rome's well-known brutality to its enemies and sustained in peaceful times by the sanguinary entertainments of the amphitheater, was a factor.[27] So was the absence of conditions that would have enabled the mobilization of regional or national opposition.[28] But here I would like to focus briefly on another set of factors. One thing the Romans appear to have done with at least limited success was to co-opt and domesticate localized networks of social dependency (conditions were very different in the east and the west, but for my purposes mainly the east is relevant). This does not mean that the empire constituted a neat pyramid of dependency with the emperor at its peak, as *padrone di tutti padroni*. But it does mean that in the absence of a truly effective bureaucracy and a sufficiently large army, the Roman Empire had to govern through networks of local intermediaries. What distinguished Rome from its Hellenistic and Iranian predecessors was its success in shaping those mediators culturally and politically and in introducing some specifically Roman or Greco-Roman norms even into highly localized social institutions.[29] In many places, traditional institutions of social dependency acquired the trappings of Roman patronage and clientele, and cities, whatever their cultural background, tended to work through euergetism, the name modern scholars have given to the practice whereby wealthy citizens absorbed a disproportion of the public expenses of their cities and were reciprocated with public displays of gratitude and honor.[30] This is what I mean by domestication.

What does this all have to do with mediterraneanism, and, more to the point, what does it have to do with the Jews? The Roman imperial period is the only period in history when the Mediterranean basin (and adjacent areas) demonstrably shared elements of a single culture, and that culture had a recognizable affinity with ethnographic mediterraneanism, though

---

[26] See P. Brunt, "Did Rome Disarm Its Subjects?" in *Roman Imperial Themes* (Oxford: Oxford University Press, 1990), 255–81.

[27] Hopkins, *Death and Renewal*, 1–30.

[28] See G. Miles, "Roman and Modern Imperialism: A Reassessment," *CSSH* 32 (1990): 629–59. I return to this issue presently.

[29] See R. Saller, *Personal Patronage under the Early Empire* (Cambridge: Cambridge University Press, 1982); A. Wallace-Hadrill, ed., *Patronage in Ancient Society* (London: Routledge, 1989); and P. Veyne, *Le pain et le cirque: Sociologie historique d'un pluralisme politique* (Paris: Editions du Seuil, 1995; first edition 1976).

[30] On the function of honor as currency in Roman reciprocity-based institutions, see the account of Lendon, *Empire of Honor*.

it was not identical with it. To be sure, Roman patronage was diverse in its political, social, and economic functions. At higher social levels it was not unlike forms of patronage characteristic of eighteenth-century England or of France in the reign of Louis XIV—mainly a key to political and, to a lesser extent (at least in Rome), commercial advancement.[31] At lower social levels or in rural environments, it might still be a way of gaining access to officials, but it might serve more basic redistributive functions as well. But in either case, at its core the relationship bears a family resemblance to the range of ethnographic versions of patronage (the likes of which could also be found outside the Mediterranean basin).[32] Whether or not we accept some of the more extreme claims made about its importance, the Romans and many of the people under their rule certainly had conceptions of something like honor, and honor certainly was an element in the practice of euergetism, even though the vendetta and the blood feud—important components of ethnographic Mediterranean honor, though not every version of it—were of little ascertainable importance to the Romans in historical times, perhaps owing to the availability of a more or less effective court system; why murder when you can sue?

In this sense, my interest in the Jews' integration in the Roman state in various periods is a historically specific case of my investigation of the Jews, reciprocity, and the Mediterranean. But obviously politics makes a huge difference: Ben Sira, Josephus, and the Palestinian rabbis all struggled with notions of honor and reciprocity. The tension I am interested in, between institutionalized reciprocity and pious corporate solidarity, was systemic in premodern Judaism, as it was in Christianity. But the valence of this tension—its social effects, its political implications—was constantly changing: very different things were at stake in 180 BCE, 85 CE, and 300 CE. That is the interesting part of the story.

The Jews' Nonintegration in the Roman Empire

The Jews' integration into the Roman system was especially fraught. Objections to this claim may certainly be made: true, the Jews rebelled, but

[31] See Saller's argument that patronage was how administrative and military posts got filled. It thus fulfilled the function of the civil service exam, characteristic of imperial China and modern states. For the classic sociological analysis of patronage as intermediation and access, see S. N. Eisenstadt and L. Roniger, "Patron-Client Relations as a Model of Structuring Social Exchange," *CSSH* 22 (1980): 42–77.

[32] See E. Gellner and J. Waterbury, eds., *Patrons and Clients in Mediterranean Societies* (London: Duckworth, 1977), and the useful but rather odd discussion in Davis, *People of the Mediterranean*, 132–50.

provincial revolts were not uncommon in the Roman Empire, and the Roman state crushed them ruthlessly wherever they erupted. Furthermore, there has long been a tendency among historians, both Roman and Jewish, to assume the "abnormality" of the Jews. Roman historians have tended to regard the Jews as such eccentric Roman subjects that they are best ignored, whereas Jewish historians have often written the history of the Jews under Roman rule, especially after 135 CE, as if the Jews were not living under Roman rule at all but continued to constitute a fully autonomous or at least culturally self-enclosed entity. But these positions are, it may be argued, manifestly the products of bias, both of the historians and of their sources. It is thus necessary to strive to "normalize" the Jews, to provide them with a recognizably human history, to scrutinize their writing for hitherto overlooked evidence precisely of their normal and successful integration into the Roman Empire. Claims about the atypicality of the Jews must be regarded with utmost skepticism.

In fact, though, the Jews were inarguably unusual in various ways, and though in the final analysis they had to learn to cope with Roman rule, just as every other subject population did, the terms of their accommodation remain open for discussion. Meantime, let us recall several indisputable facts. No provincial population rebelled as many times and as disastrously as the Jews. The first hundred and thirty years of Roman rule in Palestine, beginning with Pompey's entry into Jerusalem in 63 BCE, featured the standard series of small uprisings and disturbances—for example, those that followed Herod's death in 4 BCE or that accompanied the census of Quirinius in 6 CE, or the sudden profusion of messiah figures (some of them armed) in the 30s and 40s. The Great Revolt, which began in the late spring of 66, was not wholly unlike other provincial revolts. It was generated in part by the cruelty of an amateurish Roman administration struggling to impose order, was led initially by a small group of partly Romanized elites, can thus be plausibly viewed as a by-product of an acculturative process, and was never universally popular in its province.[33] But in other ways it stood out: it was unusually durable—seven or eight years passed from the initial outbreak of disturbances in Jerusalem and Caesarea in 66 to the fall of Masada[34]—and was quelled with remarkable severity even by Roman standards. Jerusalem met the fate

---

[33] See the still suggestive though Western-focused S. L. Dyson, "Native Revolts in the Roman Empire," *Historia* 20 (1971): 239–74, and "Native Revolt Patterns in the Roman Empire," *ANRW* II.3, 138–75. T. Rajak preferred to compare it to early modern revolutions: *Josephus: The Historian and His Society* (London: Duckworth, 1983), 104–43.

[34] Which occurred either in 73 or, perhaps less likely, 74. See H. Cotton, "The Date of the Fall of Masada: The Evidence of the Masada Papyri," *ZPE* 78 (1989): 157–62.

that Carthage and Corinth had endured more than two centuries earlier—utter destruction.[35]

To be sure, there were several reasons apart from the unassimilability of the Jews in the Roman state for the peculiar features of their treatment. One reason the rebellion lasted so long was that it coincided with the final tumultuous years of Nero's reign and the year of chaos that followed his assassination; once affairs at Rome were settled, in July 69, the main part of the Jewish War was over within just over a year. The temple of Jerusalem and its priesthood had played a disproportionately large role in the revolt, and the siege had dragged on for several months—facts that partly explain the fate of Jerusalem at the hands of Titus. Another element was that the Flavians, the short-lived dynasty (69–96 CE) whose founder, Vespasian, commander of the Roman forces in Palestine, ascended to the throne in 69, needed a decisive victory to help establish their legitimacy (they were usurpers). The destruction of Jerusalem, the display of its rich plunder, both at the triumph and in the form of the reliefs decorating Titus's triumphal arch at the southern entrance to the Roman forum, and the construction of the massive Amphitheatrum Flavianum (better known as the Colosseum) just beyond the arch, on the site of Nero's scandalous Domus Aurea, from the spoils of the revolt (and possibly also the reconstruction of the temple of Jupiter Optimus Maximus on the Capitol using the revenues of the tax to the "Jewish fisc") all played crucial roles in confirming the credibility of Vespasian and his family as emperors.[36] Another factor was that by the later first century the emperors were finding indirect rule, through local institutions, increasingly unattractive; even without a rebellion the Herodian kings and aristocrats and the Jerusalem priesthood might eventually have gone the way of the Nabataean kings and the score of local princes of Syria and eastern Asia Minor. What then would have happened to the Jerusalem temple we can scarcely guess. What role would it have played after it ceased to serve as the center of the partly autonomous Jewish *ethnos* (nation), peaceably deconstituted by a shift in Roman policy, and after its priests lost their political power?

But these factors cannot explain why the Jews, this time mainly in the Egyptian and north African diasporas, rebelled again, in 116 and 117, and, having once again been crushed, rebelled yet again, in parts of Palestine,

---

[35] Unlike those cities, though, Jerusalem was looted, that is, it was never declared *sacer*. See W. V. Harris, *War and Imperialism in Republican Rome 327–70 BC* (Oxford: Clarendon Press, 1979), 234–44.

[36] See the important account of F. Millar, "Last Year in Jerusalem: Monuments of the Jewish War in Rome," in *Flavius Josephus and Flavian Rome*, ed. J. Edmondson, S. Mason, and J. Rives (Oxford: Oxford University Press, 2005), 101–28.

including but not necessarily limited to the district of Judaea, between 132 and 135—the so-called Bar Kokhba revolt. We know relatively little about these events, since no history comparable to Josephus's history of the Great Revolt survives for them, but in both cases their consequences seem fairly certain. There is next to no evidence for Jews in Egypt or Cyrenaica (roughly modern Libya) from 117 to the end of the third century, and for its part, the Bar Kokhba revolt seems to have ended with something like the depopulation of the district of Judaea. Aelia Capitolina, the new Roman city founded on the ruins of Jerusalem (probably in 130),[37] was never more than a tiny backwater; Jerusalem and its Judaean hinterland did not begin to recover until the fourth century, when they benefited from their theological importance to Christians: eventually Jerusalem became a major ecclesiastical and Christian pilgrimage center, and Judaea served as home to thousands of monks.[38]

Though the Roman state was not above treating *all* its subjects with brutality if it felt it needed to (Tacitus could have the Caledonian rebel leader Calgacus say of the Romans, *solitudinem faciunt, pacem appellant*—they make a wilderness and call it peace; *Agricola* 30), it is clear that the Jews were different, an observation much less banal than one might think.[39] It will not do to follow one recent account in attributing the entire calamitous mess that was the first century of Roman-Jewish relations to a series of accidents.[40] After all, the Jews had on the whole adapted as well as anyone to the rule of earlier Near Eastern and Mediterranean empires, and small groups of Jews seemed to cope adequately in the Roman diaspora. Clearly, something was distinctively wrong with the relations between the Jews qua national group and the Roman state, and whatever these problems consisted of, they did not persist in quite the same way later. After 135 there was no major Jewish rising against Rome, not even when the Jewish population, which was drastically reduced throughout the Roman Empire in the aftermath of the three revolts (a fact I did not

---

[37] On the diaspora revolt, see M. Pucci Ben Zeev, *Diaspora Judaism in Turmoil, 116/117 CE: Ancient Sources and Modern Insights* (Leuven: Peeters, 2005), and P. Schäfer, ed., *The Bar Kokhba War Reconsidered: New Perspectives on the Second Jewish Revolt Against Rome* (Tübingen: Mohr Siebeck, 2003).

[38] See Y. Hirschfeld, *The Judean Desert Monasteries in the Byzantine Period* (New Haven, CT: Yale University Press, 1992).

[39] Especially in light of the laudable and proper effort by more enlightened scholars—Goodman, discussed below, is an excellent example—to "historicize" the Jews, that is, to describe them as recognizable human beings, explicable as more or less conventional historical agents. But it is incorrect to infer from this that they—to the extent that the Jews persisted in constituting a group, as opposed to individual Jews—can be described as conventional Roman subjects. As I show later, Goodman tried to do this but failed.

[40] See Goodman, *Rome and Jerusalem*, and the discussion below.

emphasize sufficiently in *Imperialism and Jewish Society*), apparently began to recover to some extent in the third and fourth centuries.[41]

In sum, the problem apparently transcended the circumstances that led to the outbreaks of the three revolts. Although each had its locally specific causes, when we step back from the events we can see that each was to some extent a manifestation of a deeper, structural problem, one that was in effect solved once the third revolt was crushed. (This having been said, though, it seems legitimate to focus on the first revolt, to treat it as in some measure diagnostic of the deeper problems; in fact, such a focus is inevitable because the first revolt is so well attested.) To my knowledge the issue has rarely been framed at so high a level of abstraction (I discuss an exception below), and to the extent that scholars have, usually in passing in the course of detailed monographic studies, wondered why the Jews were so difficult to integrate into the Roman system, they have resorted to truisms in place of explanation.

Now, truisms are not always completely false; they are just too pat and simplistic. Thus, the idea that ancient Judaism validated organized and sustained resistance to foreign rule (an idea that reached its apogee in the massively detailed work of Martin Hengel)[42] is now generally dismissed: Judaism was possibly created and certainly sustained by the Achaemenid rulers of the Near East (539–332 BCE) and by some of their Macedonian successors. By contrast, another common idea, that the Jews' monotheism stood in the way, must in broad terms be partly correct but requires fleshing out to have any real explanatory power. It is in any case perfectly plausible to search the Jews' religion, and not some set of social or economic contingencies, for the structural aspects of the Jews' nonintegration, though such a religion-based hypothesis must confront the fact that Judaism in some measure survived the Jews' successful integration into the Roman state after 135.

Another approach was adumbrated by Brent Shaw, one of the very few historians who actually asked and tried systematically to answer questions about the Jews' failed integration before 66 CE. He argued that for the Jews, all power was mediated through individuals, in ways that precluded any ability to deal with the unusually institutionalized and depersonalized Roman state.[43] Personal power was important in first-century

---

[41] Notwithstanding the obscure hints dropped by some Christian chroniclers about a Jewish uprising against Gallus Caesar in 352. See G. Stemberger, *Jews and Christians in the Holy Land: Palestine in the Fourth Century* (Edinburgh: Clark, 1999), 161–84.

[42] See M. Hengel, *Die Zeloten: Untersuchungen zur jüdischen Freiheitsbewegung in der Zeit von Herodes I. Bis 70 n. Chr.* (Leiden: Brill, 1976).

[43] B. Shaw, "Josephus: Roman Power and Jewish Responses to It," *Athenaeum* 83 (1995): 357–90.

Jewish Palestine, as Shaw argues, but there was much more to Judaean politics and social relations than that, as I discuss in chapter 4.

In what follows I briefly analyze the best extended treatment of the background of the first revolt that I am aware of, that of Martin Goodman, who focused on the social and economic impact of Judaism on the life of the Jews, especially in Judaea.[44] For Goodman, Roman rule empowered groups of Jews, especially members of the Herodian family and leading priests of the Jerusalem temple, whose rise generated a social and economic crisis. They, and the temple they controlled, accumulated vast quantities of wealth in a way that tended to push Judaean smallholders off their land and into lives of debt, penury, and brigandage. The Jews lacked the practices of rural patronage and urban euergetism, which might have provided a measure of social stability for some farmers and artisans, and instead practiced charity, which kept the poor alive, numerous, unhappy, and socially unmoored.

Goodman's more or less explicit intention was to rescue first-century Judaea from theologians by normalizing the Jews as Roman subjects. Goodman wished to attribute the Jews' rebellion precisely to locally specific causes and not to deeper structural problems (while not absolutely excluding the importance of religious issues in the background of the revolt, pp. 11–2).[45] By replacing the standard theologizing, or ideologizing, accounts of the ancient Jews with an account rooted in specific material, economic, and social conditions, he set out to demonstrate that there was no essential misfit between Judaism and Roman rule, only an accidental crisis generated primarily by the Romans' improvident promotion of Jewish *novi homines* ("new men"—recently created aristocrats).

Despite his declared intentions, though, Goodman's Judaeans seem far less normal, and to have much more in common with the theologians' Jews, than he supposed (as he practically concedes, pp. 97–108); he came close to admitting that Judaism—and so the Jews, to the extent that they persisted in adhering to it—was in some sense systemically unassimilable in the Roman state. Indeed, in Goodman's view (though not in his language), the only thing actually integrating the Judaeans internally was ideology, a shared devotion to the Jerusalem temple and to the Torah.

---

[44] M. Goodman, *The Ruling Class of Judaea: The Origins of the Jewish Revolt Against Rome A.D. 66–70* (Cambridge: Cambridge University Press, 1987). The view presented here is greatly expanded in Goodman's *Rome and Jerusalem: The Clash of Ancient Civilizations* (London: Penguin, 2007), but fundamentally little altered. For fuller discussion, see S. Schwartz, "*Sunt Lachrymae Rerum*: Martin Goodman's *Rome and Jerusalem*," *JQR* 99 (2009): 56–64.

[45] Erich Gruen's approach to the Jewish-Greek mini-war in Alexandria (38–41 CE) is even more dismissive of the possibility of structural problems: *Diaspora: Jews amidst Greeks and Romans* (Cambridge, MA: Harvard University Press, 2002).

They had no networks of social dependency, reciprocity having given way to the contract as the basis of exchange (as if these were mutually exclusive; see the previous chapter), and patronage to charity. If all states are in some measure imagined communities,[46] Judaea, with its overcentralized economy but fundamental lack of materially based social cohesion, constituted a community far more imagined than most. In fact, it proved to be remarkably fragile, shattering under Roman pressure into competing little groups of extremists, since religious sectarianism and ideological extremism offered the only realistic forms of social cohesion available. Goodman's account, then, explores the dark, dysfunctional side of the Pentateuch's utopian legislation.

To be sure, viewing the situation of the Jews in first-century Palestine through the prism of the failed revolt and the destruction encourages an emphasis on dysfunction. Still, we may wonder whether, in arguing for the Jews' normality as Roman subjects, Goodman paradoxically did not greatly overstate their abnormality.[47] In particular, much of Goodman's ethnography or religious history, especially in *Ruling Class* but to a surprising extent even in *Rome and Jerusalem*, proceeds by treating prescriptive texts as descriptive: the Jews' holy books were obsessed with purity; ergo, real-life Jews were so obsessed; the Torah enjoins charity and disapproves of patronage, so the Jews did, too; and so on. But this prejudges the question of the relation between the Jews' core religious ideology and their culture—their workaday attitudes, practices, and social institutions.

In chapter 4 of this book I try to provide a more nuanced account of some of these issues by reading Josephus, not primarily for what he has to say about the causes and course of the Jewish revolt against Rome but for his own attitudes about issues that have seemed of peripheral interest to most Judaic scholars who have studied Josephus's works but may have been of crucial importance for Josephus's Roman and Greek contemporaries and patrons, and fateful for the ancient Jews themselves. Josephus provides a surprising amount of information and editorial comment, much of it hitherto little noticed, about what modern scholars since Veyne have called euergetism, the cultural practice of benefaction, memorialization, and honor characteristic of urban life in the Hellenistic

---

[46] See B. Anderson, *Imagined Communities: Reflections on the Origins and Spread of Nationalism* (London: Verso, 1991; first published 1983).

[47] See B. Shaw, Review of Goodman, *JRS* 79 (1989): 246–7, partly conceded in M. Goodman, "Current Scholarship on the First Revolt," in *The First Jewish Revolt: Archaeology, History and Ideology*, ed. A. Berlin and J. A. Overman (London: Routledge, 2002), 15–25. Yet the same approach is pushed even farther in *Rome and Jerusalem*.

world and the early and high Roman Empire. Euergetism was a reciprocal relationship—the benefactor shouldered his (or more rarely her) city's public expenses and was repaid with honor and commemoration by the citizens—an adaptation of patronage to the communitarian ideology of the later Greek and Roman city, or alternatively a kind of synthesis of oligarchy and democracy whose ceremonial manifestations contained features of both.

Euergetism, as a creator of ties of corporate dependency, as a highly conformist culture (since euergetism, often fuelled by intercity competition, tended to produce cities that were essentially carbon copies one of the other, with the same sorts of buildings and monuments, the same sorts of public entertainments, the same general sorts of socioeconomic behaviors, the same standards of elite education and deportment), was one of the fundamental building blocks of the Roman political pyramid. Josephus's comments on the subject are of special interest not only because they have never really been studied before but also because he himself was surprisingly opposed, or partly opposed, to the practice, and claimed the Jews were, too, a claim partly—but only partly—confirmed by archaeology and epigraphy.

Rome and the Rabbis

We may pause at this point to consider a minor paradox: Jewish writers and intellectuals who lived to see the disastrous unraveling of relations between Rome and the Jews—most important among them Philo of Alexandria and Josephus—tended to be highly integrationist. Admittedly, this is a simplification: unlike his Ptolemaic-era and strongly pro-royal spiritual forebear, the Alexandrian Jewish writer who posed as the courtier Aristeas, Philo freely acknowledged his doubts about the benefits of Roman rule and the possibility of Roman-Jewish coexistence. Nevertheless, he remained firmly committed to Jewish-Greek integration at Alexandria even after the strife between Greeks and Jews there in 38 CE. Philo's much younger Jerusalemite contemporary, Josephus (37 CE–ca.100), insisted that Judaism was reconcilable with Roman rule, but the only model he had for Roman-Jewish coexistence was one that even in his lifetime may have come to seem outdated: Roman support for the autonomy, the "ancestral laws," of the Jews, a regime that had in reality come to an end in 70. It is furthermore striking that, unlike other Greek writers who were also Roman citizens, Josephus viewed the Romans primarily as powerful and fearsome, not as beneficial; even in the more pro-Roman *Jewish War*, he did not fully identify with his Roman overlords.[48] Nevertheless, Josephus never abandoned his essentially pro-Roman orientation, even in his later, more pro-Jewish, works, written, not coincidentally, after he had lost imperial patronage.

By contrast, the Palestinian rabbis, who, once the Bar Kokhba revolt was crushed, are not known to have offered any material (as opposed to symbolic) resistance to Rome, and whose attested existence largely coincided with the pax romana at its height, never concealed their hostility. Furthermore, unlike Philo and Josephus, whose very literary style was an aspect of their embrace of cultural and political integration in the hellenophone Roman east, the rabbis produced a set of writings that, first of all, were in Hebrew and Aramaic, never Greek, and second, were fundamentally unlike anything else ever written in the Roman world. The rabbis *performed* their political and cultural marginality in their teaching and writing.[49]

In both cases, we are entitled to ask what was happening behind the cultural performance. In the cases of Philo and Josephus, we happen to know, because the authors more or less tell us: Philo's integrationism was intellectual and aspirational; he was genuinely devoted both to the Torah and to Greek philosophy and really believed not simply in their reconcilability but in the fundamental identity of their teachings. For all that, and for all his wealth and social distinction on top of it, he did not deceive himself about the nature of the real-life relations between Jews and Greeks in Roman Alexandria, or about whose side the emperors Gaius and Claudius were really on. Josephus for his part was a cultural and political shape-shifter, the sort of unscrupulous colonial product much beloved of contemporary theorists, who in his time had not hesitated to fight the Romans, and admitted that he had joined the Roman side to save his own skin. Yet even while living in Vespasian's house in Rome he could never bring himself to identify with his captors (at least not politically; his personal adulation of Titus is a different matter).

---

[48] See M. Goodman, "Josephus as a Roman Citizen," in *Josephus and the History of the Greco-Roman Period: Essays in Memory of Morton Smith*, ed. F. Parente and J. Sievers (Leiden: Brill, 1994), 329–38.

[49] I thus differ sharply from those who, in the wake of Saul Lieberman's brief English books, *Greek in Jewish Palestine* and *Hellenism in Jewish Palestine*, argued for the essential cultural normalcy of the rabbis in a Roman imperial context: see S. Schwartz, "Historiography on the Jews in the 'Talmudic Period,' 70–640 CE," and "The Rabbi in Aphrodite's Bath: Palestinian Society and Jewish Identity in the High Roman Empire" in *Being Greek under Rome: Cultural Identity, the Second Sophistic and the Development of Empire*, ed. S. Goldhill (Cambridge: Cambridge University Press, 2001), 335–61.

In the case of the rabbis, we know much less about what underlay the cultural performances, and I do not believe it will ever be possible to provide a full account. However, some basic historical points may be emphasized. As I have suggested above and argued elsewhere,[50] in the aftermath of the revolts the Jews were so drastically reduced, numerically speaking, that the activities of a handful of self-proclaimed Jewish sages were probably of little interest to Rome. In the middle and later second century, the rabbis were probably nearly invisible to the authorities, and presumably as long as they refrained from the suicidal advocacy of further revolt, they probably had a certain paradoxical freedom (as the qualifications suggest, this is speculative). But once the Jews' demographic and political recovery began to gain force, in the third and especially the fourth century, the rabbis were again confronted with a dilemma. Serious opposition was by this time probably no more an option for most rabbis than it was for most Christian bishops, or at any rate its cost would have been much higher than earlier: a truly marginal existence on the fringes of society, flight, imprisonment, death. The only reasonable alternative was some kind of accommodation. In practice, some, or even many, rabbis were employed as members of the patriarchal retinue and staff, or as judges or religious functionaries. This meant they were part of what by the middle and later third century was beginning to emerge as a Jewish quasi-government in Palestine, headed by a Jewish dynast who was thoroughly romanized and whose descendants in the fourth century would be the first and only known Roman senators who were "professing" Jews (there had been senators of remotely Jewish origin, descendants of Herod, already in the early second century). The rabbis' growing ambivalence toward the patriarchal dynasty in the course of the third century has been amply demonstrated by others.[51]

Even those rabbis who lacked patriarchal patronage were still (after 212) city-based Roman citizens normally of prosperous, not necessarily very wealthy, background. In the final sections of the book I show that the rabbis struggled with some Roman values and quietly appropriated others. Honor and patronage, centrally important Roman ideas and institutions, as well as crucial components of ethnographic mediterraneanism, turn out to be important issues in rabbinic literature, too.

---

[50] S. Schwartz, "Political, Social, and Economic Life in the Land of Israel, 66–c.235," in *Cambridge History of Judaism*, ed. S. Katz vol. 4 (Cambridge: Cambridge University Press, 2006), 23–52.

[51] See, for example, L. Levine, "The Jewish Patriarch in Third Century Palestine," *ANRW* II 19.2 (1979): 649–88.

CHAPTER THREE

A God of Reciprocity

Torah and Social Relations

in the Wisdom of Jesus ben Sira

The Text of Ben Sira

The Wisdom of Jesus ben Sira (Sirach; Ecclesiasticus) is an "apocryphal" book (that is, one not included in the Jewish or Protestant biblical canons) composed at Jerusalem around 180 BCE. About three-fifths of the book survives in some approximation of the original Hebrew,[1] courtesy of six fragmentary high medieval manuscripts discovered in the 1890s in the *genizah* (damaged book depository) of the Ben Ezra Synagogue in Fustat (Old Cairo), Egypt.[2] The qualification is necessary because, while there is now no doubt that the Genizah manuscripts reflect the original Hebrew and are not a retranslation from later Greek or Syriac versions, as some once believed, the manuscripts, where they overlap, often preserve very different texts, all of them differing in significant ways from the Greek (which itself exhibits very wide divergences between manuscripts), and all of these differ in turn from the ancient fragments of the text discovered on Masada in 1964 (though the latter are close enough to the Genizah texts to demonstrate the latter's fundamental authenticity).

---

[1] For an introduction to Ben Sira, see J. J. Collins, *Jewish Wisdom in the Hellenistic Age* (Louisville, KY: Westminster John Knox Press, 1997), 21–111; the text is discussed on pages 42–44. All the texts quoted below were translated by me from (where relevant) the Hebrew text of M. Z. Segal, *Sefer Ben Sira Ha-Shalem* (Jerusalem: Mossad Bialik, 1972; first published 1953), corrected against and supplemented by P. Beentjes, *The Book of Ben Sira in Hebrew: A Text Edition of All Extant Hebrew Manuscripts and a Synopsis of All Parallel Hebrew Ben Sira Texts* (Leiden: Brill, 1997), 57–59, and otherwise from the Greek text of J. Ziegler, *Sapientia Iesu Filii Sirach* (Göttingen: Vandenhoeck-Ruprecht, 1965). The best commentaries by far remain those of Segal (a judgment some specialists may find eccentric but is in my view defensible) and of R. Smend, *Die Weisheit des Jesus Sirach, hebräisch und deutsch* (Berlin: Georg Reimer, 1906).

[2] For an account, see S. Reif, "The Discovery of the Cambridge Genizah Fragments of Ben Sira: Scholars and Texts," in *The Book of Ben Sira in Modern Research: Proceedings of the First International Ben Sira Conference, 28–31 July 1996, Soesterberg, Netherlands*, ed. P. Beentjes, BZAW 255 (Berlin: de Gruyter, 1997), 1–22.

Ben Sira is thus the only book of the apocrypha demonstrably copied and read by Jews deep into the Middle Ages; the Genizah manuscripts were written in the twelfth century. In fact, Ben Sira's status was anomalous: it is also the only nonbiblical book to have been quoted approvingly in the Talmud (providing an additional collection of early textual witnesses).

For those sections of the book of which no Hebrew manuscripts survive, we rely on a Greek translation produced (according to its prologue) by the author's grandson, who can, however, be shown to have altered Ben Sira's Hebrew wisdom in ways great and small.[3] The state of the text of Ben Sira thus constitutes a hermeneutical problem in an unusually basic and direct way. For this reason, and because of my conviction that my reading of Ben Sira is novel and needs to be argued, I decided to present the texts and to lay out as clearly and briefly as possible my arguments about their interpretation, including, where relevant, and normally in footnotes, brief discussion of textual and philological problems. Many of the texts I comment on are brief, but those on which the discussion of the social hierarchy are based (see pp. 66–70) consist of full chapters or more, and so cannot be conveniently presented in the text. These, and the accompanying philological and textual discussions, are consigned instead to appendix 1.

The Sage and His Book

Ben Sira is the only Hebrew text from the time of the Israelite prophets down to the Middle Ages whose author is apparently nonpseudepigraphic and appears also to tell us something about himself—for example, his occupation (sage or teacher) and his social position (middling). He also identifies himself as a contemporary (and probably also as a compatriot) of the Jerusalemite high priest Simon, known to have lived around the year 200 BCE. The brute fact of the book's unusually precise contextualizability, and the further fact that it was written immediately preceding the Maccabean Revolt, lend it a particular historical importance. But this has

---

[3] Ben Sira's Hebrew is exceptionally difficult, both archaizing and eccentric. Though there is uncertainty in many individual cases, it would be uncontroversial to say that frequently the author of the Greek text simply misunderstood his grandfather ("grandfather"?), and that in other cases the changes were conscious, leaving aside those cases where his Hebrew text differed. See in detail—with a focus on the Greek translator's Hebrew *Vorlage*—B. Wright, *No Small Difference: Sirach's Relation to Its Hebrew Parent Text* (Atlanta, GA: Scholars Press, 1989). On both the incomprehensibility of the Hebrew text and the Greek translator's misunderstandings, see also M. Kister, "A Contribution to the Interpretation of Ben Sira," *Tarbiz* 59 (1990): 303–78; esp. 306.

been to some extent undermined by a tradition of generalizing and de-contextualizing translation and interpretation, exemplified in the recent past by the Anchor Bible Ben Sira.[4] By contrast, I argue that while the book cannot easily be situated in a speculatively specific political or cultural context—a debate about the reception of Greek culture, for example—many of its teachings are very unlike the blandly commonplace sentiments attributed to it by so many translators and commentators.

The book of Ben Sira is animated by a literary and ideological tension that mirrors the social tension between reciprocity and solidarity described in the first chapter of this book. To be sure, if read selectively, the book seems to constitute a conservative reaction to the radicalism of such slightly earlier or near-contemporary Israelite wisdom or wisdom-associated books as Job (sixth to fourth centuries BCE?), Ecclesiastes and the older sections of the compilation modern scholars call 1 Enoch (both third century BCE)[5]: the first responds to the problematic presence of evil in the world by imagining God to be transcendent and inscrutable, basically dismissing the human search for an answer to the problem of evil as useless; the other two follow in Job's footsteps conceptually but are more radical; for the former, the world, both natural and human, is in a condition of amoral stasis, while the author of the Book of Watchers (1 Enoch 1–36), acknowledging the mysteriousness of God's ways, nevertheless claims knowledge of and seeks to reveal the mysteries, and supposes they consist of the sort of basically polytheistic cosmological mythology the author of Genesis 1–11 had been careful to avoid: evil was introduced into the world by subordinate deities as an act of rebellion against the authority of their divine overlord. Ben Sira, though, rejected, more or less explicitly, both the sophistication of Job and Ecclesiastes and 1 Enoch's audacious revival of myth, and apparently advocated a return to the piety of the Deuteronomist: no evil befalls those who fear the Lord and observe his commandments.[6] This simplistic-seeming piety, which rests on the conviction that God's creation is well-ordered and just, is in tension with

[4] P. W. Skehan and A. A. di Lella, *The Wisdom of Ben Sira* (Anchor Bible 39) (New York: Doubleday, 1987).

[5] For this characterization of Ben Sira, see A. A. di Lella, "Conservative and Progressive Theology: Sirach and Wisdom," *CBQ* 38 (1966); 139–54. For discussion of the date of Job see M. Pope, *Job* (Anchor Bible) (New York: Doubleday, 1965), xxxii–xl; the issue is unresolved. The earliest Qumran fragments of the earliest components of 1 Enoch, "Watchers" (ch. 1–36) and the "Astronomical Book" (ch. 72–82), are dated paleographically to ca. 200 BCE: see A. Y. Reed, *Fallen Angels and the History of Judaism and Christianity: The Reception of Enochic Literature* (Cambridge: Cambridge University Press, 2005), 16–23. On Qohelet's date, see T. C. Vriezen and A. S. van der Woude, *Ancient Israelite and Early Jewish Literature* (Leiden: Brill, 2005), 459–60.

[6] Ben Sira 3.20–24 is normally understood as a rejection of apocalyptic speculation, but notes that it does not question the desirability of secret knowledge but rather claims (if we follow the

a hardheaded practicality about social relations that takes for granted a very different view of the world: when Ben Sira is not advocating an optimistic Pentateuchal piety, he is offering advice about coping with a world in which the poor and the suffering are frequently righteous, the rich and powerful are unjust, and very few people can be trusted—a world, in sum, closer to that imagined by Qohelet than to that of the Deuteronomist.

In fact, the Wisdom of Ben Sira consists of much more than a reassertion of Pentateuchal piety; it contains the following elements: (1) hymns to and praises of wisdom, repeatedly identified with fear of God; (2) exhortations to piety, study of the Torah and observance of its laws, both general and specific (especially cult-related, and charity [see below] but not, for example, the Sabbath or food laws)[7]; (3) advice on relations to one's fellows, including friends, social superiors, hosts, guests or parasites (dining figures prominently in the book), dependents, family members, slaves, and women; reciprocity is a near-constant theme, and gift exchange is mentioned frequently; (4) there are two long hymns to nature (39.15–35; 42.15–43.33), the second of which rivals the nature Psalms in its majesty; (5) the book concludes (ignoring chapters 51–52, which may not be an original part of the book) with a poem recounting the *aretai,* the glorious achievements, of the fathers of the Jewish nation (44–50).

One of the striking peculiarities of the book is that almost every pericope in the third category of passages contains an exhortation to piety or wisdom or fear of God, or asserts that the pious man will succeed socially. Similarly, and equally problematically, Ben Sira makes it clear that he regards his social advice as a component of wisdom, but it is very difficult to reconcile this with the repeated identification, throughout the book, of wisdom with Torah and fear of the Lord. The mood of the passages that provide social instruction is generally very remote from that of their pious tags. Indeed, whether or not we accept the common hypothesis that in his social teachings Ben Sira was indebted to the first book of elegiac poems attributed to the archaic Greek sage Theognis (a hypothesis that is far from absurd),[8] an eccentric Greek city seems an appropriate setting for much of this material.

Hebrew rather than the Greek of 3.20) that God grants such knowledge only to the humble, and not to the hubristic pursuers of mysteries.

[7] Though Sabbaths and festivals are in a single passage adduced as demonstrations of God's wisdom: 33.7–9. On Ben Sira and the cult, see B. G. Wright III, "'Fear the Lord and Honor the Priest': Ben Sira as Defender of the Jerusalem Priesthood," in *The Book of Ben Sira in Modern Research: Proceedings of the First International Ben Sira Conference, 28–31 July 1996, Soesterberg, Netherlands,* ed. P. C. Beentjes, BZAW 255 (Berlin: de Gruyter, 1997), 189–222.

[8] For a balanced discussion, see J. T. Sanders, *Ben Sira and Demotic Wisdom* (Chico, CA: Scholars Press, 1983), 29–38.

I would like to suggest two solutions to this anomaly. The first is internalist and draws attention to a remarkable though not unambiguous passage that at least may help explain how Ben Sira was able to identify correct social behavior as part of Torah (and see the "grandson's prologue"); the second does not rely on the first. It involves more detailed discussion of the content of Ben Sira's social teaching and will suggest that the literary-ideological tension found throughout the Wisdom of Ben Sira constitutes an attempt to resolve the social tension I described in the previous chapters.

My suggestions are not meant to exclude other possibilities. John Collins and David Winston have written of Ben Sira's "nationalization of wisdom" through its identification with Torah or, to put it differently, his universalization of Torah, and, rejecting Hengel's extreme contention that this constituted a frontal attack on Hellenism, they see it with more subtlety as a declaration of competition. "In an age when Hellenic wisdom dominated the civilized world, [Ben Sira] did his best to broaden the borders of the Mosaic law so that it would encompass every manifestation of wisdom".[9] Still more interestingly, Winston notes that Ben Sira shared with and probably borrowed from the Stoics the notion that the universe consists of the harmony of opposites—an idea perhaps implicit in the jarring juxtapositions and incoherent combinations that form the topic of this chapter.[10] While Winston is concerned with their philosophical foundations, I am concerned with the sociopolitical work they perform.

Solution 1: God's Three Laws

In the following pages I argue that Ben Sira 16.24–17.23 constitutes the author's attempt to provide a hermeneutical solution to the problem just described, by showing how God gave a Torah to all humanity—in addition to those given to all creation and to Israel alone—that contained rules for correct social interaction. Here Ben Sira argues from biblical narrative that etiquette *is* piety, or Torah.

[9] G. Sterling, ed., *The Ancestral Philosophy: Hellenistic Philosophy in Second Temple Judaism. Essays of David Winston*, Brown Judaic Studies 331, Studia Philonica Monographs 4 (Providence, RI: Brown Judaic Studies, 2001), 35–36.

[10] On the other hand, the fullest extant Stoic, or Stoic-tinged, account of reciprocity, Seneca's massive treatise on benefits, idealizes it, and while recognizing that it can be abused, regards liberality—and its recompense—as a high social ideal, not, in a Sirachian vein, as a peril to be managed. Seneca's view seems basically traditionally Stoic, in a way that problematizes Ben Sira's relationship with Stoicism. On Seneca's debt to Stoicism, including his idealization of reciprocity, see Inwood, "Politics and Paradox in Seneca's *De beneficiis*," and Griffin, "*De Beneficiis* and Roman Society."

Ben Sira 16.24–17.23 (preserved mainly in Greek) reads[11]:

16.24. Hear me, son, and learn knowledge
and attend to my words in your heart (=mind).

16.25. I will disclose instruction by measure
and in precision [Geniza MS A: "with modesty"] will I
announce knowledge.

16.26. When the Lord created His works in the beginning
from [the time of] His making of them did He divide
them in parts.

16.27. He set in order their works for eternity
and their reigns for [all] their generations;
they grew neither hungry nor weary
nor did they leave off from their works.

16.28. None of them oppressed his neighbor
and for all eternity they will not disobey His word.

16.29. And after these things, the Lord observed the earth
and filled it with all his good things.

16.30. He covered its face with the spirit of every living thing
and into it is their return.

17.1. The Lord created man from earth
and returned him again into it.

17.2. He gave to them days of number and a final time [kai-
ros]
and He gave to them authority over all things on it
[earth].

17.3. Like Himself, He clothed them in strength and in His
own image did He make them.

17.4. He placed fear of him [man] on all flesh
so that he ruled over beasts and birds.

17.6.[12] Deliberation [diaboulion; Segal tr. yetzer] and tongue
and eyes
ears and heart did He give to them so that they might
have understanding.

17.7. He filled them with the knowledge of wisdom
and pointed out good and wicked things to them.

17.8. He set the fear of Himself into their hearts
to show to them the greatness of His deeds.

17.9. And they will praise His holy name

[11] All translations in this chapter are mine unless otherwise indicated.
[12] Verse 5 is omitted in most manuscripts.

17.10. that they might retell the greatness of his deeds.

17.11. He placed before them knowledge, and a law of life
[*nomon zoes*] did He grant to them as an inheritance.

17.12. He established with them an eternal covenant
and its decrees did He show to them.

17.13. Their eyes saw the greatness of His glory
and the glory of His voice did their ears hear.

17.14. And He said to them, "Keep apart from all injustice";
and He instructed them each concerning his [behavior
toward his] neighbor.

17.15. Their paths are before His eyes always they will not be
concealed from His eyes.

17.17. For each nation He appointed a ruler,
and Israel is the portion of the Lord.

17.19. All of their deeds are as the sun before Him,
and His eyes are perpetually on their paths.

17.20. Their injustices were not concealed from Him,
and all their sins are before the Lord.

17.22. The charity [*eleemosune*—surely *zedaqah*, righteousness,
as Segal] of a man is as a seal before him
and he will guard a person's *charis* [=*hesed*] like the
pupil of his eye.

17.23. After these things He will rise up and repay them;
and He will repay their recompense on their heads.

This poem describes three divine laws, of ascending importance, but also progressively more difficult to observe.[13] First are the laws God gave at Creation to all nature (16.27)—laws observed by the elements of nature in complete internal harmony and with no disobedience to the divine command (16.28)—with the clear implication, as in Psalms 148.6 and 1 Enoch 2–5, that nature's behavior is meant to serve as an example for humanity. The second law (17.1ff.) is that given to mankind as a whole. Ben Sira here is following the biblical narrative fairly closely, moving through Creation to the primordial history of humanity, with the covenant of 17.12

---

[13] In the "praise of the fathers" (44–50), too, Ben Sira emphasizes a multiplicity of covenants, and may have regarded them, or some of them, as progressively more important; cf. R. Horsley and P. Tiller, "Ben Sira and the Sociology of the Second Temple", in *Second Temple Studies III: Studies in Politics, Class and Material Culture*, JSOT Supplement Series 340, ed. P. R. Davies and J. M. Halligan (Sheffield, UK: Sheffield Academic Press, 2002), 74–107. Argall, *I Enoch and Sirach: A Comparative Literary and Conceptual Analysis of the Themes of Revelation, Creation and Judgement* (Atlanta, GA: Scholars Press, 1995), 136–68, believes the passage describes two torahs, one given to nature and one given to humanity and Israel.

referring perhaps to God's covenant with Noah and his sons (Gen 9.1–17), though according to one widespread interpretation 17.12 refers to the covenant with (the as yet unmentioned) Israel. The Noachide covenant, like this one, was also meant to be eternal (Gen 8.21–2; 9.8), and is in fact called *berit 'olam* (9.16), precisely the *diatheke aionos* of Ben Sira 17.12 (both terms mean eternal covenant). The covenant with Noah, like that of Ben Sira 17.11ff., requires humanity to observe certain laws, such as prohibitions against the consumption of live animals and murder, though the list is not the same. But the differences between the lists are not a conclusive argument against the identification of Ben Sira 17.11ff. as somehow connected with the Noachide covenant: the rabbis later would propose a list—or, rather, lists, since several different versions exist—of "commandments of the sons of Noah" that also diverges from the scriptural list by including laws derived from rabbinic-style exegesis of Genesis 9 and other biblical texts, but also by considering what sorts of norms—law courts, for example—might be indispensable to human society in general, and regarding them as implicit in the biblical account.[14] Or, even more strikingly, and more chronologically relevant to Ben Sira, Jubilees 6.1–38 seems to present the solar calendar of 364 days as one of the terms of God's covenant with Noah, demonstrating, like the rabbinic sources, that some ancient Jewish writers could treat the biblical episode with considerable freedom.

Ben Sira strikingly calls God's law for humanity not just an eternal covenant, following Genesis, but also *nomos* (note: no definite article) *zoes*—literally, "a law of life," an expression that, for all its resonances with later Jewish texts, where *torat hayyim* means more or less "the living Torah," has no biblical antecedents.[15] Here, however, *torat hayyim* may perhaps be understood as "instruction for life," rather like the later rabbinic *derekh eretz*, but with an intentional and even bold designation of this universal law as Torah, implying that it is comparable in importance

[14] For a recent survey, see M. Bockmuehl, "The Noachide Commandments and New Testament Ethics with Special Reference to Acts 15 and Pauline Halakhah," *RB* 102 (1995): 72–101. Bockmuehl is the only scholar I have found so far who regards Ben Sira 17.11ff. as addressed to all humanity (80 n. 16); note also the somewhat unsystematic discussion in D. Novak, *The Image of the Non-Jew in Judaism: An Historical and Constructive Study of the Noahide Laws* (New York: Edwin Mellen Press, 1983), 3–51. Collins, *Jewish Wisdom*, 59–60, suggests that Ben Sira "admits no distinction between the covenant of Noah and that of Moses."

[15] The closest is Prov 13.14, "The instruction of a wise man [*torat hakham*] is a source of life [*meqor hayyim*]." Collins, *Jewish Wisdom*, 59, suggests that *torat hayyim* is derived from Dt 30.11–20 and so definitely refers to the Mosaic covenant. On these verses, see also L. A. Schökel, "The Vision of Man in Sirach 16.24–17.14," in J. G. Gammie et al., eds., *Israelite Wisdom: Theological and Literary Essays in Honor of Samuel Terrien*, other eds. W. Brueggemann, W. Lee Humphreys, J. M. Ward (Missoula, MT: Scholars Press, 1978), 235–45.

to the Torah of the Jews.[16] Ben Sira tells us what this universal Torah contains: the exhortation to avoid all injustice, and rules governing man's
behavior toward his fellows (precisely the content of Ben Sira's teachings
about social relations)—a peculiarly partial account of the contents of
the Israelite Torah, if that is what is meant here, but not a bad description of a hypothetical Torah for humanity.

Verse 17 should be seen as an introduction to the next stage of the
story, the separation of humanity into distinct nations, each ruled by its
own god (or perhaps human rulers are intended—so Anchor Bible and
Smend), who are all subordinate to God, who rules Israel directly. These
verses suggest that while nature observes its Torah perfectly, and humanity, granted understanding and choice, (generally) chooses to observe its
social Torah, Israel has a much harder time: apart from its obligation to
observe the Torah of all humanity, its own Torah is still more difficult to
observe, the temptation to evade is stronger, and God's supervision is much
more direct and relentless. This explains the emphasis of verses 19–23,
while 24–26 reassure the (Jewish) reader that even for sinners, doom is
not inevitable, since God accepts the penitent.

This remarkable capsule retelling of the first book and a half of the Hebrew Bible can also be understood as a summary of Ben Sira's wisdom. It
accounts for the contents of the book nearly completely, at least until "the
praise of the fathers," starting in chapter 44, since it explains how wisdom
can include praise of nature, advice about social behavior, *and* exhortations to observe the commandments of the Torah. It also explains how Ben
Sira was able so consistently to conflate piety or fear of the Lord, Torah,
wisdom, and the cautious, effective, advantageous management of social
relations. All except the Israelite Torah are part of the Torah of life, a set of
rules God gave to all humanity, along with the senses, understanding, and

---

[16] Against this view, however, is the use of the identical expression—*torat hayyim/nomos
zoes*—at 45.5 to refer to the Israelite Torah, though it may be significant that Ben Sira there makes
emphatically certain that there is no ambiguity about the connotation of the expression, especially the fact that it is meant for Jews alone. 45.4-5, Hebrew MS B:

45.4. For his trust and his humility
       He chose him from all [flesh].
45.5. And He caused him to hear His voice
       and drew him near to the storm-cloud ['*arafel*]
       and placed in his hand commandment
       a Torah of life and understanding
       to teach His laws in Jacob
       and His testimonies and judgments to Israel.

By contrast, in the "praise of the fathers" (Ben Sira 44–50), Noah's covenant is emphasized, and it
is, at least according to the Greek text, designated a *berit 'olam*, as in chapter 17, and Genesis 9,
but its content is said simply to be that all flesh would not be destroyed (44.17-18).

the ability to distinguish between good and evil and to recognize the greatness of God's deeds.

What this passage shows, if I have interpreted it correctly, is that Ben Sira was himself aware of the tension in his work and so strove to provide a theological, or rather exegetical (since Ben Sira's Torah of humanity seems related to or derived from the biblical account of the Noachide covenant), rationale for those parts of his wisdom that seem so remote from the ethos of the Torah. The *torat hayyim*—Torah of life—is thus the mechanism by which the tension is resolved. But it does not explain why the tension is present in Ben Sira's book to begin with: we are still entitled to wonder what, on the structural level, Ben Sira's advice not to treat slaves too well, or never (really) to trust anybody, or not to overeat or be outspoken at dinner parties, is doing in a book that professes to have the Torah and fear of God as its main theme (1.1–20).

Solution 2: Ben Sira's Sociology

In what follows, I cite extensively from and examine carefully a selection of Ben Sira's social teachings, especially those concerned with the reciprocal exchange of benefits and social dependency, for the obvious reason that they constitute the core problematic of ancient Jewish (indeed, probably of all premodern Jewish) social ideology and praxis. These items, however, are part of a larger Mediterranean cultural nexus, and Ben Sira is in fact demonstrably concerned with all the elements of the construct. Some of these issues I discuss only in passing: though honor and shame in Ben Sira have not yet received a comprehensive discussion, Claudia Camp's conclusions, though based on only part of the evidence, seem to me compelling and generally applicable, and are discussed below[17]; memory, too, has been extensively discussed because it is the central theme of the "praise of the fathers" (ch. 44–50)[18]; and friendship, a topic almost completely ignored in the Hebrew Bible, not to mention in the scholarship on Ben Sira before the 1990s, has now received two monographic treatments. However, both books are concerned with text criticism and with the philological and theological exegesis of a rather artificially delineated corpus of

[17] C. Camp, "Honor and Shame in Ben Sira: Anthropological and Theological Reflections," in *The Book of Ben Sira in Modern Research: Proceedings of the First International Ben Sira Conference, 28–31 July 1996, Soesterberg, Netherlands*, ed. P. C. Beentjes, BZAW 255 (Berlin: de Gruyter, 1997), 171–87.

[18] See especially B. L. Mack, *Wisdom and the Hebrew Epic: Ben Sira's Hymn in Praise of the Fathers* (Chicago: University of Chicago Press, 1985).

"friendship pericopae" (whereas *ahabah* and *re'ut* are in fact pervasive themes in Ben Sira's work) and offer little or no analysis of the sociohistorical, sociological, and socioanthropological aspects of Ben Sira's comments on the subject.[19] In sum, though honor, memory, and friendship are not ignored in what follows—indeed, Ben Sira's appropriation of honor, his claim that honor is the province of the wise or pious man, is one of the central messages of his book—I do not discuss them discretely, or as extensively as reciprocity (which includes friendship) and dependency.

It may also be worth observing that my theme here is not the extraction of a sociology of early second-century BCE Jerusalem from Ben Sira's social teaching. This interesting and valuable enterprise has often been undertaken in the past, but even in the best cases—for example, the work of Richard Horsley and Patrick Tiller[20]—it suffers from several problems. Most relevant for the present purposes, it is far too positivistic. Horsley and Tiller's work, to be sure, has the great merit of recognizing that there was more to Judaean social life around 180 than arguments about Hellenism, but I would argue that we have to be far more cautious and subtle. For example, Horsley and Tiller think that if only we could figure out who the various great men—*nedivim* and *gedolim* and *megistanes* and *dynastai*— were, whom Ben Sira warns his audience to treat carefully—what their

---

[19] F. V. Reiterer, ed., *Freundschaft bei Ben Sira: Beiträge des ersten Symposions zu Ben Sira, Salzburg, 1995*, BZAW 244 (Berlin: de Gruyter, 1996); J. Corley, *Ben Sira's Teaching on Friendship*, Brown Judaic Studies 316, (Providence, RI: Brown Judaic Studies, 2002). The more or less discrete friendship pericopae are: 6.5–17 (be wary of run-of-the-mill *'ohabim*—the standard biblical Hebrew word for friend is *'oheb*, though sometimes *re'a* is used—but an *'oheb 'emunah*, a trustworthy friend, *pistos philos*, is worth more than money—practically a quotation of Theognis 1.77–78, who specifies, however, that he is talking about periods of *stasis* (on friendship in Theognis, see W. Donlan, "Pistos Philos Hetairos," in *Theognis of Megara: Poetry and the Polis*, ed. T. Figueira and G. Nagy [Baltimore, MD: Johns Hopkins University Press, 1985], 176–96]—and will be found by a fearer of God); 9.10–16 (old friends are best, great men are dangerous, it is best to associate with the wise); 19.13–17 (rebuke a friend, and observe [thereby] the Torah of the Most High); 22.19–26 (*'ahabah* can recover from physical attack, but not from verbal humiliation, revelation of secrets, or betrayal; support your *re'a* in bad times and he will reciprocate); 27.16–21 (*re'im* flee from the revealers of confidences); 37.1–6 (*'ohabim* stand up for each other in battle, and do not forget each other when the loot is distributed). Almost all these themes are discussed below, since they are commonplace in Ben Sira's teachings about social relations, the exception being secrecy, a unique characteristic of friendship for Ben Sira. We note in passing that friendship here is presented in nonaffective terms, primarily as a system of exchange—of goods, *'emunah* or *pistis* or trust, information, and that, unlike the friendship of David and Jonathan (whose affective component is very prominent), it is informal rather than contractual. Finally, the friendship passages display the same pattern as the rest of Ben Sira's social teaching, a pattern that is explored below. One of them seems simply to expand on a Pentateuchal command, several provide entirely nonbiblical advice about friendship, and several try to adapt friendship to Jewish norms by claiming that the pious or wise are and find the most trustworthy friends.

[20] Horsley and Tiller, "Ben Sira and the Sociology of the Second Temple," 74–107.

roles were, what the differences between them might have been, and so on—then we would have useful, if not necessarily absolutely complete, information about the identity of the ruling class of pre-Maccabean Judaea. Perhaps, but it is at least worth observing that Ben Sira refers repeatedly to institutions, most significantly the *qahal* or *'edah*—apparently some sort of assembly or assemblies[21]—whose existence is not attested elsewhere and that seem to have a confusing variety of functions: we should not assume, without external confirmation, that the sociopolitical world Ben Sira constructed in his books has any definite—and certainly not any simple—relationship to the one in which he actually lived.

What I propose to do instead is to investigate Ben Sira's social imagination, to try to reconstruct, if only partially, not a sociology from Ben Sira but the sage's own sociology, paying special attention to its gaps and inner tensions and to its problematic failure to cohere adequately with the rest of the book.

It is first of all odd that Ben Sira can be said to have had a sociology at all, at least in the form of a fairly extensive set of observations about—if no meaningful theoretical analysis (in contrast to, say, Aristotle) of—how society and the systems of human relations that constitute it work. Serious interest in social relations distinguishes it sharply from its most obvious antecedent, the book of Proverbs, which is mainly concerned with the pious, wise, or ethical behavior of the individual and, though there are some exceptional pericopae containing Ben Sira-like social advice, seems not to be extrapolating his teachings from a totalizing or near-totalizing view of human social behavior.[22] Job, Qohelet, and 1 Enoch seem barely more concerned, though Qohelet may be said to have had a general view of human society if only because he viewed it as incompletely differentiated from the rest of nature: while the rest of the Israelite or Jewish wisdom tradition viewed nature as exemplarily law-abiding, Ecclesiastes viewed it as being in blind thrall to a wearisome amoral regularity, the prototype of human wickedness, not virtue. Job and Enoch, for their part, seem to have similarly pessimistic views of the human condition, but they too are distinguished from Ben Sira by their failure to elaborate their sociologies or to offer realistic instructions about how to cope, though perhaps this was because they thought coping impossible.

---

[21] For the relevant passages, see D. Barthélemy and O. Rickenbacher, *Konkordanz zum Hebräischen Sirach* (Göttingen: Vandenhoeck and Ruprecht, 1973), 288, 346.

[22] For example, Proverbs 27.10: Your friend [*re'a*] and the friend of your father do not abandon / and do not come to the house of your brother on the day of your disaster; / better a close neighbor than a distant brother. On the "individualism" of Proverbs, see N. Whybray, *The Book of Proverbs: A Survey of Modern Study* (Leiden: Brill, 1995), 112–13.

Ben Sira probably drew not only on Israelite-Jewish but also on late Egyptian sources, the most important of which were the Demotic Wisdom of P. Insinger[23] and perhaps also Onkhsheshonq (or at any rate on Egyptian texts that resembled them), texts that in their prevailing ethos of sour practicality bring us a bit closer than Proverbs or the other Jewish wisdom texts (which have the sourness but not the practicality) to the thought of Ben Sira.[24] However, the Egyptian texts are explicitly directed to apprentice scribes. Their advice narrowly concerns the nontechnical aspects of the scribal profession, such as how to avoid offending powerful and malicious employers and humiliating weak but vengeful petitioners, and so is less an expression of a totalizing view of the human condition than the ancient equivalent of a modern corporate staff manual, which may also engage in a bit of formulaic moralizing.[25] The archaic Greek Theognidea—also possibly a source of Ben Sira, as I mentioned earlier—has a rather more universalizing tone. But much of it concerns, or was shaped by, the conditions of *stasis*, the political strife that wracked many late Archaic Greek cities, conditions in which advice about distinguishing true friends from false, for example, had an urgency and specificity it may have lacked in Ben Sira's Jerusalem.[26] So, Ben Sira has generalized or universalized a Near Eastern and Greek tradition characterized by a hardheadedly realistic but very limited view of some aspects of human behavior into a full-blown account of human interaction (which does not contradict the fact that his teaching remains anchored in history, in a specific cultural, social, political, and literary environment; the reason why it is necessary to harp on this point is that the theologizing and universalizing tradition of reading Ben Sira, as enshrined in the Anchor Bible translation and the commentary of Alexander Di Lella and Patrick Skehan, is still a significant component of the scholarship).

[23] Sanders, *Ben Sira and Demotic Wisdom*, called this text "Phibis," a name that has caught on in Ben Sira scholarship, but this appears to be based on an incorrect reading of the name of the papyrus's scribe, Phebhor, not the text's author. See J. Ray, review of Sanders, *Ben Sira and Demotic Wisdom*, *VT* 35 (1985): 383–84.

[24] See Sanders, *Ben Sira and Demotic Wisdom*; M. Lichtheim, *Late Egyptian Wisdom Literature in the International Context: A Study of Demotic Instructions*, Orbis Biblicus et Orientalis 52 (Freiburg: Universitätsverlag, 1983). For the texts, see Lichtheim, *Ancient Egyptian Literature, vol. III: The Late Period* (Berkeley and Los Angeles: University of California Press, 1980), 159–217. M. Goff, "Hellenistic Instruction in Palestine and Egypt: Ben Sira and Papyrus Insinger," *JSJ* 36 (2005): 147–72, argues that P. Insinger is likely to be later than Ben Sira and that both texts draw on a common fund of wisdom sayings, but the similarities seem to me substantial enough to suggest that the texts are related—a formulation I am leaving intentionally vague; see J. T. Sanders's response, "Concerning Ben Sira and Demotic Wisdom: A Response to Matthew J. Goff," *JSJ* 38 (2007): 297–306.

[25] Note the nice irony of the "Enron Code of Ethics," published in July 2000: see *The New Yorker*, July 4, 2005, 30–31.

[26] Which is not unsurprising in a book composed only ten years or so before the reforms of the high priest Jason, themselves commonly thought to have generated *stasis*.

Gift Exchange

Exchange of gifts and benefactions is a pervasive theme in Ben Sira's account of social relations, and the language and imagery associated with gift exchange are an important source of metaphors elsewhere in his work.[27] Ben Sira takes it for granted throughout that the exchange of benefits constitutes the foundation of most institutionalized nonfamilial relationships, but, in contrast to Aristotle, Cicero, and Seneca,[28] he does not evince a consistent attitude toward the gift; rather, he shifts from rejecting the ethical and social value of the gift outright to regarding the gift as effective in conferring well-being and security on the giver but inferior to piety or wisdom, to regarding it as an inevitable though highly dangerous component of human relations whose rules the wise man had best master, to regarding it as both a social and ethical asset, at least for the man who disposes of surplus; on occasion, he tries to conflate it with Pentateuchally mandated poor relief. Proverbs, to contrast Ben Sira with its main "intertext," proposes, in the four verses that mention *matanot* (gifts), a much simpler view: the gift is deadly (15.27) and equivalent, or at least comparable, to bribery (21.14), an equation incidentally not infrequently made in classical Athens, and probably in both the latter and in the perhaps contemporaneous Israel of Proverbs, one that betrays resistance to reciprocity as a foundation of society.[29] Ben Sira's careful distinction, at 32(35).10–17, between the (legitimate) gift, made with *tuv 'ayyin* (literally, goodness of eye; more or less, generosity of spirit; cf. *megalopsychia*), and

[27] On gift exchange in general, see the discussion in chapter 1. This is one of the sociological topics to which the editors of *Semeia* dedicated a special volume. See especially G. Stansell, "The Gift in Ancient Israel," *Semeia* 87 (1999): 65–90, and V. H. Matthews, "The Unwanted Gift: Implications of Obligatory Gift Giving in Ancient Israel," *Semeia* 87 (1999): 91–104: both articles proceed by constructing a model on the basis of the classic sociological literature on the topic and then applying the model deterministically to various episodes of biblical narrative as a way of "forcing" the episodes to conform: in reality, though, narratives evince a range of attitudes to the gift, including strong opposition (for example, Gen 37.3). Another flaw some of the papers share is a tendency to slip from Bible stories, to the ideology of the biblical texts in general, to "ancient Israel." But in reality, biblical narratives, laws, hymns, and wisdom sentences tell very different stories from each other, and any appropriately cautious and sophisticated reading would preclude their unproblematic transformation into a social history of ancient Israel.

[28] See Griffin, "*De Beneficiis.*"

[29] Since gift giving, when regarded as generating enduring reciprocal relationships, is fundamentally inegalitarian, as Proverbs itself emphasizes (18.16; 19.6). By contrast, peripatetic and stoic writers expressed an ideology-driven resistance to this view: see Inwood, "Politics and Paradox." On the inegalitarianism inherent in gift exchange, see above and G. Herman, *Ritualised Friendship and the Greek City* (Cambridge: Cambridge University Press, 1987), 73–81. On the other hand, 15.27 (The maker of profits destroys his house [*beyto*], but the hater of the gift will live), at least in its first hemistich, seems to preserve a trace of an aristocratic contempt for money and trade, not fully shared by Ben Sira (see below).

the bribe, made from illicit profit to secure further illicit gain, may be meant as a criticism of Proverbs' teaching (see below).

We may illustrate the range of Ben Sira's attitude to gift exchange by citing several passages.

> 3.17. [from Geniza MS A] My son, in your wealth comport yourself with modesty[30]
> and you will be more beloved [*vete'aheb*] than a giver of gifts.
> 3.18. Diminish yourself from all the great things of the world and before God you will find mercy.
> 3.20. For many are the mercies of God and to the humble will He reveal His secret.[31]
> 3.21. That which is too marvelous for you do not seek and that which is concealed from you do not investigate.
> 3.22. Contemplate [rather] that which is permitted to you and have no dealing with[32] hidden things.

Like much of the social teaching in the first third of Ben Sira, this passage is basically antireciprocal, warning against the utilization of wealth to maximize influence (in the form of *'ohabim*, or friends) and applying the same advice to the cosmic political economy: just as wealth should not be used for the acquisition of social control,[33] so too wisdom should not be used to acquire power in the divine realm. God rewards obedience (3.22a) and modesty. (This is in a way a translation to human-divine relations of the modesty Ben Sira recommends in dealing with the human grandee: keep a respectful distance and he will draw you near [13.9]) Ben Sira here admits that gift giving is the conventional way of collecting friendships[34] and does not condemn it per se, but asserts that the man

[30] Greek: Son, in gentleness perform your work. . . . Kister, "A Contribution," 314–15, observes than Ben Sira may be using the word *mel'akhah*—normally, work—as a substantive of the verb *halakh*, to go. This has little impact on the meaning.
[31] The Greek is very different: For great is the power of the Lord, and by the humble is He glorified.
[32] Or, make no claim over: see Kister, "A Contribution," 315–16.
[33] Cf. 5.1–7 (Do not rely on wealth: it will not save you from divine wrath), or, along slightly different lines, 7.4–7 (Do not seek political power—but here the advice takes a practical turn: unless you are strong [or rich?] enough not to fear the "*nedivim*" and the damage they might do you in public assemblies). As suggested above, it is difficult to know what sort of real-life situations, if any, Ben Sira is referring to here.
[34] The verb *'hb* in both the Hebrew Bible and in Ben Sira often conveys the sense of "to establish a friendship," or more generally, "to establish a relationship of personal dependency." See Corley, *Ben Sira's Teaching on Friendship*, esp. 219–27; on the meaning of *'hb* in the Bible, see W.

who is modest in his wealth (or who behaves mildly) will be even better loved, that is, he will make more friends.

Ben Sira, 12.1–6, evinces a rather different attitude toward gift exchange[35]:

> 12.2. Bestow a favor on a righteous man and find
> reciprocation
> if not from him then from the Lord.
> 12.3. There is no bestowal of a favor for one who supports an
> evil man
> nor has he [even] performed a righteous deed [or, ful-
> filled the commandment of charity].
> 12.5.[36] Twice the evil will he receive in the time of need
> for every favor that reaches him.[37]
> [Surely] give him no weapons
> lest he set them up against you!
> 12.6. For God too hates the wicked
> and to the evil He responds with vengeance.
> 12.4. Give to the good man and withhold from the wicked.
> 12.5. Honor[38] the pauper; give not to the scoundrel.

L. Moran, "The Ancient Near Eastern Background of the Love of God in Deuteronomy," *CBQ* 25 (1963: 77–87), who shows that *'hb* and its cognates are the terms normally used in ancient Near Eastern literature to characterize the relation between lord and vassal or between allies and thus is surely in the background of Deuteronomy's oft-repeated insistence that Israel love God (and vice versa), a love not necessarily without emotional content but in practice primarily a matter of loyalty and obedience on the vassal's part and the obligation to protect on the lord's part. (On the combination of the political and the emotional in *ahabah*, see P. R. Ackroyd, "The Verb Love—*Aheb* in the David-Jonathan Narratives: A Footnote," *VT* 25 [1975]: 213–14; S. Ackerman, "The Personal Is Political: Covenantal and Affectionate Love ('aheb, 'ahaba) in the Hebrew Bible," *VT* 52 [2002]: 437–58). In the ancient Near East such relationships were legal and contractual, or, we might say, covenantal, so that the *ahavah* of God and Israel in Deuteronomy is still another aspect of the well-known resemblance of that book to Assyrian alliance or subjection treaties. In Ben Sira, by contrast, the term *'oheb* has lost its contractual aspect and describes an informal relationship, comparable to Greek *philia* (The noncontractual character of Greek *xenia* and *philia* is assumed by Herman, *Ritualised Friendship*, 1–34; and see D. Konstan, *Friendship in the Classical World* [Cambridge: Cambridge University Press, 1997], who goes even further, regarding classical friendship not as exchange-based but as more or less exclusively sentimental, in a way that excludes the possibility of a contractual basis; but Konstan's account is idealizing.)

[35] I leave verse 1, which begins the pericope, untranslated in view of its difficulty; see Smend and Segal for attempted explanations.

[36] Smend and Segal, followed here, change the order of verses 4–6.

[37] The sense is manifestly that anyone who does a good thing for a wicked man receives as his reciprocation a bad thing, doubled.

[38] Following Segal (deriving *hqyr*—vocalized *hoqeyr*—from *yqr*, "honor") against Smend, who vocalizes *haqeyr* and derives the word from *qwr*, translating, "provide satisfaction [*qorat ru'ah*] for."

This passage merges gift exchange with charity and piety. It begins with a sentiment repeated later in the book, which may be paraphrased as righteous men know and follow the rules of gift exchange, whereas wicked men do not; therefore, confer benefits on righteous men, who can be counted on to reciprocate; for the wicked will repay your generosity with evil. The last point here is given a remarkably concrete twist: do not lend your weapons to a wicked man, who is liable to use them against you! But the passage is careful to maintain some ambiguity about its intentions. Is it offering pious (though somewhat unexpected: the Pentateuch never distinguishes between "deserving" and "undeserving" poor) instruction about charitable distribution (one who gives to the wicked has not given charity; God himself offers the wicked nothing but vengeance but can be counted on to reward one who is generous to a good man; one should honor the *makh*—pauper—with gifts—possibly implying that the whole passage really concerns charity to the righteous poor) or sensible advice about reciprocal exchange (the good person will reciprocate if he can, whereas the bad person will misreciprocate, even to the point of attacking you with your own weapons—implying that the whole point is not to help a helpless pauper but, if possible, to enter into a relationship based on reciprocal exchange)? We might say that conceptually, Ben Sira here is suspended somewhere between Leviticus 25, with its insistence on unreciprocated poor relief, and the idealization of reciprocity found in such texts as Seneca's *De Beneficiis*.

Elsewhere, Ben Sira renounces even the ambiguous biblicism of the above and straightforwardly identifies the wise man as one who knows the rules of gift exchange (20.13–17, extant only in Greek). Indeed, nowhere in the remainder of his book does Ben Sira try to reconcile gift exchange with Pentateuchal piety:

20.13. The wise man makes himself beloved with little
but the favors of fools will be poured out [i.e., squandered].

20.14. A gift of the foolish man will not profit you
for his eyes are many in return for one.[39]

20.15. He will give few things and reproach much
and will open his mouth like a herald [Segal: a crow]
Today he will lend and tomorrow he will demand repayment:

---

[39] Which manifestly means, following Smend and Segal, that the fool expects too much reciprocation for his gift; contrast the Anchor Bible. There are Aristotelian and Stoic parallels to the theme of the fool's or the base man's misunderstanding—and the sage's mastery—of the rules of reciprocity; see Inwood, "Politics and Paradox," 249–53.

Hated is such a man as this.

20.16. A fool will say: I have no friend,
I receive no gratitude for my favors;
those who eat his bread are coarse in tongue
how much and how often do they mock him!

Here Ben Sira lays out with what seems to me complete transparency a basic account of how gift exchange operates without making any attempt to reconcile it with biblical piety (except implicitly, in light of the knowledge that wisdom in Ben Sira is normally equal to piety), in the form of a warning of what befalls the foolish man who is ignorant of the rules: such a man wastes his resources on unwise or unnecessary gifts, and also expects too much in return, and is impatient to receive it—with the possible implication that he misconstrues the benefit as a loan (Ben Sira here agrees with Seneca that the wise man must never think of reciprocation when offering a benefit). Because such a man has no grasp of the rules, he is hated; that is, he has no real *ohabim* (thus Ben Sira makes explicit once again the relationship between gift exchange and *ahabah*). Rather (and here Ben Sira could be offering a capsule summary of the Trimalchio's Feast section in Petronius's *Satyrica*), he has parasites, people who eat at his table but are no true friends, whom he holds in contempt because they fail to reciprocate his benefits in a way he deems appropriate, while the parasites, for their part, in the words of an old *Simpsons* episode, repay his abuse with raw hatred.

Several chapters earlier, Ben Sira had discussed complementarily some of the etiquette of gift giving (18.15–18, extant only in Greek)—or so it seems, for in fact the passage is quite difficult to understand.[40] In general, though, it seems to be taking up one of the other great themes of Ben Sira, the social power of speech, and exploring some of its tensions with material exchange:[41]

18.15. Son, when conferring benefits[42] do not give reproach
and in every gift pain of words.

[40] For it is this, and not charity, as Skehan and di Lella in the Anchor Bible ad loc. assert, that is most likely the topic of the pericope (contrast Segal and Smend).

[41] See A. A. di Lella, "Use and Abuse of the Tongue: Ben Sira 5,9–6,1," in *'Jedes Ding hat seine Zeit . . .': Studien zur israelitischen und altorientalischen Weisheit. Diethelm Michel zum 65. Geburtstag*, ed. A. A. Diesel et al., BZAW 241 (Berlin: de Gruyter, 1996), 33–48, according to whom Ben Sira has more to say about speech than any (other) biblical book. The fullest account of the issue is in J. Okoye, *Speech in Ben Sira with Special Reference to 5.9–6.1* (Frankfurt am Main: Lang; 1995).

[42] *En agathois; agatha* invariably translates *tobah* = favor or benefaction, as Segal and Smend note.

18.16. Will not dew calm a burning wind?
       Thus is a word better than a gift.
18.17. Lo, is not a word better than a gift?
       Both may be found in a man upon whom favor has
       been bestowed.[43]
18.18. A fool reproaches without bestowing a favor[44]
       and the gift of a stingy man wears out the eyes [?].

If in the above the exchange of benefits was understood as a basic feature of society, for the most part morally neutral (it is difficult not to see
an implicit polemic with Proverbs here), whose well-defined rules the
wise man will take care to master, elsewhere Ben Sira's attitude to gift exchange seems still more positive. Thus, Ben Sira 14.10–13:

14.10. The eye of the stingy man will hover over his bread
       even if there is nothing[45] on his table. [14.10c–d are per-
       haps not original]
14.11. My son, if you have, serve yourself
       and if you have, bestow a favor on yourself
       if you are successful, indulge yourself [lit., eat until you
       grow fat].
14.12. Remember that in Sheol there is no luxury [ta'anug]
       and death does not tarry
       and the decree of Sheol has not been disclosed to you.
14.13. Before you die bestow a favor on a friend [heteb
       le-'oheb]
       and give him what you have acquired.

While exchange of benefits is only an implicit theme of this passage, it
serves the important role of transforming the lesson of the passage from
the conventional "eat, drink and be merry, for tomorrow you die," to one
whose closest parallels may be found in Greek funerary epigrams of the
Hellenistic and Roman imperial eastern Mediterranean worlds. The
point of these poems is often to celebrate the nexus of surplus, generosity, and display that formed so central a part of the economy and culture
of the later Greek city (a culture that, like Ben Sira's imagined social

---

[43] *Kecharitomeno*. The meaning is not obvious. Segal, perhaps following the Syriac, which
translates, *kashira*, has *hasid*; Smend suggests, *tob ayin*—that is, a generous man, more or less
followed by the Anchor Bible.

[44] Segal translates, *belo' hesed*, but this seems forced.

[45] Following Smend in taking *mehumah* as equivalent to (or mistaken for) *me'umah*; Segal's
interpretation is forced.

world, idealized both community and reciprocity).[46] The main difference is that Ben Sira paradoxically focuses far more on death than do his epigrammatic parallels.[47]

Perhaps the most remarkable passage on gift exchange appears at the culmination of a very long and complex pericope (31[34].1–32[35].26) that seems to concern primarily the right and wrong ways to relate to God. The passage begins with a rejection of dream interpretation, soothsaying, and the like, unless—in a significant qualification—the dreams, omens, and so forth, are known to have been sent by God. (Experience is a better source of knowledge; 31[34].9–13) God protects those who fear him, and his *ohabim*. What good, Ben Sira continues (31[34].21–31), is sacrifice or prayer or fasting if they are combined with sin or a lack of righteousness? Rather, the performer of righteous deeds is as if he has offered many sacrifices (32[35].1–5). Not that Ben Sira is advocating the abolition of the sacrificial cult. On the contrary, he sees generosity to God as the cosmic counterpart to generosity to (good) humans[48]:

> 32[35].6. Do not appear before God empty-handed (=Dt 16.16),
>   7. for all these are for the sake of the commandment.
>   8. The sacrifice of the righteous man makes the altar fat
>   and its pleasing aroma is before the Lord.
>   9. The meal offering of the righteous man will be accepted
>   and its remembrance will not be forgotten.
>   10. With generosity [*tub 'ayyin*] respect the Lord,
>   and do not diminish the donation of your hand.
>   11. In all your [sacrificial] deeds be cheerful
>   and with joy sanctify the tithe.
>   12. Give to Him as is His gift to you [*ten lo ke-matnato lakh*]
>   with generosity and in accordance with what you have
>   acquired [*be-tuv 'ayyin uve-hasagat yad*].[49]

---

[46] For the texts, see R. Merkelbach and J. Stauber, eds., *Steinepigrammen aus dem griechischen Osten*, vol. 5 (Munich: Saur, 2004), 339, under entry "Geniesse das Leben." I have discussed some of these texts in *IJS*, 151–53.

[47] 30.18–22 lacks both the focus on death and the advice to share your abundance with your friends:

> 30.18. A good thing [tobah—here probably not benefit] poured out
>   on a closed mouth
>   is an offering presented before an idol.
> 30.19. What good will it do the idols of the nations which do not eat and do
>   not smell.
>   Likewise one who has wealth and derives no pleasure from it.
> 30.20. As when a eunuch embraces a girl and sighs.

[48] For a slightly different approach, see Kister, "A Contribution," 308.

[49] An adaptation of Dt 16.17: *ish ke-matnat yado, ke-virkat YHWH elohekha asher natan lakh.*

13. Because He is a God of reciprocity [*tashlomot*]/
    and He will repay you seven fold.
14. But do not bribe Him because He will not accept it.
15. And do not rely on a sacrifice [paid for from the pro-
    ceeds] of oppression
    for He is a God of justice
    and with Him there is no currying favor [God protects
    the weak and takes revenge on His enemies].

This pericope is first of all an adaptation of the Deuteronomic laws of pilgrimage (Dt 16.16–17), but one that amplifies the reciprocal aspect of the laws (nowhere else in ancient Jewish literature is God called *eloah tashlomot*!), applying to sacrifice or pilgrimage the language and conceptual baggage of gift exchange. In this way it balances 12.1–6, in which the reciprocal relationship based on exchange of benefits is partly assimilated to the Pentateuchal language of poor relief. Likewise, passages that discuss gift exchange with no effort to assimilate it to biblical norms are balanced by other passages, such as 29.1–20, which preach the value of poor relief simply as a *mitzvah*, a commandment, without any reference to the (competing) norms of gift exchange. In sum, Ben Sira's approach to the gift runs the gamut, from a biblically based rejection of reciprocation as the foundation of social relations to its unhesitating embrace to various attempts at reconciling the two views.

One of the implicit assumptions of the passages on exchange of benefits is that without assiduous attention, one is likely to slip: the wise man tries zealously to maintain his place in both the social and the cosmic orders, a status that depends on a careful balance of individual self-sufficiency and the exertion of the maximum possible control over ones' inferiors, equals, and superiors. Hence the warnings above against seeking more power than you can effectively exercise, lest you be crushed by the *nedivim*, and of maintaining a kindly and modest demeanor to your beneficiaries, lest they turn into parasites who consume your surplus while mocking you; likewise, the warning to cultivate generosity toward your equals, so that they help you even in bad times, and a fortiori to God, who is the most generous reciprocator of all but, like the human benefactor who prefers his gifts to be combined with kind words and friendly attitudes, accepts only gifts accompanied by righteousness and piety (not to mention cheerfulness). If all this wise advice is ignored, then one is a fool, and in God's case, guilty of bribery as well: hated by men and punished by God, in no position to exert control over one's social environment and so, through the mishandling of social reciprocity, sure to lapse into danger.

The Social Hierarchy: Domination and Honor

In another set of passages, Ben Sira's concern with the maintenance of position in the social hierarchy takes much more explicit form. In its first
appearance, the theme is merely adumbrated, in a way that has led commentators to think that the pericope concerns only charity (4.1–10; see
appendix 1, part A). Like some of the texts discussed in the previous section, this too is a highly complex passage that merges the language and
ideology of poor relief with those of institutionalized personal dependency. The protection of the poor and the weak is clearly presented as a
divine command and at the same time as part of a general strategy for the
maintenance of social position: one should be kind to the poor, a friend
(ha'aheb) to the 'edah (and whatever precisely this means, it probably refers to some group of social equals), and deferential to rulers. But though
kindliness to the poor may be part of a social strategy—a way of prevent-
ing the poor from taking revenge on you by cursing you—it is also motivated by a religious concern: God will surely hear their cries (see Ex 22.22;
Dt 24.14; Ps 9.13; cf. Job 34.28). And conversely, if you care for the poor,
God will care for you, but even here, Ben Sira seems to recommend an
approach to poor relief that deviates to some extent from Pentateuchal
norms: he seems, though one should perhaps not press the point, to recommend reducing the poor to a state of enduring personal dependency
on oneself (v. 10).

The topic is dealt with more comprehensively at 7.18–8.19 (appendix 1,
part B), but here Pentateuchal norms are not merged with social rules but
are incorporated into the picture in a different way, by presenting God and
his priests as the pinnacle of the social hierarchy, and also, perhaps still
more interestingly, by making the poor and weak their neighbors. Even
apart from its standard pious coda, this passage offers still another specifically Pentateuchal revision of the list of relationships that is practically a
topos in Ben Sira. It begins with social equals—friend, brother—proceeds
to a variety of dependents—slave, hired laborer, livestock, sons, daughters,
wives—and concludes with superiors—parents, God, the priests. The pov-
erty-stricken, the dead, mourners, and the sick are appropriately placed
here, next to God and the priests, rather than next to, say, slaves, laborers,
and livestock, because, though their social status may be similar to the latter's, the standard Israelite's obligation to the pauper strongly resembles
that to the priest (both must be supported from the agricultural production of Israelite landowners, both are specially protected by God)[50] and is

---

[50] And note Dt 14.28–19: every third year, the tithe—which the rabbis later interpreted as a
poor tithe—is given to the Levite, the resident alien, the orphan, and the widow.

quite different from his purely contractual obligation to slaves and labor-ers.[51] This is in fact not Ben Sira's typical list, as we will see: aside from the brief mention of the *oheb* at the very beginning,[52] the list mentions no one who is not in some sense formally bound to the listener, whether by a commandment of the Torah or by a contractual obligation. These are, except for the *oheb*, all relationships that the Torah and other biblical lit-erature acknowledge and of which they approve. Indeed, though some elements of reciprocity have crept into Ben Sira's account here, for exam-ple, in the exhortations about parents and the sick, in general, the pas-sage is more concerned with how to perform a divine command (31) and how to achieve a state of complete blessedness (32). It thus adapts a topos, the hierarchical list of relations, from the social Torah to organize a set of teachings derived mainly from the Israelite Torah.

This pericope should probably be read together with the one that fol-lows it (8.1–19), which contains advice about the sorts of relationships to avoid. It seems to have been composed in part as a kind of photographic negative of chapter 7. So, for example, chapter 7 begins with the exhorta-tion to value relation more than money, and chapter 8 begins by pointing out the dangers of money. It also exclusively concerns relationships that have no legal or contractual foundation. Indeed, one wonders whether one of the points of chapters 7 and 8 read as a unit might not be that rela-tionships in which the mutual obligations of the two parties are defined by law are better, morally, religiously, socially, than informal relationships, mastery of whose complicated, subtle, and dangerous rules is the exclu-sive province of the wise.

Ben Sira 10.19–11.1 (appendix 1, part C) plays out the tension between social and biblical norms in a slightly different way still. The ostensible main point of this pericope is one that to my knowledge is not closely paralleled in biblical texts, though it is perhaps adumbrated in several verses in Proverbs and in Ps 112.9: the fearer of God or the observer of the commandments or the wise man is truly honored.[53] As suggested above,

[51] See P. Brown, *Poverty and Leadership in the Later Roman Empire* (Lebanon, NH: University Press of New England), 2002.

[52] Indeed, the first verse of the pericope seems anomalous: not only does *oheb* not belong, but it is not clear how one can exchange an *ah* (brother; admittedly the reading is problematic). Fur-thermore, the rest of the passage concerns how to deal with your relations, not whether or not it is wise to keep them or whether or not relationships are better than money. It is tempting to relo-cate this verse to the beginning of the next chapter. Alternatively, this pericope has the logical structure of an analogy, like many other pericopae in Ben Sira: just as you should not exchange a friend for money, so too you should not loathe a wise wife—both will bring you much profit—and so on. The logic remains problematic.

[53] Proverbs is the only biblical book that seems to reckon seriously and repeatedly with the possibility that human Israelites might possess *kabod*. But Proverbs does not generally attribute

honor may be, among many other things, a perquisite of domination or sociopolitical control or superiority; it may automatically belong to the superior party in a relationship of asymmetrical exchange. For the Pentateuchal legislators, one of the points of the covenant between God and Israel seemed to be that by making God the only true sovereign (as Ben Sira himself noted [17.17])—Israel's only lord, king, father and friend—it extricated Israelites, in ideology if not in practice, from the entire nexus of dependency and honor. Thus, to say that the observer of the commandments is truly honorable may sound blandly pious but actually involves the collision of two mutually exclusive systems of values.

There is more to the passage than this, though, for in fact it also affirms the same Mediterranean system of values it is trying so hard to subvert or surpass.[54] Ben Sira admits the honorability of the wealthy man, the ruler, and the judge, and accepts the standard belief of aristocrats (though he was probably not one himself)[55] in agrarian societies that labor is dishonorable. But he also rejects the option of taking the aristocratic notion of the honorability of idleness to its logical conclusion, by arguing that it is better to work, at the expense of honor, than to have nothing. He also asserts that fear of God, even more than wisdom, confers honor even on the most dishonorable—several different categories of foreigners, and slaves. Verse 25 seems intrusive; at least it muddies the point of the pericope, by apparently referring to the familiar figure of the clever (as opposed to pious) slave, and by rehabilitating a power-based conception of honor— the slave's intelligence leads to his acquisition of influence even over free people (and so honor), a fact about which no free person should complain.

As was true also in connection with gift exchange, here too Ben Sira concentrated his more Torah-oriented teaching in the earlier chapters of his book. In chapter 13 (appendix 1, part D), by contrast, he warns his audience against falling into a state of dependency on the wealthy without any allusion to Pentateuchal norms or much significant use of biblical

---

kabod to the observer of *mitzvot*, and its relationship to the Pentateuch is controversial. In Ps 112.9 honor may be the reward of the righteous man, or specifically, perhaps significantly, of the man generous to the poor; on this verse and its relation to Proverbs, see A. Hurvitz, *Wisdom Language in Biblical Psalmody*, (Jerusalem: Magnes, 1991), 96–98 (I thank Ben Sommer for this reference.)

[54] Contrast D. A. de Silva, "The Wisdom of Ben Sira: Honor, Shame, and the Maintenance of the Values of a Minority Culture," *CBQ* 58 (1996): 433–55, who, following di Lella, reads the pericope as stating that "people are honorable only when they fear the Lord," and then adds arbitrarily, "If riches could only be acquired through assimilation to the Hellenic culture and transgression of the Torah, then for Ben Sira poverty would be more honorable" (444–45).

[55] See Wright and Camp, "Ben Sira's Discourse of Riches and Poverty," esp. 162 ff.

language except in the very first verse, which opens with an idea (do not befriend sinners) that is immediately abandoned, to be taken up again in slightly different form only in the final hemistich of the pericope. As Wright and Camp have well observed,[56] much of this passage concerns not the relations between the rich and the poor but the more subtle and complicated issue of how the moderately well-to-do should negotiate their social relations with the powerful. Ben Sira warns against *haberut* or *hithabrut*—which I assume is synonymous with or at least very similar to *ahabah* or *re'ut*, and like them primarily refers to a relationship between equals—with a social superior: there is no room for a pretense of equality in such a relationship (v. 11), which can only end in the exploitation of the poorer partner by the richer (a point emphasized in parabolic form in the poem that begins at v. 15). Not that such relationships are not necessary, but the poorer party should be properly deferential (8); it is wise to keep a certain distance from the rich man, so as to allow him to take the social initiative (9). In sum, Ben Sira here offers advice, based on a keen sense of its inherent danger, about the proper management of a social institution he did not yet have a separate name for but that following Roman precedent, we would call patronage.[57]

Still more explicitly concerned with the maintenance of social rank, and even less concerned with reconciling this concern with pentateuchal norms is 30(33).28–40 (20–33) (appendix 1, part E). Though Ben Sira in general warns against dependency here and, in a way that might be drawn from a textbook of social anthropology, draws a direct link between domination and honor, his exemplification of this principle—his exhortation to retain lifelong control of one's property, and not hand it over to relatives or friends (as a gift? a loan? rental?) in a way that may result, rather paradoxically, in one's dependence on them—is interesting for its apparent conviction that social supremacy relies on land ownership (or at any

---

[56] Ibid., 162–65.

[57] On the existence of which in the Near East in the Bronze and Iron Ages, in the absence of a dedicated vocabulary, see R. Westbrook, "Patronage in the Ancient Near East," *JESHO* 48 (2005): 210–33, a cautious and minimalistic account vastly preferable to that of N. P. Lemche, "Kings and Clients: On Loyalty Between the Ruler and the Ruled in Ancient 'Israel,'" *Semeia* 68 (1994/1996): 119–32. Lemche's views are accepted without question by R. Simkins, "Patronage and the Political Economy of Monarchic Israel," *Semeia* 87 (1999): 123–44.

The dangers inherent in such relationships and advice for their cautious management are also the theme of the second of Ben Sira's sympotic poems, 34[31].22–35[32].13: like Roman-era authors but unlike classical Greek ones, Ben Sira saw the symposium not as a celebration of the egalitarian ethos of the aristocratic *hetaireia* (fellowship) but as a performance of social domination and submission. I treat this issue separately in "No Dialogue at the Symposium? Conviviality in Ben Sira and the Palestinian Talmud," in *The End of Dialogue in Antiquity*, ed. S. Goldhill (Cambridge: Cambridge Univeristy Press, in press).

rate on some kind of ownership, since land is not specified),[58] a sentiment not found elsewhere in the book as far as I am aware (see below for further discussion of this issue). At first glance the second half of the pericope, on the treatment of slaves, seems only loosely related to the first half, but it is possible to read it as continuing the same line of argumentation: it is bad to be controlled or dependent (cf. 40.28–30) and good to control (and one means of attaining such control is through the unencumbered ownership of land) in a way that may cause your social equals to become dependent on you. Another way of exercising control is through the ownership and successful, which is to say very cruel, management of slaves (though without, Ben Sira adds, rather weakly, going overboard).

Money, Trade, Honor

The archaizing ring of much of Ben Sira's teaching, his manifest debt to such earlier texts as Proverbs, the sources of P. Insinger, perhaps Theognis, and the traces of what seems at first glance a Greek-style oligarchic ideology scattered throughout his work, might lead us to expect Ben Sira to replicate the hostility to money and trade typical of eastern Mediterranean landowning aristocrats throughout antiquity (which did not necessarily prevent them from engaging in trade and accumulating money) but was literarily important especially in an earlier period.[59] Ben Sira might also have had a motivation his Egyptian and Greek predecessors lacked: it was not simply that money tended to fall into the wrong hands, that those who had it felt, incorrectly, that it bestowed honor on the dishonorable, that is, that it subverted the moral and sociocultural economy of the world. He might have hated money for specifically Jewish reasons. Like the authors of Proverbs or Psalms or the prophetic books, Ben Sira might have hated money because of its nearly inextricable connection with sin, which it all too often generated and of which it was all too often the consequence. The oppression of the poor by the rich was a favorite theme of many Israelite and Jewish authors, and, as we have seen, Ben Sira was among them.

[58] Kister, "A Contribution," 333, notes that the verbs that here denote dominance, the aramaism ShLT and its biblical Hebrew equivalent MShL, are used in legal documents to connote a state of absolute legal mastery over a plot of land. Since Ben Sira is using the words metaphorically, their sense in documentary texts does less to pin down the precise referent of the text than Kister suggests.

[59] This, broadly speaking, is the topic of Kurke, *Coins, Bodies*.

Competing with these considerations, though, was what Max Weber famously called the theodicy of good fortune, the belief that prosperity is a divine blessing and that the prosperous must ipso facto deserve their state. And though there might be an as it were empirical correlation between money and sin, there was no reason money had to be used for wicked purposes.

I have already presented passages that illustrate several of these themes:[60] 3.17–18 warns against using wealth to acquire power; 7.18, in true oligarchic style, claims that relationship is more valuable than money (also 6.15); chapter 13 notes the sinfulness and, especially, the rapaciousness and exploitativeness of the rich; 10.21–11.1, however, admits that wealth is honorable and poverty dishonorable but argues that piety or wisdom can subvert—or perhaps rather supplement or surpass—this standard system of values; 14.10–13 is one of several passages that celebrate wealth, which as a gift of God it would be sinful not to enjoy. We may also note the following (26.29–27.3)[61]:

> 26.29. With difficulty can a merchant be saved from
>   wrongdoing,
>   nor will a petty trader be justified from sin.[62]

---

[60] More illustrations could easily be added, for example, on the theme of the superiority of relation to wealth, already encountered, not to mention a basic conviction about the dishonorability of poverty and the at least potential honorability of wealth, 25.1-2:

> 25.1. Three things my soul loves, and these are beautiful before the Lord and men:
>   the harmony of brothers, the friendship [philia] of neighbors, and a wife and husband who are appropriate for each other [vel sim.].
> 25.2. Three types my soul hates, and I am enraged at their life:
>   a haughty pauper, a lying rich man, and an adulterous old man without wisdom.

[61] According to Segal, the pericope continues down to verse 7, with verses 4ff. Meaning roughly as follows:

> 27.4. When the sieve is shaken the husks remain
>   so also a man's excrement [=sins] in his business dealings.
> 27.5. The utensils of the potter does the furnace test,
>   so a man by means of his business dealings.
> 27.6. The fruit reveals the care of the tree,
>   so too do business dealings reveal the desires of a man's heart.
> 27.7. Before you have done business with him do not praise a man,
>   for this is the test of men.

However, the Greek word *logismos*, or *dialogismos*, which Segal takes to mean business deals, is highly ambiguous, and other commentators have understood it differently. It is more likely to mean "speech" or "conversation," the morally diagnostic power of which is a common theme in the book.

[62] It is unclear whether the first hemistich is meant to refer to a large-scale merchant; if so, Ben Sira is denying the customary Greek distinction between honorable *emporia* (large-scale trade) and dishonorable *kapeleia*; see Kurke, *Coins, Bodies*, 6–23.

27.1. On account of money [*mehir*] many have sinned,
and the one seeking to grow great will turn away his eye.[63]
27.2. In the joint between stones will the wedge be stuck,
between purchase and sale will sin be crushed [?]
27.3. If he does not hold fast to fear of the Lord,
quickly will his house be destroyed [cf. Prov 15.27].

While this denunciation of trade (as opposed to wealth more generally) is isolated in Ben Sira, it still requires an explanation. The ideological conflict between land ownership and trade, between traditional aristocrats and new men who made their fortunes as merchants, is one of the stock themes in the history of classical antiquity. Although its significance has sometimes been posited for Israelite and ancient Jewish history as well, the issue seems far murkier there, and to the best of my knowledge has never been responsibly investigated. This is in part an evidentiary problem: the sources overwhelmingly preserve the teachings of priests, prophets, and scribes, who, however much land they may actually have owned, derived their authority not from land tenure (or trade, for that matter), in the manner of a traditional aristocracy, but from their ancestry or from acquired skills. Certainly the laws these men made and perpetuated were intended to inhibit the accumulation of landholdings at least as much as profits from trade and other commercial activities.[64] The marginal persistence of the "nomadic ideal" (perhaps, however, to be considered an effect rather than a cause of the biblical ambivalence to landholding) may also have offered some Israelites an alternative to an ideology based on land ownership. The existence and importance of a lay gentry in partial competition with the clerisy of priests, scribes, and so forth have been posited, and at least for some periods the existence of a lay gentry is not unlikely—by the first century it was extensive and diverse, but the fact remains that we know precious little about whatever ideology its members may have constructed as an alternative to the priestly one extensively preserved in the written sources.[65] So a comprehensive understanding of the full ideological freight of land ownership

---

[63] Apparently (so Segal): anyone seeking to improve his profits must ignore the sins involved in doing so.

[64] For a survey of the sources, see A. Hakham, "Mishar Ve-khalkalah Ba-miqra," *Mahanaim* 2 (1991): 20–39. While in general, biblical writers may have thought that all land belonged to Yahweh, at least in the land of Israel, they also described, and validated, the intense devotion of the smallholder to his ancestral plot (and condemned—indeed, rendered theoretically impossible—the long-term accumulation of landholding): see R. de Vaux, *Ancient Israel: Its Life and Institutions* (London: Darton, Longman and Todd, 1961), 164–67.

[65] The classic attempt to reconstruct the ideological position of the Israelite-Jewish gentry from its alleged traces in the Hebrew Bible is Morton Smith, *Palestinian Parties and Politics That*

(and so, as a corollary, of trade) among ancient Jews will necessarily remain elusive. Furthermore, trade may in most periods have been less fraught for Palestinian Jews than for Greeks and Romans simply because (at least, again, until the first century) they did proportionally much less of it, living as they did away from the coast and off the main trade routes.[66] Unlike in archaic Greece or Republican Rome, there may never have been a discrete Palestinian Jewish mercantile class large enough to compete with the priesthood and the gentry.[67] And for this reason, money, the all too liquid mercantile equivalent of land, the object of so much critical scrutiny by Greek sages, may have seemed to their Israelite and Jewish counterparts simply another type of wealth, no different from unstamped metal, gems, good textiles, or indeed fertile fields.[68]

In any case, it seems clear that Ben Sira generally did not follow his hypothetical Greek sources in distinguishing between (good or honorable) wealth derived from agricultural surplus and (bad or dishonorable) wealth derived from trade. The pericope just quoted does indeed preserve a trace of such an idea, since it regards trade and sin as closely linked, just as a few other texts may hint at the idea that agricultural work is inherently honest (7.15; 20.28),[69] or even that there might be some connection between (land?) ownership and honor (see above on 30 (33).28–40). More ambiguous is 34 (31).5–7, the culmination of a long, complex pericope on wealth, part of which has been discussed above:

34.5. The pursuer of gold will not be declared innocent,
and the lover of money [*mehir*] will err on its account.

34.6. Many have been shackled by gold, and trust in pearls,
but they were not able to be rescued from evil or to be
saved on the day of wrath.

34.7. For it is a stumbling block for the unwise,
and every fool will be ensnared by it.

Shaped the Old Testament, 2nd ed. (London: SCM Press, 1987; first published 1971 by Columbia University Press)

[66] A point made already by Josephus, *Against Apion* 1.60–8.

[67] Related to this may be the implication of some biblical texts that at least at certain times in the Iron Age, trade in Judah (or Yehud) was controlled by "Tyrians" or "Canaanites" (probably Phoenicians); see Y. Dan, "Seher Penim ve-Seher Hutz be-Eretz Yisrael Biyemei Bayit Sheni," in *Commerce in Palestine Throughout the Ages*, ed. B. Z. Kedar, T. Dothan, and S. Safrai (Jerusalem: Yad Ben Zvi, 1990), 91–107.

[68] Coins also had dramatically different political connotations in old Greece, where they embodied the authority of the citizen body over all forms of exchange, and Persian and Hellenistic Palestine, where they embodied the authority either of the imperial ruler and his local agent or of a local king. See C. Howgego, *Ancient History from Coins* (London: Routledge, 1995), 12–18, 39–61; S. von Reden, *Exchange in Ancient Greece*, 178–81.

[69] See Wright and Camp, "Ben Sira's Discourse of Riches," 157, whose analysis I adopt.

The pericope continues with a brief exposition of the theme of verse 7, commending the wise as those able to avoid the pitfalls associated with the pursuit of wealth, concluding (v. 11): "Therefore his wealth[70] is strong / and his praise will the assembly [*ekklesia*/*qahal*] tell." Until this conclusion it was possible to read the pericope as arguing that the wise, in their zeal to avoid sin, reject the value of wealth tout court. Instead it recapitulates a theme already encountered, a slight variation of Weber's theodicy of good fortune, with a hint of an idea explored above: the wise man knows the rules of effective benefaction; the wise man can possess wealth without becoming embroiled in the sinfulness with which wealth is normally associated. The same man's wealth is stable, not fleeting, and he uses it in a way that earns him public praise.

It is worth emphasizing that any contrast between honorable/unsinful agriculture and dishonorable/sinful trade, any tendency to see money as a uniquely problematic form of wealth, are, if present at all, no more than trace elements in Ben Sira's book; even 26.29ff. does not actually declare trade itself a sin. In any case, Ben Sira regarded all work as, if not inherently dishonorable, then as less honorable than the occupation of the sage or scribe: in addition to 10.25, discussed above, the point is made most strikingly in a long pericope (38.24–39.14), manifestly borrowed from the Egyptian gnomic tradition best preserved in a text called the Instruction of Duauf, with many parallels in other Egyptian texts, in which Ben Sira describes a series of artisanal trades (emphasizing their physical difficulty, dirtiness, and so forth), noting that though these trades are necessary for civilized life (38.32), their practitioners "will never be sought to advise the nation / and will not be exalted in the *qahal*" (33).[71] He then contrasts tradesmen with scribes or sages (incidentally providing a hint as to the sorts of background such people normally came from), who (4) "serve among leaders and appear before great men."

Hellenism

The Wisdom of Ben Sira was probably composed at Jerusalem, only a few years before the accession to the Seleucid throne of Antiochus IV. Its author was a wise man who was a supporter, if not a member, of that priestly aristocracy soon to be destroyed by a combination of civil war

---

[70] "*Tubo*"—Greek: *ta agatha*; Segal compares 44.14, where the word seems to mean something approximating "property." If Ben Sira means here to contrast money, pursued by fools, with land, possessed by the wise, he is doing so with great subtlety and indirection.

[71] See Sanders, *Ben Sira and Demotic Wisdom*, 61–63.

and rebellion at least one of the causes of which was internal disagreement over the role of Greek culture in Jerusalem. It is therefore common, as well as plausible, to try to interpret Ben Sira's Wisdom in light of a controversy that was perhaps already beginning to rage in or near Ben Sira's social milieu, even though Ben Sira wrote not a single word about Hellenism, at least not explicitly.

I do not wish to deny the possibility that some passages in Ben Sira were meant to respond to this issue. Perhaps Hengel was right to argue that Ben Sira's insistent identification of wisdom and Torah was directed against Greek education, though to follow Hengel in calling Ben Sira's claim "a declaration of war against Hellenism" (see note 9 above) overstates the case, since Ben Sira's Torah manifestly contained much wisdom derived from sources other than the Pentateuch, probably including some "Greek wisdom," too.[72]

But the culture of reciprocity that Ben Sira appropriated should not be viewed as an artifact of hellenization. Almost all the institutionalized relationships Ben Sira discusses are already mentioned in (probably) pre-Hellenistic biblical texts, and the specialized vocabulary Ben Sira uses when writing about it all likewise seems biblical or indigenous Hebrew.[73] The Hebrew Bible may not have approved of friendship, vassalage, and other forms of institutionalized reciprocity, may have imposed restraints on guest-friendship, may have been indifferent to parasitism and military comradeship, and may have had profound reservations about the gift itself; it may furthermore have denied to honor any legitimate role in human social and political relations and prohibited the vendetta; nevertheless, the Hebrew Bible indubitably acknowledged the existence of such institutions among the Israelites and their neighbors. The relationships Ben Sira wrote about were part (though precisely what part is very unclear, and for the moment unnecessary to specify) of the native social praxis and ideology of the Jews of Judaea.

Indeed, what distinguishes Ben Sira from other texts discussed in this book is the near invisibility of foreign rule. There is no reason to think

[72] For an attempt to situate Ben Sira in a less schematic cultural and political setting than the one implied by the standard Judaism-Hellenism divide, see J. Aitken, "Biblical Interpretation as Political Manifesto: Ben Sira in His Seleucid Setting," *JJS* 51 (2000): 191–208.

[73] The exception seems to be the word *tashlomet*, which gave this chapter its title. Is it a calque of the Greek *antapodoma*? Or of *amoibe* or *tisis* in their Theognidean senses (see J. Hewitt, "The Terminology of 'Gratitude' in Greek," *CP* 22 [1927] 142–61, at 149–51)? In any case, Ben Sira uses many other less recherché words to denote the return of a favor or benefit, most of them attested in biblical Hebrew.

On the relation of (noncontractual) patronage to (contract-based) vassalage in the pre-Hellenistic Near East, see Westbrook, "Patronage"; on honor, see Olyan, "Honor, Shame."

that the oppressive great men and fickle friends who form such an important part of the book's worldview are anything other than Judaeans. Though the book is not wholly devoid of the "universalism" that was a traditional component of Israelite wisdom, it does contain a curiously context-free couplet tacked on to the end of the concluding section of the book, the "praise of the fathers," which expresses anger at and contempt for "the residents of Seir and Peleshet, and the foolish people that dwells in Shechem" (50.25–26). This is an archaizing or biblicizing way of referring to Idumaeans, possibly culturally Greek residents of the city territories of the Palestinian coast, and Samaritans, here regarded as unambiguously non-Israelite. This particularism may suggest that Ben Sira would have mentioned it if his *nedivim* and so on were non-Judaeans—it would have added some piquancy to their oppressiveness—though it may be meaningful that, like traditional Israelite particularism, Ben Sira's was aimed more at the Judaeans' neighbors than at their foreign rulers. Nevertheless, it should be remembered that before the reign of Antiochus IV, the Seleucids seem to have ruled Palestine almost entirely through such local intermediaries as the Zadokite high priests (whom Ben Sira admired); if the kings or their courtiers maintained any presence in Jerusalem at all, it would have been very limited and probably outside the experience of such middling "retainer" types as Ben Sira or his expected audience. Ben Sira's wisdom thus reflects a political regime unlike the far more interventionist and centralizing one that Josephus and the rabbis later endured, and his social and cultural observations and lore bore correspondingly less political freight, at least in terms of imperial politics.

This is not to say that the social institutions Ben Sira discusses were unaffected by a century and a half of Macedonian rule. The most important case for my purposes is the (hypothesized) transformation of what are described in the Bible as, and seem generally in the Iron Age Near East to have been, contractual relations into the nonlegal though still highly formal and institutionalized relations they seem to be in Ben Sira's book (one may even step out on a historicist limb here and say that this shift explains the practical need for advice like Ben Sira's—people were no longer certain how to behave—though it does not explain Ben Sira's insistence that such lore counts as Torah or wisdom).

Conclusion: Adaptation

There is a long standing and rather sterile debate about how to characterize the Wisdom of Jesus ben Sira: are the biblical or Deuteronomistic elements—the exhortations to fear God and observe the laws of the Torah, the apparent conviction that God can be counted on to reward the righteous and punish the wicked, the hymns to nature as a demonstration of God's majesty and absolute lordship, the even longer hymn praising God's glory as made manifest in the biblical heroes and ancestors of the Jews—primary, with the rest being just a bit of window dressing, a late reflex of the "worldliness," itself traditional, of Israelite wisdom, or a gesture of half-hearted adaptation to a perhaps hellenizing society, by no means successfully concealing a firm loyalty to an unusually conservative version of the Israelite theological tradition? (The rather pietistic, theologically oriented scholarship definitely tends to prefer this option.)[74] Or is the Wisdom of Ben Sira primarily a guide for practical young men trying to get ahead in a surprisingly "secular" and lively Jerusalemite high society, a guide in which traditional piety is a secondary element, present because it could hardly be absent from a book pretending to continue the tradition of Israelite wisdom, or perhaps because before the high priesthood of Jason the Oniad (son of Ben Sira's hero Simon, and introducer of the hellenizing reforms that eventually and indirectly led to the Maccabean Revolt) lip service still had to be paid to biblical norms?[75]

I would argue that what is primary in the Wisdom of Ben Sira is neither the Deuteronomic-biblical nor the worldly pessimistic element. What is primary is the tendency to adaptation. We have seen repeatedly how Ben Sira tried to adapt his advice about navigating the complexities of reciprocity-based relationships of personal dependency to Torah-based norms by asserting that wisdom (or fear of God, or observance of the Law) is a fundamental component of such relationships, or that the wise man has a better chance of being successful at them. Sometimes the exhortation to piety is simply tacked on at the end, not infrequently as a

---

[74] See, for example, W. O. E. Oesterley, *An Introduction to the Books of the Apocrypha* (New York: Macmillan, 1935), 232–44; at greatest length, M. Hengel, *Judaism and Hellenism: Studies in Their Encounter in Palestine in the Early Hellenistic Period* (London: SCM Press, 1974), 1.131–53, following Smend in construing Ben Sira's traditional piety as "a declaration of war against Hellenism" (138). It is not entirely clear to me how he understands the other elements of Ben Sira's teaching—he seems to regard them as the result of Greek influence, since "one can be influenced by one's opponent precisely in warding off his language and thought forms" (150), which implies that these teachings are in some sense meaningless. Certainly for Hengel they have little or no relevance to our understanding of what matters about Ben Sira, his theology.

[75] This is a rather crude presentation of the view of the refreshingly nontheological E. J. Bickerman, *The Jews in the Greek Age* (Cambridge, MA: Harvard University Press, 1988), 161–76; in general, the debate I am describing is a version of the debate among theologians as to whether "fear of the Lord" or "wisdom" is primary in Ben Sira, surveyed by Sanders, *Ben Sira and Demotic Wisdom*, 16–17.

clumsy non sequitur.[76] We have also seen how often Ben Sira phrases his exhortations to piety or to Torah observance in the language of social reciprocity. In fact, though, the incorporation of the two competing value systems, the one based on the valorization of reciprocal exchange and the other on that of solidarity—the Mediterranean and the Pentateuchal—in Ben Sira's work is much more profound. For Ben Sira, wisdom or piety and social dominance are parts of a single package, since the former completes, perfects, guarantees, and ensures the latter. If my interpretation of Ben Sira 16.24–17.23 is correct, he even managed to find some exegetical justification for this view in the conviction that rules of socialization are part of the Torah God gave to all humanity, probably through his covenant with Noah.

I would suggest that through this process of adaptation Ben Sira is trying (and it should go without saying that both the hypothesis of authorship and the language of intention here must be understood as metaphorical) to resolve the social-ideological tension discussed in the previous chapter. He is trying, that is, to provide a Jewish, Torah-based justification for a set of social and cultural norms that in reality were radically at odds with the norms and ethos of the Torah. To put it in less formal terms, he is striving to advise the observer of the Torah how to behave as social agent, but in a world that fails to conform with the irenic vision of the Deuteronomist. He thus accepts an ethos of reciprocity while repeatedly reminding his reader or listener of the transcendent value of covenantal piety. Unlike the Stoics, though, he stopped short of transforming reciprocity into a social ideal. For Ben Sira, reciprocal exchange, though he episodically celebrated it, never lacked a dangerous edge. He did not fully disagree with the core biblical view, usually implicit, that reciprocity led in-

---

[76] For example, 37.10–12 (following Geniza MS D):

> 37.10. Do not take counsel with your father-in-law
> and from someone jealous of you conceal a secret.
> 37.11. [Do not take counsel] with a woman about her co-wife
> with a conqueror about war
> with a merchant about his merchandise [following Gk]
> with a purchaser about his purchase
> with a stingy person about acts of kindness
> with a cruel person about physical indulgence
> with a hired [day?] laborer about his work
> with a laborer hired by year about expenditure for seed.
> 37.12. Rather, frequent a man who fears [God]
> one you know to be an observer of the commandment . . .

Here, the pious tag is a non sequitur because the body of the pericope concerns the interestedness, not the moral character, wisdom, or piety, of the adviser. The clumsiness of the grafting procedure in such cases reflects its importance, and Ben Sira's zeal to introduce piety even into discussions in which it has no obvious place.

exorably to, or was inescapably always characterized by, inequality and oppression. He differed from most biblical books—though not, of course, from Qohelet—in regarding such relationships as fundamentally inescapable, and he differed from Qohelet in regarding them as manageable.

In fact, it could be argued that Ben Sira was to sociology as his older near contemporary who wrote parts of the First Book of Enoch was to cosmology. Both shared a view of the world as pervaded by unfairness, evil, disorder—for Ben Sira primarily social, for Enoch primarily cosmic. Yet both transformed and mitigated the views of their Israelite predecessors: Enoch softened Job as Ben Sira softened Qohelet. And both did so in similar ways, by arguing that piety offers a shield from the wickedness of the world, or rather a means of coping with it. In this way both seem to reflect the impact on traditional Israelite thought of the increasing importance of the Torah. Ben Sira and Enoch both show, however, that one way for the Torah to achieve its hegemonic status, or enhance it, was for its interpreters and mediators to acknowledge the seriousness of the challenge posed by competing ideological systems, and to strive somehow to incorporate them. In the process, coherence and simplicity were sacrificed to internal tension, complexity, and the potential for fragmentation.[77]

[77] Cf. Schwartz, *IJS*, 74–91.

CHAPTER FOUR

Josephus

Honor, Memory, Benefaction

Unlike Ben Sira, the historian Josephus (37/38 CE–ca. 100) only rarely paused to offer his readers abstract consideration of the tensions between reciprocity and the pious solidarity enjoined on the Jews by the Torah: the handful of passages, largely neglected in scholarly tradition, explicitly on this theme are discussed in this chapter. But much of Josephus's narrative, especially of recent history, is profoundly concerned with the reciprocal relations between the Roman state and Jewish grandees, and the way the latter tried to impose themselves on the Jews—in Josephus's account, usually unreceptive—by using Roman practices of benefaction and honor.[1] Josephus in fact presents the Jews, especially in his later work, the *Jewish Antiquities* and *Against Apion*, as starkly countercultural, radically resistant to Roman or Greco-Roman norms. In this chapter I explore Josephus's presentation of these issues, though without the aspiration to comprehensiveness of chapter 3, since Josephus wrote thirty books, not one. Unlike the age of Ben Sira, that of Josephus is rich in Palestinian archaeology, and some of the cultural practices Josephus was concerned with, especially the construction of public buildings funded by individuals whose generosity might be commemorated in the form of public monumental inscriptions, leave material traces. This means that we have the rare opportunity, and one it would be perverse to neglect, to test Josephus's claims about the Jews against another body of evidence. This will show that Josephus described the Jews' behavior somewhat simplistically, but that he was basically nearly correct: the Jews' culture of public benefaction, especially in Judaea, was from the Roman perspective problematically transgressive,

---

[1] Cf. Shaw, "Josephus," especially on Josephus's *Autobiography*. In Shaw's account such practices are precisely characteristic of the Jews, who for this reason were unprepared to confront, or even comprehend, the institutionalized and depersonalized power of the Roman state—a challenging and original argument, not wholly invalid but greatly overstated. See below.

The following abbreviations are used in this chapter: *Jewish War* (*Bellum Judaicum*) = *BJ*; *Jewish Antiquities* (*Antiquitates Judaicae*) = *AJ*; *Autobiography* (*Vita*) = *V*; *Against Apion* (*Contra Apionem*) = *CAp*.

and remained so even when the Jews came under more direct Roman rule after the death of Herod in 4 BCE.

Josephus is the pivotal figure for the concerns of this book, as the most important early translator of traditional Israelite or Jewish anxieties about reciprocity and related practices into a Roman world where such practices were beginning to assume fundamental political importance. By contrast, Ben Sira had lived at a time when emperors often showed greater cultural flexibility (though the sage's younger contemporary Antiochus IV obviously showed much less), or at any rate less active concern. Ben Sira's struggles with institutionalized reciprocity had no obvious implications for the relations between Judaeans and their Seleucid rulers. For their part, the rabbis of the Yerushalmi, who are the subject of the next chapter, were heirs to centuries of corporate Jewish compromise with Rome. The pangs of accommodation, though indubitably present in rabbinic literature, were less painful and raw than they necessarily were for Josephus, who had personally witnessed the disastrous collapse of Roman-Jewish relations.

A few introductory words about Josephus and his writings are in order. By his own account, Josephus came from a well-to-do landowning priestly family of Jerusalem, allegedly remotely related to the Hasmonean family, which had ruled Judaea until the accession of Herod in 37 BCE (*V* 1–2). Beyond some adolescent dabbling in the religious factionalism that was so important a feature of life in first-century Judaea (*V* 9–12), and a trip to Rome to try to rescue some priestly friends who were being held there (*V* 13–16), Josephus reported nothing about his adult life before the outbreak of the Great Revolt against Rome in 66, when he was about twenty-nine years old. Perhaps this was in part because he did not have much to do; if so, then Josephus's case can be taken as symptomatic: the tremendous popularity of the Jerusalem temple, expressed in the great triannual pilgrimage festivals ("They shall not appear before the Lord empty-handed," Dt 16.16), and enabled by the stability, prosperity, and support of the Roman state, had a powerful inflationary effect on the economy of the city and its surrounding district, and tended to enrich people like Josephus while leaving them underemployed. Priests and other religious officials derived their wealth and prestige not from their access to or their ability to mediate the power of the imperial center, but from the temple and the Torah.[2] They had a vested interest in Jewish piety and a necessarily

---

[2] This paragraph abbreviates and refines an argument I first made in *IJS*, 87–99. And see Shaw, "Josephus," 360: "power [in the segment of Jerusalemite society into which Josephus was born] was seen to derive not just from wealth, some of which derived from priestly status itself, but also from the control of sacred knowledge."

fraught and ambivalent relationship with Rome. Hence the flirtations with sectarianism, and, in the case of Josephus's friends being held at Rome, possibly with political extremism as well. Just for the sake of an illustrative comparison one may think of the paradoxical political, cultural, and religious impact of the tremendous influx of Western money into the petroleum states of the Persian Gulf in our own time.

Whatever its explanation, the enthusiastic participation of large segments of the upper class, mainly priestly, youth of Jerusalem in the revolt against Rome appears to be a fact, extensively documented by Josephus, himself one of the participants.[3] The nature of Josephus's participation may also be diagnostic: even his own cautiously and defensively presented accounts of his revolutionary activities in Lower Galilee make it clear that he was motivated not only by hostility to Rome (which he tries to obfuscate in the circumstantially richer and in other ways more plausible account in the *Autobiography*) and by devotion to Jewish institutions heightened to the point of desperation. He was motivated at least as much by desire for adventure—or at any rate something to do—and profit: even in his own account many of his activities seem less like those of a revolutionary general, or more accurately a guerilla leader, than like those of a private entrepreneur. This is precisely the intention Josephus attributed to a competitor and critic of his named Justus (*V* 340–42), and it seems fair to suppose that many of the rebel leaders, especially the wealthier ones, had similarly mixed, perhaps often little analyzed, motivations.[4]

When Nero finally sent a large army, commanded by a senior senator named Titus Flavius Vespasianus (Vespasian) and his son, commonly known as Titus, the Galilean revolt quickly collapsed, and Josephus defected to the Roman side (summer of 67).[5] He spent the following three years traveling with and occasionally working for the Roman army in Palestine, a period that culminated in his presence at the siege and destruction of Jerusalem in the summer of 70. By this time Josephus was no longer a common captive: the previous summer Vespasian had been declared emperor by his troops and had marched off to Rome, freeing Josephus and apparently granting him Roman citizenship as a member of the *gens Flavia* before he left. This may have been recompense for Josephus's

---

[3] This is also extensively discussed in the literature: S. Cohen, *Josephus in Galilee and Rome: His Vita and Development as a Historian* (Leiden: Brill, 1979), 181–99; in greatest detail, Goodman, *The Ruling Class of Judaea*; see also J. Price, *Jerusalem Under Siege: The Collapse of the Jewish State, 66–70 C.E.* (Leiden: Brill, 1992), 27–38.

[4] On Justus, see T. Rajak, "Justus of Tiberias," *CQ* 23 (1973): 246–68.

[5] *BJ* 3.392–403. For a discussion of Josephus's life after 67, see S. Schwartz, *Josephus and Judaean Politics* (Leiden: Brill, 1990), 4–21.

infamous prophecy that Vespasian would be emperor, supposedly uttered at the time of his surrender, as Josephus says (*BJ* 4.622–29). Or perhaps, as those who are skeptical about the prophecy might prefer to think, it was merely a kind of amnesty Vespasian offered to Josephus among other helpful captives at the time of his still theoretical accession.

In any case, Josephus soon made his way to Rome, where he lived in a house Vespasian owned (*V* 422–23) and began to write a history of the Jewish revolt, first in Aramaic, intended for a readership of Jews and other inhabitants of the Roman Empire's eastern frontier (*BJ* 1.3–6; this work is lost), and then in Greek. This second version, the one that survives, was probably completed around 80 (it contains seven books).[6] There is a tendency in very recent scholarship to take Josephus's claim that he intended the second version of the *Jewish War*—he said the same of his later *Jewish Antiquities* as well—for a Roman and, perhaps, also a "Greek" (upperclass non-Jewish mainly urban inhabitants of the eastern part of the empire) audience at face value, but this is an unsustainable oversimplification, since so much of the work is intended to demonstrate that Vespasian and, especially, Titus wished only to protect the Jews and their city and temple, not to harm them—an argument, among others in the book, manifestly aimed at a Jewish readership.[7]

Be this as it may, Josephus's early work, the *Jewish War*, and his later work, the *Jewish Antiquities* (twenty books, completed ca. 93–94), the *Autobiography* (ca. 95), and *Against Apion* (two books, ca. 95?), have, uncontroversially, rather different orientations. The *Jewish War* is much like a normative piece of imperial Greek historiography manifestly inspired by Thucydides. Surprisingly often it assumes a Roman point of view, or perhaps it would be more precise to call it an imperial point of view, since its argument is that the emperors were usually well-intentioned, whereas the Roman administrators in Judaea were venal and corrupt. As Martin Goodman has noted, Josephus's assumption of a pro-imperial perspective can make for uncomfortable reading: can he really have been as pleased to witness Vespasian's Judaean triumph as the account in the *Jewish War*,

---

[6] I have adopted the dates proposed by C. P. Jones, "Towards a Chronology of Josephus," *SCI* 21 (2002): 113–21, which reflect the revival of an early dating for the death of King Agrippa II.

[7] Steve Mason has been the most influential proponent of an intended elite Roman audience, exclusively, a position that is a priori unlikely and has gained little plausibility from having been repeatedly argued; see, for example, S. Mason, "Of Audience and Meaning: Reading Josephus' Bellum Judaicum in the Context of a Flavian Audience," in *Josephus and Jewish History in Flavian Rome and Beyond*, ed. J. Sievers and G. Lembi (Leiden: Brill, 2005), 71–100. For a view close to that advocated here, see, in the same volume, J. Price, "The Provincial Historian in Rome," 101–18; on the audience of *AJ*, see P. Höffken, "Überlegungen zum Lesekreis der 'Antiquitates' des Josephus," *JSJ* 38 (2007): 328–41.

book 7, suggests?[8] On the other hand, Josephus also argues that the "official" Jewish leadership and most of the people wanted peace, even if inef-
fectually so; only some highly motivated individuals lower in the social
hierarchy were hostile to Rome. The *Jewish War* thus also seeks to defend
the Jews. Accordingly, it downplays as far as possible the distinctiveness
or exoticism of the Jews. Unlike so much imperial Greek writing, though,
the *Jewish War* never describes Rome as a generally beneficent power and
never expresses its author's identification with Roman imperial aims. Despite the unattractive toadying, Josephus, at least in his writing, never
identified himself as a Roman. In his view, Rome is to be submitted to because it is extremely powerful, and failure to submit is, as the case of the
Jews demonstrates, suicidal. Under the bluster of the *Jewish War*, it is easy
to see the work of a crushed and frightened provincial.[9]

The later work tends to strike most readers—and has struck many
scholarly commentators—as more "Jewish." Here Josephus tends to emphasize, and also to defend, the Jews' distinctiveness. He makes more use
of biblical language and concepts and correspondingly less use of ideas
borrowed from popular Greek philosophy and classical literature, though
these are certainly not absent. One of the central ideas of the *Antiquities*—when the Jews observe their laws God rewards them, and when they
do not, he punishes them—is simply taken over from the biblical Deuteronomic historian.[10] And other ideas that were important in the *Jewish
War*, for example, that God has gone over to the Romans, are here omitted. All of Josephus's later work is manifestly much more concerned than
the *Jewish War* to defend the validity of the Torah, of the Jews' "ancestral
laws," often with a surprising degree of militancy. Indeed, the first half of
the *Jewish Antiquities* consists of a paraphrase of the Hebrew Bible and includes long sections featuring summaries of pentateuchal laws[11]; for its
part, *Against Apion* is explicitly apologetic, defending the antiquity and
peculiar lifestyle of the Jews from their pagan detractors. The *Jewish War*
had not rejected the validity of the Torah (though one may wonder about
the implications for the covenant of God's having joined the Roman side),

---

[8] Goodman, "Josephus as a Roman Citizen," *Josephus and the History of the Greco-Roman
Period: Essays in Memory of Moron Smith* , ed. F. Parente and J. Sievers (Leiden: Brill, 1994), 329–38.

[9] See Goodman, "Josephus as a Roman Citizen"; cf. A. Eckstein, "Josephus and Polybius: A
Reconsideration," *CA* 9 (1990): 175–208; M. Stern, "Josephus and the Roman Empire," in *Josephus
Flavius: Historian of Eretz-Israel in the Hellenistic-Roman Period*, ed U. Rappaport (Jerusalem:
Yad Ben Zvi, 1982), 237–45.

[10] See my *Josephus and Judaean Politics*, 170–208.

[11] The most incisive comparison of *BJ* and *AJ* remains Cohen, *Josephus in Galilee and Rome*,
48–66; also still fundamental is H. St. J. Thackeray, *Josephus the Man and the Historian* (New
York: JIR Press, 1929), 23–74.

any more than *Antiquities* or *Against Apion* preached hostility to Rome. But the themes are given very different sorts of emphasis. In analyzing the writings of Josephus it is worth retaining the cautious practice of considering his earlier and later works separately.

Benefaction and Memory

This chapter concerns evidence from Josephus and from archaeology for two overlapping but not coextensive practices. The first of these is private benefaction to corporate entities, nowadays generally called euergetism (from the Greek *euergetes*, benefactor), especially if the beneficiary was a Hellenistic or Roman city.[12] This practice could be seen as constituting a resurgence of oligarchic ideology in a still notionally democratic political environment: wealthy citizens were expected (in some places and at some times this expectation approximated a demand) to pay for a disproportionate amount of the public expenses of their cities, but in return for this they won the approbation and loyalty of the citizen body as a whole. The act of benefaction thus served the rich as a way of celebrating their wealth and dramatizing and institutionalizing their civic pride and civic dominance. The citizen body reciprocated by voting to pass decrees honoring its benefactors, by providing them with symbolic gifts such as gold crowns, the right to sit in the front row in the municipal theater, and monumental statues erected in the public marketplace or another public space, accompanied by an inscription commemorating the community's gratitude. The practice of euergetism thus also allowed the citizenry to display its own civic pride, in addition to its corporate solidarity and its enduring self-conception as an egalitarian or democratic body, not to mention its careful maintenance of classical Greek traditions. In the first century of the Roman Empire, which corresponds to the last century of the Second Temple period, euergetism emerged as a major political tool; Rome relied increasingly on its alliance with city councillors, especially in the urbanized east, whose hold on their fellow citizens depended to a large extent on the practice of municipal benefaction and on the prestige and political leverage they secured thereby.

The fact that reciprocation to benefaction frequently though not invariably (see below) took the form of commemoration in plastic form suggests that another objective of benefaction might be perpetuation of

[12] The term was popularized but not invented by Paul Veyne. On the history of the term, see P. Garnsey, "The Generosity of Veyne," *JRS* 81 (1991): 164–68.

the fame and memory of the donor. Euergetism was one of several ways of achieving this goal in the early Roman imperial world. Josephus claims that Herod built and named certain fortresses and other settlements as ways of memorializing himself, his friends, and his relatives. People not in the position to found cities or build fortresses had more affordable ways of perpetuating their memories, through inscribed dedications in temples, funerary monuments, and the like. What these had in common was the assumption that the subject could somehow secure immortality or at least enhance his postmortem longevity by having his (or her) name written, perhaps on some object symbolizing him- or herself, and displayed in a public or semipublic space. In the early and high empire, Romans were obsessed with public writing. For this reason, scholars frequently speak of them as having had an "epigraphical culture." In a premodern setting, in which literacy rates were certainly much lower than ours, the prominence of writing should not be taken for granted.[13] How, then, can it be explained?

The desire to be named and remembered links most of the major categories of early imperial Roman epigraphy: honorary, dedicatory, and funerary. In fact, it has recently been argued that Roman culture of the early empire was unusually concerned with memorialization. In this view, the first century was characterized by a profound anxiety about the individual's place in the world, a consequence of the social upheavals produced by Roman expansion. People responded to this anxiety in two ways: first, with monumental construction, and second, by constantly writing their names in public and semipublic spaces. The tombs of the citizenry and the writing that decorated them, the dedicatory and honorary inscriptions posted in temples and marketplaces, all reflected efforts by citizens and the communities they supported to mark their places in an alarmingly unstable world.

This is a rather reductive account of Greg Woolf's attempt to explain the rise of the epigraphical culture in the early Roman Empire.[14] It seems obvious in retrospect that one should be cautiously skeptical about the ascription of moods or states of mind—in this case anxiety—to abstractions like society, however heuristically useful such abstractions may be, in a way that flirts with the pathetic fallacy. Still, even if we think that large-scale cultural shifts are not so easy to explain, we can admit their reality and ask some questions of our own about them. Something did

---

[13] See W. V. Harris, *Ancient Literacy* (Cambridge, MA: Harvard University Press, 1989).

[14] G. Woolf, "Monumental Writing and the Expansion of Roman Society in the Early Empire," *JRS* 86 (1996): 22–39.

change under the early empire; the Mediterranean-wide spike in monumental construction and lapidary writing is real and meaningful, and, like so much writing from the ancient Mediterranean world starting sometime in the Iron Age, whether carved or painted on stone or inscribed in books, it was meant at least in part to secure the memorialization of the people named.[15] In this way, study of a specifically Greco-Roman epigraphical culture intersects with the cross-cultural study of social memory, the ways in which groups of people construct and memorialize their corporate past.[16] A broader study of social memory in first-century Jerusalem would be a fine project, able to draw on unusually rich documentation by the standards of premodern Jewish history. Susan Alcock's recent essay on the Athenian agora in the first century could provide an excellent model.[17] But the question I am concerned with here is somewhat different.

Given the cultural, social, and political importance in the Roman world of the overlapping practices of memorialization and euergetism, I ask instead whether or how Jews in the century preceding the Jewish revolt against Rome, especially those of Jerusalem, where both the evidence and the political impact are concentrated, participated. In fact, the core idea of this chapter was based on a moment of intuition I had while thinking about predestruction Jerusalemite epigraphy: when considered as an example of early imperial municipal inscriptional practice, Jerusalem's epigraphical culture is surpassingly odd. Specifically, surviving texts are overwhelmingly very brief graffiti. There is little monumental epigraphy and few or none of the building or honorary inscriptions typical of cities in the eastern Roman Empire.

Now, this anomalous fact *could* be reconciled with a hypothesis of Jerusalem's fundamental cultural normalcy—for example, by arguing that the remains give a skewed impression of the actual material culture of first century Jerusalem—or at least its partial normalcy—partial because even normalizers can scarcely overlook the fact that in important ways, first-century Jerusalem was *not* a normal eastern Roman city: it was not just a pilgrimage

---

[15] See M. Beard, "Writing and Religion: *Ancient Literacy* and the Function of the Written Word in Roman Religion," in *Literacy in the Roman World*, ed. J. Humphrey, *JRA* Suppl. 3 (1991): 133–43; H. Mouritsen, "Freedmen and Decurions: Epitaphs and Social History in Imperial Italy," *JRS* 95 (2005): 38–63.

[16] See especially J. Fentress and C. Wickham, *Social Memory* (Oxford: Blackwell, 1992), and for a bibliographical survey, J. Olick and J. Robbins, "Social Memory Studies: From 'Collective Memory' to the Historical Sociology of Mnemonic Practices," *Annual Review of Sociology* 24 (1998): 105–40.

[17] S. Alcock, *Archaeologies of the Greek Past: Landscapes, Monuments, and Memories* (Cambridge: Cambridge University Press), 2002, 51–86.

center, a status it shared with several other Mediterranean cities, but also the metropolis of a nation,[18] a nation united, if only symbolically, by professed adherence to a separatist, exclusivistic religious ideology. But it is equally impossible to deny that Jerusalem was in other ways a fairly typical eastern Roman city. After all, the city and the *ethnos* as a whole required the support of its rulers and also friendly relations with its political, social, and cultural environment; without these, it could hardly survive. So, Greek was widely used, emperors, generals, and other grandees were warmly flattered and supported, and the public architecture and private lifestyles of the elites bore a more than passing resemblance to those of their counterparts elsewhere in the region.[19] Hence we can never know a priori whether to expect to encounter items from the standard repertoire of Greco-Roman culture among the Jews. The challenge for the historian is to pin down in as precise a way as possible the details of Jerusalem's civic compromise, to borrow Richard Gordon's phrase[20]: how far did it buy into the system, what did it reject, and what did it accept, but only with adaptations?

Josephus's treatment of the practices for which inscriptions can serve as a tracer—benefaction, its reciprocation, and memorialization—can help explain Jerusalem's epigraphical remains by revealing to us something of the Jews' ambivalences toward these practices. In other words, the epigraphical remains, if understood properly, give a correct impression of the

[18] As emphasized by V. Tcherikover, "Was Jerusalem a 'Polis'?" *IEJ* 14 (1964): 61–78; see also M. Stern, "'Jerusalem, the Most Famous of the Cities of the East' (Pliny, Natural History V, 70)," in *Jerusalem in the Second Temple Period: Abraham Schalit Memorial Volume*, ed. A. Oppenheimer, U. Rappaport, and M. Stern (Jerusalem: Yad Ben Zvi, 1980), 257–70.

[19] Use of Greek (the vagueness of this formulation is intentional: greater—and correspondingly more misleading—specificity is unnecessary for my purposes): see the material gathered by L. Y. Rahmani, *A Catalogue of Jewish Ossuaries in the Collections of the State of Israel* (Jerusalem: IAA, 1994); discussions of the issue in J. N. Sevenster, *Do You Know Greek? How Much Greek Could the First Jewish Christians Have Known?* (Leiden: Brill, 1968); less satisfactorily, J. Barr, "Hebrew, Aramaic and Greek in the Hellenistic Age," in *Cambridge History of Judaism*, ed. L. Finkelstein and W. D. Davies (Cambridge: Cambridge University Press, 1989), 2:79–114; S. Schwartz, "Language, Power and Identity in Ancient Palestine," *Past & Present* 148 (1995): 3–47; P. van der Horst, "Greek in Jewish Palestine in Light of Epigraphy," in *Hellenism in the Land of Israel*, ed. J. Collins and G. Sterling (Notre Dame, IN: University of Notre Dame Press, 2001), 154–74. On foreign grandees, see Schürer-Vermes 2:309–13; D. Schwartz, "On Sacrifice by Gentiles in the Temple of Jerusalem," *Studies in the Jewish Background of Christianity* (Tübingen: Mohr Siebeck, 1992), 102–16. The architecture of Jerusalem is surveyed by L. Levine, *Jerusalem: Portrait of the City in the Second Temple Period* (Philadelphia / New York: JPS / JTS, 2002), 313–50; on material culture, see H. Geva, ed., *Jewish Quarter Excavations in the Old City of Jerusalem conducted by Nahman Avigad 1968–1982*, vol. 2 (Jerusalem: IES, 2003); and idem, "Jerusalem," *NEAEHL* 2.717–57.

[20] R. Gordon, "Religion in the Roman Empire: The Civic Compromise and its Limits," in *Pagan Priests: Religion and Power in the Ancient World*, ed. M. Beard and J. North (Ithaca, NY: Cornell University Press, 1990), 235–55.

city's extremely fraught and limited reception of these crucial elements of Roman culture. I continue therefore with a brief survey of the inscriptions of Jerusalem in the last century before its destruction in 70 CE.

The Epigraphical Culture of Jerusalem

The epigraphical remains of Jerusalem from the period between the reign of Herod and the destruction (37 BCE–70 CE) are unlike those of most other cities of comparable size (however precisely we calculate it) and importance in the eastern Roman Empire.[21] In brief, the overwhelming majority of instances of public or quasi-public writing consist of graffiti scratched on limestone ossuaries.[22] These inscriptions, of which there are several hundred, normally record only the name of the deceased, usually either in Aramaic letters or in Greek (a handful are in Palmyrene), without so much as a *hic iacet*, though there are exceptions.[23] Inscriptions of

[21] It is generally agreed that under Herod the city covered about 90 hectares—a bit under twice the size of the average city of high imperial Roman Gaul (see below). Subsequently an additional tract of land was incorporated into the city, through the construction of a "third wall." But the location of this wall is controversial: either it roughly followed the course of the current northern wall of the Old City, or it passed through the modern Sheikh Jarrah neighborhood several hundred meters to the north. If it followed the northern route, the city's area was nearly doubled. But the land newly annexed to the city, in this view, is generally regarded as having been sparsely populated. See Geva, "Jerusalem," and Levine, *Jerusalem: Portrait of the City*, 313–18.

Population size has been much more controversial: one should resist the temptation of averaging out the extreme estimates, which seems to be more or less Levine's method (340–43), yielding a figure of perhaps 70,000–100,000. Price's aporia (*Jerusalem Under Siege*, 208–9) is, strictly speaking, correct, given the uncertainties involved in estimating average population densities of built-up areas—the only truly respectable technique for calculating population sizes of ruined cities—but there is still some utility in such estimates, if carefully done, because they may provide figures likely to be correct within an order of magnitude. Broadly parametric figures are the best to be hoped for, in any case, and are also extremely useful (it is important to know that figures like 300,000 or 10,000 are practically impossible for the population size of Jerusalem in 66 CE). The best such accounts are by M. Broshi, "La population de l'ancienne Jérusalem," *RB* 82 (1975): 5–14, and, more recently, idem, "The Inhabitants of Jerusalem," in *The City of the Great King: Jerusalem from David to the Present*, ed. N. Rosovsky (Cambridge, MA: Harvard University Press, 1996), 9–34, esp. 15, who suggests a figure of 60,000. Woolf's discussion of the population density of Gallic cities (he proposes a maximum of 150 per hectare) suggests a figure closer to 30,000 for pre-revolt Jerusalem, though Broshi's reasons for positing a population density of more than 300 per hectare are not completely unconvincing; see G. Woolf, *Becoming Roman: The Origins of Provincial Civilization in Gaul* (Cambridge: Cambridge University Press, 1998), 137–38.

[22] For bibliography, see V. Fritz and R. Deines, "Jewish Ossuaries in the German Protestant Institute of Archaeology," *IEJ* 49 (1999): 222–41, esp. 237–39, updating Rahmani, *Catalogue*.

[23] For summaries, see H. Misgav, "The Epigraphic Sources (Hebrew and Aramaic) in Comparison with the Tradition Reflected in Talmudic Literature," PhD dissertation, Hebrew University, 1999, 19–20; Rahmani, *Catalogue*, 11–19.

similar type have been found in burial caves and monumental *nefashot*, or mausolea, scattered around the outskirts of the city. Even here, though, writing is much less common than in the earlier Palestinian burial caves of Marisa (Tell Sandahanna), or the later ones of Bet Shearim.[24] As examples of what *is* there, there is an enigmatic, very roughly carved graffito from the Tomb of the Kings, and a longer graffito, interestingly in Hebrew, listing the names of the members of the priestly clan of Hezir buried in their famous mausoleum in the Kidron Valley (CIJ 1388, 1394).[25]

Several nonfunerary inscriptions have turned up, too, for example in the Jewish Quarter excavations, but these are similar in character to the funerary, very brief, often graffiti, often apparently simply marking possession of an item. Aside from the *benei* Hezir inscription just mentioned and a very enigmatic Aramaic inscription from Givat Hamivtar, north of ancient Jerusalem,[26] the few relatively long texts from Jerusalem are all in Greek: the epitaph of Nicanor (CIJ 1400); the warning inscription from the Temple, explicitly addressed to gentiles; the dedicatory inscription of the synagogue of Theodotus (1404), a synagogue explicitly built in part to serve the needs of pilgrims from the Mediterranean diaspora.[27]

In sum, one might fairly characterize the epigraphical culture of first-century Jerusalem as largely informal and consisting overwhelmingly of personal names and little else. The exceptions to this generalization usually reflect in a fairly transparent way the epigraphical practices of places other than Jewish Palestine.

Now, as already suggested, an argument can be made that Jerusalem's epigraphical culture was actually much more normal than the surviving

[24] Cf. Misgav, "Epigraphic Sources," 19–20, emphasizing that the overwhelming majority of ossuaries and graves of the Second Temple period are anepigraphic.

[25] On the Tomb of the Kings, see M. Kon, *The Tombs of the Kings* (Tel Aviv: Dvir, 1947); on the Kidron Valley monuments, see now Barag, "The 2000–2001 Exploration of the Tombs of Benei Hezir and Zechariah." According to Barag, the monument of the Benei Hezir was built in the later second century BCE and remained in use until 70 CE.

[26] See J. Naveh, "An Aramaic Tomb Inscription Written in Paleo-Hebrew Script," *IEJ* 23 (1973): 82–91; and E. S. Rosenthal, "The Givat Ha-Mivtar Inscription," *IEJ* 23 (1973): 72–81. Note also the Aramaic inscription marking the alleged burial place of Uzziah, king of Judah: E. L. Sukenik, "An Epitaph of Uzziahu King of Judah," *Tarbiz* 2 (1931): 288–92, with the additional comments of E. Ben-Eliahu, "The Source of the Tombstone Inscription of Uziah," *Cathedra* 98 (2000): 157–58, curiously unaware of A. Schremer, "Comments Concerning King Uziah's Burial Place," *Cathedra* 46 (1987): 188–90. And note also the brief, fragmentary Hebrew text discovered by Mazar near the Temple Mount, apparently a kind of street sign directing the (priestly?) pedestrian to the "Bet Ha-Teqi'ah" (literally, 'house of the [shofar ?] blowing'), whatever that may be: B. Mazar, "A Hebrew Inscription from the Temple Area in Jerusalem," *Qadmoniot* 3 (1970): 142–44.

[27] The standard dating to the first century is compellingly defended by J. S. Kloppenborg-Verbin, "Dating Theodotos (CIJ II 1404)," *JJS* 51 (2000): 243–80. He also provides a bibliography of inscriptions from ancient Jerusalem not carved on ossuaries.

evidence indicates, for the evidence has been skewed by the repeated destruction and rebuilding of the city: there must have been the sort of dedicatory and building inscriptions found in every city of the Roman east,
even small ones, in large quantities; the appearance of the public spaces of
Jerusalem was in this view not as transgressive as a superficial survey of
the epigraphical remains would lead one to conclude.

There is undoubtedly some truth to this argument. According to Josephus (AJ 15.267–79) Herod's theater at Jerusalem was decorated with
many inscriptions (epigraphai) glorifying Augustus. I return later to the
fact that Josephus here denounces the whole complex of cultural practices
embodied in the amphitheater as alien to Jewish customs.

Perhaps somewhat more significant is an inscription published by
Benjamin Isaac.[28] This fragmentary Greek text, inscribed on a small limestone plaque, seems to commemorate a donation made, possibly in the
reign of Herod, by someone called something like Paris son of Akeson, a
resident of Rhodes, perhaps to fund a segment of pavement, possibly in
or near the Temple precinct. To be sure, there are many uncertainties
about this text, but the small size of the plaque, and the probably modest
size of the donation (counted in drachmas, not talents, though this does
not prove much), make Isaac's suggestion that there were many other
texts like this around the Temple Mount very plausible.

Such brief commemorations of donations are not typical Greco-Roman
building inscriptions. Isaac's text, if his interpretation of it is correct, is
most closely analogous to inscriptions, mainly from a later period, commemorating the donation of a certain number of "feet" of a synagogue or
church prodromos or nave mosaic.[29] These are not so much building or
dedicatory inscriptions as commemorations of individual pious acts, conceptually similar to votive inscriptions (some of which were almost certainly to be found in the Jerusalem temple too).[30] In some contexts such
inscriptions may have had a kind of euergetistic function, as they certainly did centuries later in churches and synagogues.[31] But the supposi-
tion of such a function in this case is very much complicated by the for-
eignness of the donor and the international character of the central public
spaces of Herodian Jerusalem. An inscription like that of Paris son of
Akeson can be construed as euergetistic in only the most symbolic of

---

[28] B. Isaac, "A Donation for Herod's Temple in Jerusalem," IEJ 33 (1983): 86–92 (reprinted in
The Near East under Roman Rule: Selected Papers [Leiden: Brill, 1998], 21–28).

[29] For example, IGLS 4.1319–1337, with comments of Mouterde and Jalabert ad loc.

[30] For a suggestive discussion of the cultural significance of votive inscriptions, see Beard,
"Writing and Religion."

[31] See Schwartz, IJS, 280–89.

ways, as commemorating a benefaction not to the citizens of Jerusalem (such a concept seems not even to have existed)[32] but to the scattered, linguistically and culturally diverse *ethnos* of the Jews.

Notwithstanding these exceptions, then, the epigraphical culture of Jerusalem was in Roman terms highly eccentric. Analysis of Josephus's comments about memorialization and benefaction may help explain why.

Memory in Josephus

Josephus's *Erga*

It may be worth beginning with a basic and at first glance trivial observation. There is some reason to believe that Josephus's two main historical works, the *Jewish War* and the *Jewish Antiquities*, were written to memorialize the characters and events described in them.[33] By saying this I do not mean to exclude the alternative view, that the works were written to advance certain arguments or prove certain points. So, Josephus says in the introduction to the *Jewish War* that he wrote it to display not only the might of the Romans but also the seriousness of the Jews' resistance, and despite this to demonstrate that the Jewish nation was not actually hostile to the Romans but was forced into revolt, and the Romans into response, by *stasis*—internal factional strife—a theme borrowed from Thucydides.[34] For its part, the *Antiquities* was written to celebrate Moses, but also to show that when the Jews followed God's laws, they prospered, and when they neglected them they suffered.[35] That these really were Josephus's concerns

---

[32] Notwithstanding Josephus's allegation that the emperor Claudius addressed a letter to the Jerusalem *demos*, an entity Josephus himself frequently mentions in *Jewish War*, and the designation of a resident of Hellenistic Iasos, in Ionia, as *Hierosolymites*, which should normally imply citizenship (*CIJ* 2.749): the Jerusalem *demos* is unlikely to have existed in any technical sense, and the case of Niketas son of Jason the Jerusalemite is certainly complicated by the fact that he appears on a list of contributors to the local festival of Dionysos (see discussion in Schürer–Vermes 3.1, 25). The fundamental account remains that of Tcherikover, "Was Jerusalem a 'Polis'?" (esp. 66–67, on the Jerusalem "*demos*").

[33] Cf. Herodotos, *Histories*, 1.1.1.

[34] *BJ* 1.1–16. On Josephus's appropriation—and subversion—of Thucydidean tropes in the preface to *BJ*, see J. Price, "Josephus's First Sentence and the Preface to BJ," in *For Uriel: Studies in the History of Israel in Antiquity, Presented to Professor Uriel Rappaport*, ed. M. Mor et al. (Jerusalem: Merkaz Shazar, 2005), 131–44.

[35] *AJ* 1.14–17. On the aims of *BJ* and *AJ/V*, see Cohen, *Josephus in Galilee and Rome*, 67–180. On the deuteronomic character of *AJ*, see Schwartz, *Josephus and Judaean Politics*. For a different approach to *AJ/V*, see S. Mason, "Should Anyone Wish to Inquire Further (Ant 1.25): The Aim and Audience of Josephus's Judean Antiquities/Life," in *Understanding Josephus: Seven Approaches*, ed. S. Mason (Sheffield, UK: Sheffield Academic Press, 1998); and *Flavius Josephus: Translation and Commentary*, ed. S. Mason, vol. 3, *Judean Antiquities 1–4*, transl. and commen-

can be readily illustrated from the contents of the works. But the works show that he had many other concerns as well. Furthermore, Josephus actually writes that the *Jewish War* is meant to be a memorial of great achievements (*mneme katorthomaton*), presumably of both Jews and Romans.[36] But he evinces a certain cultural self-consciousness: Josephus says that he, "a foreigner, dedicates [*anatithemi*] to the Greeks and Romans a memorial of great achievements, made with vast expense and great labors," and continues by denouncing the "natives" (*gnesioi*, apparently meaning both Greeks and Romans) for neglecting such labors for the pursuit of money and the conduct of lawsuits. In using language pretty directly borrowed from that of honorary and dedicatory inscriptions, Josephus is obviously following the lead of Herodotus and Thucydides, but suggesting that there is something paradoxical in a foreigner (*allophylos*) producing such a piece of writing (and doing it better than the natives). Yet, though this description of a piece of historiography as *mneme* is at first glance a tired commonplace,[37] there are elements of Josephus's account that make best sense if we take the commonplace seriously and assume them to be aspects of a program of memorialization, and one of a type that, notwithstanding the self-consciousness of *War* 1.16, had been to some extent naturalized among the Jews of the first century.[38]

Now, I acknowledge the point made in the only discrete study of memory in Josephus I am aware of, published by Gabriele Boccaccini,[39] that one of chief functions of *mneme* in Josephus's works, especially *Antiquities* and *Against Apion*, is closely related to the function of *zikkaron* in Josephus's biblical sources: what Josephus repeatedly calls on his readers to

---

tary by L. H. Feldman (Leiden: Brill, 2000), xiii–xxxvi. For a less single-minded account, P. Bilde, *Flavius Josephus, Between Jerusalem and Rome* (Sheffield, UK: Sheffield Academic Press, 1988), 75–79, 99–103.

[36] A theme borrowed from Herodotos, who claimed to have presented the results of his investigation (*apodexis histories*) to ensure that "the great and marvelous *erga* of both Greeks and barbarians" not lack *kleos* (fame).

[37] See already H. Immerwahr, "Ergon: History as a Monument in Herodotus and Thucydides," *AJP* 81 (1960): 261–90; D. Lateiner, *The Historical Method of Herodotus* (Toronto: University of Toronto Press, 1989), 13–51.

[38] This may explain a feature of *BJ*'s account of the Great Revolt that as far as I know has not been explained and is unparalleled in Greek and Roman historiography (though I cannot pretend to have checked exhaustively; strikingly, even Livy features no such lists, even though his reliance on the annalistic tradition predisposed him to include many lists): Josephus's tendency to list the bravest fighters of both sides at the conclusion of accounts of battle. This issue would benefit from fuller investigation.

[39] G. Boccaccini, "Il tema della memoria in Giuseppe Flavio," *Henoch* 6 (1984): 147–63; J. Barclay, "Memory Politics: Josephus on Jews in the Memory of the Greeks," in *Memory in the Bible and Antiquity: The Fifth Durham-Tübingen Research Symposium (Durham, September 2004)*, ed. S. Barton, L. Stuckenbruck, and B. Wold (Tübingen: Mohr Siebeck, 2007), 129–42, concerns only part of Book 1 of *CAp*.

remember is the evidence of God's *euergesiai* (benefactions) to Israel, and Israel's obligation to reciprocate these benefactions with gratitude and loyalty.[40] Yet even in repeatedly stating matters in these terms, Josephus is tacitly updating the Bible's conception of memory as an element of a cultural system in which social reciprocity is institutionalized as vassalage or slavery. For Josephus, God is patron and *euergetes* (*AJ* 4.213; 4.317; 6.211; 7.206) more than he is lord. Indeed, Josephus almost never uses the terms *despotes* (master; *AJ* 1.272; 4.40) or *kyrios* (lord) for God, and, unlike many of his Christian and rabbinic near contemporaries, avoids characterizing Israel's relationship to God as one of *douleia*—'*avdut*—that is, slavery or vassalage.[41]

A more drastic innovation is that Josephus sometimes "humanizes" *euergesia* and *arete*, and so speaks frequently of, or implies, the desirability of remembering *people*, starting, in the introduction to *Antiquities*, with Moses. So Josephus supplements God's blessing to Abraham at the binding of Isaac by having God assure him that not only would he be the ancestor of many *gene* (nations, clan-groups) but also that the *genarchai* (founders of these groups, apparently not Abraham alone) would enjoy *mneme aionios*—eternal memorialization (1.235). I would suggest that for Josephus, one of the means of securing such memorialization was inscription in the biblical text itself. That is, for Josephus, any character more or less favorably mentioned in the Hebrew Bible has ipso facto attained *mneme aionios*. Note, for example, the remarkable excursus on King Saul and his sons in *AJ* 6 (343–50; appendix 2, part A). At 340, Josephus interrupts his narrative with two moralistic eulogies. In the first, he praises the witch of En-Dor for showing kindness to Saul without the hope of receiving anything in return and commends this behavior, which flies in the face of the natural human desire for reciprocation, as most noble. The second eulogy concerns Saul, who, though his death in battle had been foretold, nevertheless bravely faced up to his obligation as king to try to protect his nation. Josephus addresses "the kings of nations and the rulers of cities" about the virtue "[of] fac[ing] danger and even death on behalf of their countries, and [of] despis[ing] all terrors." For this is what Saul did, and by forgoing the possibility of honor and loyalty in his lifetime, he

---

[40] Cf. R. Hendel, *Remembering Abraham: Culture, Memory, and History in the Hebrew Bible* (New York: Oxford University Press, 2005), 32–33; M. Brettler, "Memory in Ancient Israel," in *Memory and History in Christianity and Judaism*, ed. M. Signer (Notre Dame, IN: Notre Dame University Press, 2001), 1–17; R. Clements, "ZKR," in *TDOT*, ed. G. Botterweck and H. Ringgren vol. 4 (Grand Rapids, MI: Eerdmans, 1980), 64–86.

[41] The "fourth philosophy" (the name Josephus applies to a rebel group that sinfully intruded itself into Jewish life in the Herodian period) believed that "God alone was their leader and *despotes*" (*AJ* 18.23).

secured through his death *doxa* (glory; perhaps more desirable than mere *time*) and *mneme aionios*. In other words, Saul too, like the witch of En-Dor, admirably suppressed the natural desire to have his benefactions reciprocated. Indeed, he despised even another conventional route to *mneme*—male offspring. For he encouraged his sons to join him in his doomed defense of the Israelites, knowing that the *arete* (virtue, courage) of his sons, much more than their survival, would truly secure his praise (*epainos*) and *ageros* (ageless) *mneme*. Saul knew that this was the best course of action for anyone who desires to achieve a good reputation after death (*he meta ton thanaton euphemia*).

In a speech addressed to the besieged rebels of Jerusalem in *War* book 6 (104–5; appendix 2, part B), Josephus has himself adducing the example of one of the last kings of Judah, Jehoiachin, to argue exactly the opposite point, the moral worth of timely surrender in a hopeless war, but in a conceptual framework similar to that of the encomium of Saul. Because of Jehoiachin's surrender to the Babylonians (which we might have regarded as dishonorable, but which preserved the Temple and the city), Josephus continues, "a holy *logos* hymns him among all the Jews, and memory flowing ever new transmits him immortal to those coming after him" (6.105). Of course, "holy *logos*" here is ambiguous, referring I believe both to the actual biblical text and to oral storytelling (with orality perhaps suggested most strongly by the word "transmits" [*paradidosin*], as elsewhere in Josephus's works),[42] and I would suggest that when Josephus speaks of the eternal memory of Saul and his family he intends a similar ambiguity, with an addition: there Josephus's narrative itself is a component of the flow of memorialization.

One way of understanding such passages is as a proposed solution to a kind of meta-exegetical problem: if we have been given the Pentateuchal laws to live by, and the prophecies to serve as ever-meaningful oracles (as many Jews in the first century, including Josephus, thought), why have we been given the biblical histories? Josephus may be responding here, they are to serve as monuments to the benefactions (*euergesiai*) and great deeds (*aretai*) of the founders of our nation. If so, Josephus's approach to the biblical histories bears comparison to that of Ben Sira, who almost three centuries earlier had written a poem memorializing precisely the *euergesiai* and *aretai* of (a selection of) the biblical heroes (ch. 44–49).[43] So far, then, Josephus appears to have embraced the idea of memorialization:

---

[42] On the oral *paradosis* of the Pharisees, see A. Baumgarten, "The Pharisaic Paradosis," *HTR* 80 (1987): 63–77; more recently and controversially, M. Goodman, "A Note on Josephus, the Pharisees and the Ancestral Tradition," *JJS* 50 (1999): 17–20.

[43] See Mack, *Wisdom and the Hebrew Epic*.

benefactors and saviors can reasonably expect to have their deeds remembered and their memories perpetuated. Here those doing the remembering are the general membership of the community of Israel, and such commemoration takes two forms, which in Josephus's account are scarcely distinguished from one another: oral recitation and inscription in text. To the extent that the latter refers mainly to the scriptural text, its transmission stands in for or is equivalent to the perpetuation of oral recitation. In this context the classical trope of the historiographical text as monumental commemoration is peculiarly fitting, and Josephus incorporates in his rehearsal of this trope both Greek and Jewish elements. Some of Josephus's comments about memory suggest a certain ambivalence about reciprocity, and he also has in the material surveyed so far little to say about the commemorative functions of monumental buildings and public lapidary writing. This curious silence brings us to the question of Josephus's attitude toward euergetism and toward the role of memory in it.

Josephus on Euergetism

Much of the material relevant to the topic comes from Josephus's discussions of the Herodian family, with another important episode in the story of the royal family of Adiabene. The *Jewish War* pays little attention to these episodes: the story of Queen Helena of Adiabene and her sons is omitted altogether; as far as Herod is concerned, in *War* Josephus very briefly lists the king's construction projects before moving on to his central topic, Herod's domestic and succession crises.[44] The *Jewish War* presents Herodian benefaction in a curious way. One the one hand, it is a normal and not especially noteworthy feature of the public life of all the cities of Herod's realm, including Jerusalem (*BJ* 1.401–28). On the other hand, Josephus seems intentionally to avoid characterizing these benefactions as euergetism. Rather, they were deeds of piety (*eusebeia*—1.400—perhaps applied to his gifts in general, not just the Jerusalem Temple), attempts to perpetuate "the memory and the names" of his friends (*philoi*; 1.403), to offer honor to Caesar (1.407), or to provide memorials to his relatives (417) and to himself (419). Only in the case of Herod's gifts to foreign cities does *Jewish War* utilize the typical language of euergetism, characterizing them

---

[44] On Herod's building projects—the most prominent but not the only component of his benefactions—see P. Richardson, *Herod: King of the Jews and Friend of the Romans* (Columbia: University of South Carolina Press, 1996), 174–215; A. Schalit, *König Herodes: der Mann und sein Werk* (Berlin: de Gruyter, 1969), 328–403; W. Otto, *Herodes: Beiträge zur Geschichte des letzten jüdischen Königshauses* (Stuttgart: Metzler, 1913), 77–85.

as generosity (*megalopsychia*, 422), favor or grace (*charis*, 426), and, indeed, benefaction (*euergesia*, 428)[45] in other words, as profiting Herod's clients, not his patrons (including God).

Now, it is possible that Josephus's avoidance of the language of euergetism for Herod's domestic benefactions reflects the Jews' resistance to Herod or to the culture of euergetism itself. But not all Herod's domestic beneficiaries were Jews, and his silence is perhaps more likely to reflect the *War*'s view that Herod had no need to buy his subjects' loyalty and affection. Furthermore, not all his construction projects constituted what is normally meant by euergetism. At Caesarea and Antipatris, for example, Herod might be honored more as *ktistes*, founder, than as *euergetes*, benefactor; similarly, fortresses built in the countryside did not constitute an act of benefaction. Josephus's emphasis on the commemorative aspects of these building projects is correct. In any case, Josephus certainly avoids any suggestion that the Jews or anyone else found Herod's generosity problematic; hence his silence about Herod's gift of a theater, amphitheater, and appropriately murderous games and semi-idolatrous festivals to the people of Jerusalem.

By contrast, *Antiquities* and *Against Apion* present a surprisingly though not absolutely harmonious account of the Jews' attitude to those public honorific gestures, which formed an essential part of the culture of euergetism.[46] This fact makes it useful to begin with the theoretical discussions of benefaction and its culture in *Antiquities* book 4 (the account of the Mosaic constitution) and *Against Apion* book 2 (the Jewish constitution), and to proceed with the accounts of actual benefactions in *Antiquities* 15, 16, 19, and 20.

The Jewish Constitution

Josephus provides the same basic characterization of the Jewish *politeia* (constitution) in *Antiquities* 4 and *Against Apion* 2, though in the former he calls it inappropriately an *aristokratia*, while in the latter he uses the neologism *theokratia*. One of the things Josephus means by both these terms is that there is no place in the Israelite-Jewish constitution (unlike

---

[45] See Hewitt, "The Terminology of 'Gratitude' in Greek."

[46] On the continuity of Against Apion with Antiquities, on more or less precisely this point, see T. Rajak, "The Against Apion and the Continuities in Josephus' Political Thought," in *The Jewish Dialogue with Greece and Rome: Studies in Cultural and Social Interaction* (Leiden: Brill, 2001), 195–217; along similar lines, S. Castelli, "Antiquities 3–4 and Against Apion 2.145ff: Different Approaches to the Law," in *Internationales Josephus-Kolloquium Amsterdam 2000*, ed. J. Kalms (Münster: LIT, 2001), 151–69.

in actual aristocracies) for any extralegal institution. Right after Moses calls the Israelite constitution an "aristocracy" (*Antiquities* 4.223), he exhorts the Israelites to have only the laws as their *despotai* (masters) and to do all things in accordance with them, for (Moses continues) God is a sufficient *hegemon* (leader, ruler).[47] Similarly, in *Against Apion* 2.157–63, though Moses is said to have brought about the Israelites' complete dependency on himself—a situation in which lesser men allow their polities to descend into lawlessness (*anomia*)—he used this fact not for his own aggrandizement (*pleonexia*) or as an opportunity to impose tyranny, but rather to act piously and engage in good legislation (*eunomia*). In this way he displayed his virtue and made the best possible provision for the well-being of those who had made him their leader. A few paragraphs later (175–83), Josephus remarks that the Jews conduct every facet of their lives according to their laws, the result being utter stability. What could be better, he continues, than a constitution that makes God ruler and places the priests in charge of day-to-day governance? For Moses appointed these men to positions of honor (*time*) "not because of wealth or some other incidental advantages, but because they were distinguished by their obedience (*peitho*) and moderation (or good sense, *sophrosune*— 186)." Indeed, the *oikonomia* (conduct, management) of our polity is (implicitly: nothing at all like the *oikonomiai* of the Greeks, but rather) like (what the Greeks would call) a *telete*, an initiation rite, or a *mysterion*. The states of heightened piety, purity, and religious self-control that Greeks struggle to maintain a few days a year, we sustain our entire lives (188).[48]

In sum, in these programmatic, idealizing, and summary passages Josephus describes a constitution that may resemble that of a mystery cult or of other such organizations (I think Josephus is struggling to say here that it is a *religion*). But it is completely at odds with anything familiar from Greek political thought, except for a glancing similarity acknowledged by Josephus himself to the constitution of the Lacedaemonians. Certainly the Jewish *politeia* is essentially unlike any actual Greco-Roman city. Thus, to modernize the language of Josephus's observations, the Jewish

---

[47] On *aristokratia*, see D. Schwartz, "Josephus on the Jewish Constitution and Community," *SCI* 7 (1983): 30–52; in this passage it clearly does not mean what Schwartz claims it means in general—rule by council. On *theokratia*, see H. Cancik, "Theokratia und Priesterherrschaft," *Theokratie: Religionstheorie und Politische Theologie* 3 (1987): 65–77 (exercising due skepticism about the argument that Josephus's conception was influenced by developments in Flavian politics); P. Spilsbury, "Contra Apionem and Antiquitates Judaicae: Points of Contact," in *Josephus' Contra Apionem*, ed. L. Feldman and J. Levison (Leiden: Brill, 1996), 348–68, esp. 362–67.

[48] A comment that mitigates the force of Rajak's observation ("Against Apion," 201) that one of the differences between *War* and *Antiquities* or *Against Apion* is that the latter characterize Judaism as a *politeia*, a civic constitution, whereas the former does not.

constitution is totalizing, while the constitutions of the Greeks are compartmental; the Jewish is divine in origin and nature, whereas Greeks acknowledge at least the partial humanity of theirs; the Jewish constitution grants executive power not to rich men and other local grandees, as the Greeks did in the wake of the collapse of democracy,[49] but to a priesthood chosen for its obedience and piety (in *Against Apion*, though not in *War* or *Antiquities*, Josephus plays down the fact that the priests were a hereditary class). Indeed, the Jewish constitution tries to prevent the domination of some citizens by others; Josephus may have Roman-style patronage in mind.

The main outlines of Josephus's views are thus beginning to emerge: his rejection of the social and cultural norms of the Greek and Greco-Roman city, especially in his later works, is strikingly explicit, but not absolute—hence the account mentioned earlier in which Moses, having made the Israelites his dependents (which could reflect Exodus 14.31), grants them good laws, both as recompense for their loyalty and to display his own virtue. This presentation is very remote indeed from the biblical account, and demonstrates that Josephus did not fully reject but rather adapted the culture of display and reciprocity that formed the core of Greco-Roman urban life.

This combination of rejection and appropriation is exemplified still more poignantly in Josephus's historical accounts; indeed, in *Antiquities*, unlike in *War*, benefaction is such a prominent theme that it seems legitimate to wonder whether Josephus might not have seen one of his purposes in the later books of *Antiquities* as memorializing benefactors to Jerusalem or to the nation of the Jews, or at least certain kinds of benefactors. Of course, the greatest but also most problematic benefactor of all was King Herod, and it is to him that we now turn.

Josephus reports (15.267–79; see appendix 2, part C) that Herod built a theater in and an amphitheater near Jerusalem, and established games featuring athletic, musical, and dramatic competitions, plus horse races.[50] Furthermore, the theater was decorated with inscriptions about Augustus and "trophies of the nations he had conquered." Then the king introduced

[49] And note *CAp* 2.217–19: Jews do not care for silver and gold, or for wreaths of parsley and wild olive; rather, the reward awaiting those who live in accordance with the Law is that they receive a better life in the revolution of the ages.

[50] On the theater, see most recently J. Patrich, "Herod's Theatre in Jerusalem: A New Proposal," *IEJ* 52 (2002): 231–39; Levine, *Jerusalem*, 201–6, discusses these buildings and Herod's games but contradicts Josephus by situating the events described in the amphitheater rather than the theater; see A. Schalit, *König Herodes: Der Mann und Sein werk* (Berlin: de Gruyter, 1969), 370–71. Conversation with Loren Spielman has contributed greatly to my understanding of this issue.

venationes (wild animal hunts). While foreigners were impressed by their lavishness, the "natives" (*epichorioi*) had a different reaction. In fact, Josephus seems to present several different Jewish responses to Herod's benefactions: in the first place (268), the very buildings themselves were "alien to Jewish custom" (*ethos*), for the use of the buildings and the shows or displays that went on in them *ou paradedotai*—were not part of the tradition (*paradosis*).[51] This is milder than the response to the *venationes*, described in 274 as a "manifest abrogation of the customs honored by them," "for," Josephus continues, "it is obviously impious to exchange the [Jewish] customs for foreign practices"; "worst of all were the trophies," because they seemed somehow related to idolatry (abhorrence of statues is a standard theme in Josephus's discussions of this issue).[52] In any case, Josephus says that opposition to these developments led to an uprising among the Jews—easily crushed, but enough to remind Herod of the Jews' profound devotion to their laws (291), and so of their implacable hostility to him as long as he persisted in violating them. It was for this reason, to avert open Jewish revolt, that Herod built fortifications throughout the country.

We should be skeptical about Josephus's argument here.[53] He himself says that most Jews came to accept Herod's illicit benefactions; further-

[51] Presumably, this refers to Jewish tradition in general, not to the *paradosis* of the Pharisees (contrast Schürer-Vermes 1.313)—entities that should be distinguished, notwithstanding the argument of Goodman, "A Note on Josephus."

[52] Josephus's discussions of the subject are surveyed in greatest detail by J.-B. Frey, "La question des images chez les juifs à la lumière des récentes découvertes," *Biblica* 15 (1934): 265–300, esp. 273–82 (cf., more recently, in less detail but with more special pleading, Y. [S.] Stern, "Figurative Art and Halakhah in the Mishnaic-Talmudic Period," *Zion* 61 (1996): 397–419, at 419). On statues in particular, see *CAp* 2.71–78: statues are forbidden because they are a practice useless to God and man; they so little convey honor on their subjects that the Greeks make them even of their favorite slaves. The Jewish practice of honoring the emperor by sacrificing on his behalf is more effective.

The story told at *AJ* 15.267–79 is manifestly meant to be embarrassing to the pious Jews, emphasizing the silliness of their objections and even their *deisidaimonia* (277)—a word that may neutrally denote religious devotion or scrupulosity but may also, even in Josephus's work, mean "superstition" or "fanaticism" (see K. H. Rengstorf, *A Complete Concordance to Flavius Josephus* [Leiden: Brill, 1973], vol. 1, sub v.). Yet in both the preceding accounts and the sequel Josephus repeatedly accuses Herod of violating Jewish *ethe* in a way that makes it clear where his own sympathies lie. This jarring effect is surely the result of Josephus's inept pro-Jewish, anti-Herodian revision of his source, probably Nicolaus of Damascus, which should serve as a warning against the contemporary tendency to apply to Josephus a hermeneutics of goodwill (cf. D. Schwartz, *Agrippa I: The Last King of Judaea* [Tübingen: Mohr Siebeck, 1990], 157).

[53] Schalit, *König Herodes*, 417–82, accepted and extended the implications of Josephus's account, but regarded Herod's activities as a necessary accommodation to Roman demands; for a different view, see M. Smith, "The Gentiles in Judaism, 125 BCE–66 CE," in *Studies in the Cult of Yahweh, 1: Historical Method, Ancient Israel, Ancient Judaism*, ed. S. Cohen (Leiden: Brill, 1996), 298–300.

more, Josephus lists almost all Herod's building projects in Palestine—even the city of Caesarea—among his fortifications in a way that makes it obvious that he is exaggerating Herod's need for protection, and so the Jews' hostility, and so too their single-minded devotion to their laws.

But Herod's benefactions remain an important theme in the continuation: soon after, drought struck the entire region (15.299–316). Herod's treasury was empty because of his building projects, so he stripped his palace of gold and silver and used the precious metals to buy grain in Egypt (303–7), which he then distributed with exemplary care, being especially solicitous of the needs of the aged and infirm (308–10). Josephus (or Herod himself) thereby adapts Greco-Roman euergetism—which was not especially concerned with the well-being of the poor and the weak—to the norms of biblical charity. When he had cared for his own people (that is, the Jews), he helped people in the neighboring districts, so that he distributed 80,000 koroi of grain in his kingdom and 10,000 outside it (311–14). Indeed (315), for the Jews, the hostility aroused by his alteration of *enia ton ethon* ("a few of the customs"; and note this minimizing qualification) was totally forgotten.

And so much the more so when Herod completed what he himself regarded as his greatest benefaction, the new temple of Jerusalem. The account of the celebration accompanying its completion (421–23) repays brief examination. It is generally unlike the accounts of Herod's other festivals, though it surely rivaled or even exceeded them in terms of the quantity of blood shed. In its brevity it also forms a striking contrast to the account of the dedication of Solomon's temple, which occupies approximately a quarter of *Antiquities* book 8 (50–129). Herod himself sacrificed 300 oxen, and the other great men vied to outdo each other in slaughter, though significantly, Josephus here avoids the language of competitive public benefaction. Indeed, God, not the king, was the beneficiary of the people's gratitude, and they thanked him above all for the king's enthusiasm and speed in executing the project. And there was more to it than this: the celebration coincided with the anniversary of Herod's accession, making the whole festival most splendid. In sum, *philotimia* by the king and his retainers, honor and gratitude from the people, all expressed not in terms of Greco-Roman *euergesia* but in terms of ritual and sacrifice—or so Josephus claims.

In Josephus's most extended and explicit comment on Herod's benefactions (16.150–59; appendix 2, part D),[54] he speculates that Herod was

---

[54] A passage Shaw, review of Goodman, was right to call "startling," though it has received little scholarly attention; for Shaw, this passage provides the background for Goodman's claim that euergetism was of little importance in first-century Jerusalem, an argument I am trying here to complicate.

above all motivated by passionate *philotimia* (ambitious striving for honor); he was generous as a way of securing *mneme*—memorialization—for the future and the hope of good reputation in the present (this echoes the account in *War* 1 discussed above). But his constant drive for honor made him exceedingly harsh to his relatives and his subjects, because someone had to pay for all his generosity. Herod's need to be honored was expressed both in intense deference to Augustus and his friends and through his insistence that he be similarly deferred to by his own subjects, and he was enraged if disappointed. And he was constantly disappointed, because the very thing that he regarded as most beautiful, *therapeia*—in both senses, of courting and of being courted (157)—"was alien to the nation of the Jews, who were accustomed to love righteousness more than glory." So he disfavored the Jews, since they could not flatter him by making temples and statues in his honor.

These themes are taken up again with some modifications in Josephus's comparison of Herod and Agrippa I as benefactors (*AJ* 19.328–31; appendix 2, part E). This passage amplifies the rather surprising theme of book 16 that Herod never bestowed favors on the Jews, only on the Greeks. Josephus praises his grandson Agrippa, though, as having had a kindly character and having bestowed benefits on all, but having been proportionately more beneficial to his Jewish compatriots (*homophuloi*). Now, Josephus's account itself strongly contradicts the argument that Agrippa was more generous to the Jews than his grandfather had been. In fact, Josephus is here conflating *euergesia* with character (Herod was wicked and harsh, Agrippa was kind) and more strikingly with piety: Herod neglected the laws, while Agrippa loved living in Jerusalem, observed the traditions *katharōs* (purely, meaning that he either observed them correctly or while he was in a state of ritual purity), and never let a day pass without a rite of purification or a sacrifice.[55]

So, for Josephus, true *euergesia* consists of a combination of generosity, niceness (this can be paralleled in Greek and Roman sources),[56] ethnic solidarity, and the appearance or reputation of careful legal observance,

---

[55] For discussions of Agrippa's alleged piety, and the relation between Josephus's Agrippa and rabbinic stories about Agrippas Ha-Melekh, see D. Goodblatt, "Agrippa I and Palestinian Judaism in the First Century," *Jewish History* 2 (1987): 7-32; Schwartz, *Agrippa I*, 116-34, 157-71. Both argue that Agrippa's piety was not distinctively Pharisaic (Schwartz's argument for the king's pro-Sadducean orientation goes too far; no more convincing is the claim that rabbinic stories about Agrippas Ha-Melekh are all either neutral or hostile; but his argument that Agrippa's piety was mainly a matter of trying to conform with the Jews' expectations is convincing. Why his act was more successful than his grandfather's had been is unknown).

[56] At least to the extent that a proper leader is expected to practice clemency (*epieikeia*) and mildness, or kindness (*praotes*), and to have goodwill (*eunoia*) toward his constituents.

especially, perhaps, the funding of sacrifices. This is why Agrippa, whose actual benefactions to the Jews were dwarfed by those of his grandfather, is praised as genuinely *euergetikos*, while his grandfather Herod Josephus is deprived—and successfully so, it might be added—of precisely what he most strove for, *mneme*.

A final example of the Jerusalemite style in *euergesia* is provided by the royal family of Adiabene, the story of whose conversion to Judaism in the middle of the first century Josephus tells at length in *Antiquities* 20 (17–99).[57] Though this story is not mentioned in *War*, the family is frequently mentioned there: several descendants of the royal family distinguished themselves in battle against the Romans (*BJ* 2.520). More prominently, though, the family was responsible for building at least four of the major landmarks of pre-revolt Jerusalem: three "palaces," and Queen Helena's mausoleum, apparently just outside the city walls but conspicuous or centrally located enough to have been mentioned three times in the fifth book of *War*. For our purposes it is worth emphasizing that the family's building projects in Jerusalem were monumental but private.[58] Their benefaction took a different form, or rather forms, since Josephus states that they performed many "good things" for Jerusalem, but never fulfills his promise to describe them all (20.53). Nevertheless, he does tell (49) how Helena, thankful to God for having preserved her son Izates from the many dangers she thought to be attendant on his decision to be circumcised, decided to travel to Jerusalem in order to thank God in person. But she arrived during a famine (51), and so dispatched her retinue to purchase food, which she then distributed. Her son Izates (53) also sent much money for distribution to the hungry to the "leaders of the Jerusalemites." In any case (52), Queen Helena "left behind the greatest *mneme* of her good deed to our entire nation" (note here that benefaction to Jerusalem is tantamount to benefaction to the Jews). In sum, while famine relief is on the face of it a perfectly normal type of benefaction, it was also in this case a kind of pious practice; one could think here of the resonances of "feeding the poor of Jerusalem" in other contexts. As Josephus implies in the passage just quoted, it was also an expression of ethnic solidarity, for through it Queen Helena celebrated her recently acquired Jewishness. Furthermore, popular reciprocation

---

[57] The great majority of the scholarship on this episode concerns the family's conversion and neglects its subsequent activities in Jerusalem. For some recent discussion, see D. Schwartz, "God, Gentiles and Jewish Law: On Acts 15 and Josephus's Adiabene Narrative," in *Geschichte-Tradition-Reflexion: Festschrift für Martin Hengel zum 70. Geburtstag*, ed. P. Schäfer (Tübingen: Mohr Siebeck, 1996), 1:263–83.

[58] *BJ* 4.567; 5.55, 119, 147; 252; 6.355; M Yoma 3.10 mentions Helena's votive gifts to the temple.

took initially an oral rather than a plastic form—no publicly built statues, no monuments or honorary inscriptions, but rather *mneme*, even,
according to one odd manuscript reading, *mneme eis aei diaboomene*
("memory resounding for all time"—a Thucydidean allusion; this is odd
because Josephus was writing only a generation after the gift). One could
go out on a limb and say that Josephus's story was meant to serve as part
of this memorialization, and go out still further and suggest that the surprising prominence of the family in rabbinic stories about pre-70 Jerusalem shows that Josephus's comment is no bland *hommage* but is meant
seriously: the Jews tried to remember their benefactors, and sometimes
they succeeded.[59]

One final point: though Josephus had remarked in *Against Apion* 2.205
that the Jews, as part of their general contempt for honor, eschewed lavish
funerals and grand funerary monuments, this claim is repeatedly contradicted in his historical accounts, not to mention by archaeology: as we
have seen, Josephus frequently mentions the conspicuous mausolea of Jerusalem, and some examples from the archaeological record were mentioned above.[60] Furthermore, Josephus revealingly remarks in passing,
while describing Herod's funeral rites, that many wealthy Jerusalemites
had impoverished themselves by providing excessively abundant public
funeral feasts in memory of their relatives, as Archelaus did for Herod.[61] I
would suggest that these facts, too, reflect the wealthy Jerusalemites' desire for memorialization, but again expressed somewhat differently than
among their neighbors, namely, through private if monumental construction[62] and through food distribution (which the masses would remember
as Josephus remembered Herod's funeral feast).

---

[59] Cf. the case of "Agrippas Ha-Melekh." The most comprehensive treatment of the rabbinic
material about Helena and her family remains N. Brüll, "Adiabene," *Jahrbücher für Jüdische Geschichte und Literatur* 1 (1874): 58–86; also useful is J. Dérenbourg, *Essai sur l'histoire et la géogra-
phie de la Palestine d'après les Thalmuds et les autres sources rabbiniques* (Paris: Imprimerie Im-
périale, 1867), 224–29.

[60] For a full survey, see A. Kloner and B. Zissu, *The Necropolis of Jerusalem in the Second Temple Period* (Jerusalem: Yad Ben Zvi / Israel Exploration Society, 2003), whose account furthermore demonstrates (pp. 16–22) that even relatively modest burial caves often show signs of
monumentalization.

[61] *BJ* 2.1: "But this practice [of lavish funeral banquets] is a cause of poverty among many
Jews, because they believe that if anyone omits to provide a feast for the masses—even under
compulsion—he is impious [*oukh hosios*]."

[62] This bears comparison with some contemporary Roman views, for example, Pliny the
Younger's sorrow and outrage on discovering that the tomb of Verginius Rufus, "whose memory
has gloriously spread throughout the world," remains neglected, unmarked "by inscription and
name." Still, monumental tombs do help secure the memory of the dead, just as their maintenance provides evidence of faithful friendship. But given the rarity and fragility of these com-
modities, one should build one's tomb and provide for its maintenance oneself (Epistulae

Josephus on Euergetism

In the *Jewish War*, Josephus consistently downplays the Jews' cultural distinctiveness, while in his later work, *Antiquities* and *Against Apion*, he consistently overstates it: hence his description of the Jewish constitution as being utterly at odds with the Greek. According to *Antiquities* 4 and *Against Apion* 2, the Jews do not even have anything recognizably like a politics; rather, they are like a small sectarian organization, all utterly devoted to a body of laws whose goal is to lead them to lives of piety and obedience to God, their only true ruler. These laws are administered by a priesthood that itself is not really a political class but (though Josephus did not have the language to say so) a clergy, religious functionaries distinguished for their own pious compliance with the ancestral laws. So the Jews had no use for any political or social institutions of the sort all Greek cities had, or for any of the attitudes or practices that sustained them. They had no interest in honor or wealth, or even in artistic and literary innovation. They cared only for the Law and for piety.

Even in these programmatic accounts, however, Josephus subtly adapts his view. Thus, the obligation to share goods with the poor is presented not, following the Hebrew Bible, as an aspect of *imitatio Dei*, or sanctity, or national solidarity, important as these themes are for Josephus himself in other contexts, but as an aspect of social reciprocity: we are obliged to give charity in order to secure the gratitude of the poor. And Moses is represented as a classic *euergetes*, but an ideal one, who responds to his constituents' utter dependency on him by offering them good legislation, not by lording it over them. In brief, in Josephus's more theoretical accounts of Judaism, there is little, though not precisely no, space for anything resembling such typically eastern Roman imperial political or social norms as euergetism. However, Josephus's comments about charity do reflect a tradition of adapting poor relief to norms of social dependency that goes back at least as far as Ben Sira. But they also remind us of Josephus's own zeal to acquire dependents, as revealed both in his accounts of his activities in Galilee and in his account of his behavior toward Judaean captives immediately after the destruction of Jerusalem. Brent Shaw was right to insist that real-life Judaean landowners did not refrain from accumulating *clientes*, though they were perhaps rather more hesitant about it than Shaw supposed, and perhaps in some cases understood it as a type of charity.[63]

6.10.3–5) For a discussion of Pliny's views on memorialization, see Woolf, "Monumental Writing," 25–27.

[63] See Shaw, "Josephus." Shaw's views are discussed in detail at the end of this chapter.

The narrative sections of *Antiquities* in general agree with the theoretical accounts, but nuance and complicate them. Here, too, the Jews utterly reject the normal trappings of Greco-Roman euergetism and are unresponsive and even hostile to the culture of *philotimia*, as a result of their unusually thorough devotion to their own laws. Hence their hostility to Herod's theaters and games and their refusal to honor him with statues and temples. Even the construction of the Temple they reciprocated, according to Josephus, only by thanking God, not the king. But Josephus does suggest in the later books of the *Antiquities* that the Jerusalemites did in fact possess a culture of *euergesia*, but one that was different from that of the Greeks. For the Jews, benefaction *was* important, but it was only fully acceptable if combined with mildness of character and especially with piety: while gladiatorial games were an unacceptable gift, food distribution, the provision of sacrifices (and, we are informed by other sources, supporting nazirites), and votive gifts to the temple were likely, though not absolutely certain, to be admired. And the Jews did indeed not reciprocate their benefactors with statues and temples and honorary decrees but with memorialization, apparently in mainly oral form; and monumental tombs and public funeral feasts may have been among the initiatives legitimately available to the wealthy to secure their own memorialization.

The true situation in Jerusalem was certainly still more complicated. Even according to Josephus, the real-life priests of the first century were not simply a pious clergy but had at least some trappings—land, wealth, in some cases groups of friends and dependents—of an aristocracy; not all the Jews actually opposed Herod's theaters and games, and even the exiguous epigraphical evidence available shows that the normative culture of euergetism was not unknown there, and probably not only because Jews of the Mediterranean diaspora like Theodotus the synagogue builder or Nicanor the donor of the temple gates imported it. Nevertheless, the character of the surviving epigraphical remains of first-century Jerusalem suggests that Josephus was not completely wrong: Jerusalem did not have a normal epigraphical culture because it did not have a normal euergetistic culture, and Jewish norms may indeed have been among the things hindering the development of such a culture, or rather providing it with a distinctive shape.

It is worth remembering that though the epigraphical culture and the practice of euergetism that in part sustained it were widespread in the Hellenistic and early Roman eastern Mediterranean, their local manifestations were very diverse: the Jews were not alone in producing unusual local variants. For example, Angelos Chaniotis has recently written compellingly on the peculiarities of the epigraphical and euergetistic cultures of Hellenistic Crete, which bear comparison with those of early Roman Judaea.[64] As at Jerusalem, on Crete, such euergetistic practices as existed received no epigraphical or artistic commemoration; the Cretans, like the Jews, erected no statues of their benefactors, but, Chaniotis suggests, commemorated their deeds orally. Unlike the Jews, though, the Hellenistic Cretans, like most Greeks, did have a highly developed epigraphical practice, which they used for treaties and other public documents, almost the opposite of Jerusalem's private, graffiti-dominated epigraphy. And the Cretans "normalized" their practices almost as soon as the Romans took over, whereas the Judaeans, significantly, did not (though, I have argued elsewhere, they did in the aftermath of the revolts).

The fact is, though, that Jerusalem was not simply an eccentric Greek city, like the cities of Hellenistic Crete. Nor was it a Jewish version of a Greek city, like perhaps Tiberias or Sepphoris, or in some respects Caesarea. It was not a Greek city at all. It had something Josephus called a city council (boule), but this seems to have been a very different sort of body from the boule of a Greek city; in any case, there was no ekklesia, no citizen body. Rather, Jerusalem was the metropolis of the Jewish ethnos—this, in addition to local patriotism, is why Josephus could regard a gift to Jerusalem as a gift to the Jewish people as a whole—and, especially in the first century, in effect it existed fundamentally to house the temple and support pilgrimage. It was thus a very abnormal city indeed. One reason Josephus thought that Jews cared only about piety may be that, while Jews in Tiberias may have had concerns very like those of the citizens of other Greek cities, in some sense in Josephus's native Jerusalem it was true: everything—politics, commerce, benefaction—was subsumed in piety.

Reciprocity and Integration

Brent Shaw (see note 1 above) argued that one of the Jews' crucial problems was that they were unable to adapt, cognitively or culturally, to the idea of the Roman state qua state because they failed to free themselves from the idea that all politics comes down to the personal mediation of power. This is a provocative and counterintuitive argument, and it is not entirely wrong. It is counterintuitive because, as we have seen, the core

---

[64] "From Communal Spirit to Individuality: The Epigraphic Habit in Hellenistic and Roman Crete," in Creta Romana e Protobizantina: Atti del Congresso Internazionale (Iraklion, 23–30 Settembre, 2000), ed. M. Livadiotti and I. Simiakaki (Padua, 2004), 75–87. On transitions in early Roman Crete in general, see also Alcock, Archaeologies of the Greek Past.

social and political ideology of the Jews, what Josephus called their *polit-eia*, as embodied in the Torah, was quasi-republican; it emphasized the equality of the Israelites, their unconditional solidarity, and their shunning of personal dependency. In Josephus's account, the *politeia* of Israel was also heavily institutionalized, centering as it did on the Jerusalem temple and its staff of priests. We could thus argue, against Shaw, that the Jews' problem was not their inability to conceptualize the institutionalized state as an abstraction, since they had long since embraced such a conception. Their problem was that they had a competing and exclusive set of loyalties, that while the Romans ruled by applying the metaphor and some adapted practices of institutional reciprocity to political ends—by regarding the emperor as patron- and benefactor-in-chief and by institutionalizing the euergetistic role of municipal elites—the Jews rejected those practices a priori, or at best metaphorized them differently, as applying exclusively to relations between God and Israel. The Roman state, which was far more totalizing than its predecessors in that it theoretically regarded all its constituents as potential participants in the system, could have no place in Jewish politics.

But we also learn from Josephus that this is simplistic. He claims that the Jews rejected euergetism but also, as Shaw has repeatedly observed, that they embraced something like patronage, or at any rate that personal social dependency played an important social and political role among them (its economic role is harder to specify). In story after story Josephus emphasizes the social and political importance of the big-man and his entourage. Even the chief priests behaved part of the time as pious intermediaries between the community of Israel and its God and part of the time as warlords, and it is very unclear how or whether these two roles were integrated. It may be suggested, though, that the first role made it very difficult for them to play the second in a way that worked to the long-term advantage of the Roman state.

It was inevitably the Jews, not the Romans, who were compelled to pay the price. One of the chief consequences of the three disastrous revolts that ensued was that there were far fewer Jews in the Roman Empire than there had been before their onset, though exact numbers are unavailable. A second consequence is that those Jews remaining in 135 CE had excellent reasons finally to submit to the Romans, politically, culturally, and to some extent probably even religiously. Though little statuary or (pagan) religious architecture survives from the more heavily Jewish cities of northern Palestine, especially Tiberias and Sepphoris, much circumstantial detail in the Palestinian Talmud assures us that these cities were in every respect normatively eastern Roman.[65] The same text repeatedly describes the rank-and-file Jews of the high and later Roman empires as having quite thoroughly internalized Roman values, while the zealous conservators of Jewish traditions, the rabbis, were, like their Greek counterparts in the "second sophistic," suspended between resistance and accommodation.

[65] This was a controversial but in my view not yet successfully challenged argument in *IJS*.

CHAPTER FIVE

Roman Values and the Palestinian Rabbis

The Palestinian Talmud and the Rabbis

The Palestinian Talmud (Yerushalmi, hereafter abbreviated as Y) was published in some sense sometime in the final third of the fourth century CE,
probably at Tiberias in Galilee, under circumstances and for reasons that
are entirely unknown. It is a compendious commentary, about 500,000
words long, on earlier rabbinic texts, especially the earliest one, the Mishnah (ca. 200 CE), to whose organizational structure it adheres. Like Ben
Sira, and for somewhat similar reasons, the Yerushalmi is regarded as an
unusually difficult text. In the Middle Ages it did not enjoy the same prestige and authority as the Babylonian Talmud, and so both the textual and
interpretative traditions are very poor. In fact, there is only one more or
less complete manuscript of the text, MS Scaliger 3, in the library of the
University of Leiden, which is basically identical to the text underlying
the earliest printed edition (Venice, 1523). Otherwise there are some fragmentary manuscripts, some "testimonia" (quotations) in the writings of
medieval rabbis, and, most important, a fair quantity of early fragments,
not all as yet published, found in the Cairo Genizah.[1] The classical medieval Talmud commentators neglected, though they did not completely ignore, the Yerushalmi, and the standard commentaries on the text date to
the eighteenth century, when its study enjoyed a modest revival. Useful
as these and later commentaries are (and they are frequently cited in
what follows), they are quite relentless in their tendency to interpret the
Palestinian Talmud in light of the Babylonian Talmud. This is sometimes

All translations of rabbinic texts in this chapter are my own; they strive to be as literal as the need
for comprehensibility allows.

[1] For an account of the history of the Yerushalmi text, see J. Sussmann's introduction to *Talmud Yerushalmi According to Ms. Or. 4720 (Scal. 3) of the Leiden University Library With Restorations and Corrections* (Jerusalem: Academy of the Hebrew Language, 2005). For a helpful general
introduction to the Yerushalmi, see H. Strack, G. Stemberger, and M. Bockmuehl, *Introduction to
the Talmud and Midrash* (Minneapolis: Fortress, 1996), 164–89; B. Bokser, "An Annotated Bibliographical Guide to the Study of the Palestinian Talmud," *Aufstieg und Niedergang der römischen
Welt* 2.19.2 (Berlin: de Gruyter, 1979), 139–256.

understandable: the state of the text is such that a small proportion of the Yerushalmi simply resists comprehension on even the most elementary level; hence the temptation to anchor its interpretation in the ostensible terra firma of the Bavli. In sum, here, as in the case of Ben Sira, textual and philological issues constitute core hermeneutical problems, and I perforce give them prominence in this chapter.

As to the rabbis, they began in the later first century as the battered, greatly reduced remnant of the class of judges, legal experts, and scribes who had constituted a large and important part of the bureaucracy of Herodian and post-Herodian Judaea, a class that largely overlapped with the priesthood and the sectarian groups.[2] But whereas the first-century bureaucrats, priests, and sectarians had probably numbered in the thousands, their rabbinic survivors numbered only in the dozens.[3] In the aftermath of the destruction and subsequent revolts, they were stripped of whatever official legal or judicial authority they had once possessed, and to the extent that they had residual prestige, they likely functioned mainly as arbitrators, and perhaps, especially later, as low-grade religious functionaries. The modern debate over whether the rabbis or someone else led the Jews after the destruction is rendered moot by the failure of rabbinic literature itself to claim a leadership role for its protagonists.[4] The most the rabbis ever claimed was judicial authority, not as retainers of the Roman state but as embodiments of Torah. In other words, they admitted that in real life they had only as much power, even as judges and legal decisors, as the Jews were willing to give them.

Probably in the course of the third century, the rabbis began to become an increasingly self-conscious group. This is demonstrated by the character of the earliest rabbinic document, the Mishnah, which presents itself as a corporate product of a rabbinic movement. At the same time, a dynastic

---

[2] For this view of rabbinic origins, see S. Schwartz, "The Political Geography of Rabbinic Texts," in *The Cambridge Companion to the Talmud and Rabbinic Literature*, ed. C. Fonrobert and M. Jaffee (Cambridge: Cambridge University Press, 2007), 75–96; idem, *IJS* 110–19; and C. Hezser, *The Social Structure of the Rabbinic Movement in Roman Palestine* (Tübingen: Mohr Siebeck, 1997), 55–77. All these draw ultimately on S. Cohen, "The Significance of Yavneh: Pharisees, Rabbis, and the End of Jewish Sectarianism," *HUCA* 55 (1984): 27–53.

[3] The numbers of Palestinian rabbis named per "generation" in rabbinic sources ranges from about twenty-five in the middle of the second century to about 120 in the late third to early fourth century. There is good reason to take these figures as minima, since rabbis by definition, had disciples not all of whom were named in the texts, but there is no justification for multiplying the figures by a large factor. For a sophisticated discussion, see H. Lapin, "The Origins and Development of the Rabbinic Movement in the Land of Israel," in *CHJ* 4:206–29, esp. 221–2. For sectarian numbers, see *AJ* 17.42 (6,000 Pharisees at the turn of the era); *AJ* 18.21; and Philo, *Quod omnis probus liber sit* 75 (4,000 Essenes at an unspecified date).

[4] See *IJS* 103–28; Lapin, "Origins and Development."

leadership of the rabbis, the Gamalielide patriarchate, began to emerge and by 300 had acquired considerable prestige outside rabbinic circles. The rise of the patriarchate and of its rabbinic retainers (the patriarchs also had nonrabbinic retainers, and by the later third century there were rabbis not associated with the patriarchal court) culminated in a series of imperial decrees passed in the 390s and preserved in the Theodosian Code, recognizing their authority over the religious life of the Jews, among other things.[5] The publication of the Yerushalmi coincided with this development, or preceded it by a decade or two.

There is little doubt that rabbis and patriarchs both benefited from the collapse of the high imperial regime. The patriarchs of Tiberias were not the only native dynasty to rise to power in the unstable conditions of the third century,[6] and both patriarchs and rabbis benefited in the short term from the peculiar theological status the Jews possessed in the eyes of the Christian emperors, especially before the accession of Theodosius II (reigned 402–450): now, for the first time since 66 CE, the Jews were formally, publicly, and legally practitioners of a *religio licita* (however inferior), so that the state recognized their clergy as privileged and authoritative.[7]

There is excellent evidence that the patriarchs of the fourth and fifth centuries were thoroughly romanized, and equally good evidence for their progressive alienation from the rabbis in the same period, though this was probably never as complete as the Yerushalmi seems to imply by its failure ever to mention the later patriarchs.[8] But both rabbis and patriarchs had coalesced as a group around their claim to preserve pre-Roman Jewish traditions and values, in a way that can only have problematized their relationship to the state, especially in its pre-Christian form. It is to this issue that I now turn.

Rabbis and Rome

The rabbis rejected Roman values. In this they were not unique. Some Greek writers of the "second sophistic" (second and third centuries CE)

---

[5] On the emergence of a rabbinic "movement" in the third century, see Lapin, "Origins and Development," 218–19; on the patriarchate and its relationship to the state, Levine, "The Patriarch," and idem, "The Status of the Patriarch in the Third and Fourth Centuries: Sources and Methodology," *JJS* 47 (1996): 1–32; and Schwartz, "The Patriarchs and the Diaspora."

[6] See K. Strobel, "Jüdisches Patriarchat, Rabbinentum, und Priesterdynastie von Emesa: Historische Phänomene innerhalb des Imperium Romanum der Kaiserzeit," *Ktema* 14 (1989/1994): 39–77.

[7] See Schwartz, *IJS* 179–202.

[8] See Levine, "Status of the Patriarch."

adopted an antiquarian pose that allowed them to recreate in their writing a world without Romans. Church fathers, like rabbis, protested with
remarkable frankness against Roman religious ideas and practices. On
the face of it, though, the rabbis were far more vehement than their contemporaries. Many imperial Greek intellectuals reached a quite explicit
modus vivendi with their conquerors, who reciprocated with validation
and appropriation of Greek culture: the political deck was stacked in their
favor, at least in the east. Plutarch, Roman knight and Delphic priest, not
only promoted traditional Greek religion but, in *Parallel Lives*, argued by
example for the parity and essential harmony of Greece and Rome. So too
a century later did Cassius Dio, scion of a leading Greek family of Bithynia,
a prolific Greek writer, and twice Roman consul, in his *Historical Library*.[9]
Tensions are understandably closer to the surface in Christian texts, but
even these make their case against Rome for the most part from deep
within the language and conceptual world of Greco-Roman philosophy
and rhetoric.

Rabbinic rejection of Roman values thus took at least two forms. First,
the rabbis produced a body of literature unlike anything else ever written
in the Roman world. Its alienation or self-alienation from the classical tradition is nearly absolute, which is not to deny the fact, demonstrated by
the exegetical work of Saul Lieberman and his followers, that the Palestinian Talmud and earlier aggadic midrashim are in straightforward ways
products of the late Roman urban east. The Yerushalmi is certainly much
easier to understand if the reader knows something about the high and
later Roman Empire, but expertise in the classical *literary* tradition provides diminishing returns.[10] To borrow a precise (oral) formulation from

[9] For a general discussion, see S. Swain, *Hellenism and Empire: Language, Classicism, and
Power in the Greek World, AD 50–250* (Oxford: Clarendon, 1996), emphasizing in the case of Plutarch the fact that for all his sympathy and admiration, he still regarded the Romans as essentially
foreign (135–86), whereas, not surprisingly, Cassius Dio more fully internalized Roman values
and a Roman identity while remaining self-consciously Greek (401–8). For a detailed account of
the longstanding romanization of Dio's family, see F. Millar, *A Study of Cassius Dio* (Oxford:
Clarendon, 1964), 8–27. I do not mean to reject the points argued by, for example, Greg Woolf,
among others, that this mutual accommodation was fraught, partial, and ambivalent. But it indubitably existed in a way that distinguishes Roman-Greek relations sharply from Roman-Jewish
or, say, Roman-Egyptian relations: Woolf et al. would have benefited from triangulating their investigation. See G. Woolf, "Becoming Roman, Staying Greek: Culture, Identity and the Civilizing
Process in the Roman East," *PCPS* 40 (1994): 116–43, and many of the papers collected in S. Goldhill, ed., *Being Greek Under Rome: Roman Cultural Identity, the Second Sophistic and the Development of Empire* (Cambridge: Cambridge University Press, 2001).

[10] Appropriations of and reactions to the classical literary tradition may in fact be present but
if so are well concealed. For some suggestive case studies, see J. Levinson, "The Tragedy of Romance: A Case of Literary Exile," *HTR* 89 (1996): 227–44, and idem, "'Tragedies Natural and Performed': Fatal Charades, Parodia Sacra, and the Death of Titus," in *Jewish Culture and Society*

the Cambridge Latinist John Henderson, rabbinic textuality is utterly un-Western (I would add it is not very Eastern, either). This sense of rabbinic alienation is surely heightened by the rabbis' decision to compose their texts in Hebrew and Aramaic rather than Greek, on the face of it an effective declaration of independence from classical norms. In fact, though, the rabbis were much farther from those norms than Christians who chose to write in Coptic or Syriac but whose language, rhetoric, and ideas were nevertheless suffused with literary and intellectual hellenism. The Talmud's status as Roman literature needs to be argued in ways that the status of other literary artifacts of the same time and place does not. The rabbis proclaimed their alienation from normative Roman culture in every line they wrote.

Second, the rabbis expressed their hostility toward, contempt for, and fear of Rome and its values quite openly, though to be sure, the earliest rabbinic text, the Mishnah, like Pausanias and, in much of his work, Plutarch, mainly consigns the Romans to oblivion.[11] The rabbis were ostensibly like the Jews in Josephus's accounts of them: all that mattered to them was piety—God, Torah, and commandments; they attributed no significance to power or to the sort of glory or honor that results from domination. They told story after story about how right the Torah was and how wrong the Romans were. They constantly advertised their refusal to collaborate with, and their contempt for, their rulers. On the whole their laws were based on exegesis of the Torah and other specifically Jewish sources. Unlike the Babylonian rabbis, at least some of whom regarded (some) Sasanian laws as valid,[12] the Palestinian rabbis theoretically rejected the validity of Roman law (though this statement requires some nuancing: see below), and in doing so almost explicitly denied to the Roman state a legitimate monopoly on violence. They regarded Jews' attendance of sanguinary games as tantamount to murder unless there was a chance they could save the human victims, who were often condemned criminals (T Avodah Zarah 2.7; Y Avodah Zarah 1.7, 40a), and even prohibited the sale of wild

---

under the Christian Roman Empire, ed. R. Kalmin and S. Schwartz (Leuven: Peeters, 2003), 349–82. For an evaluation similar to the one offered here, see C. Hezser, "Interfaces Between Rabbinic Literature and Graeco-Roman Philosophy," in *TYGRC* 2:161–87.

[11] See Swain, *Hellenism and Empire*, 135–86; J. Elsner, "Pausanias: A Greek Pilgrim in the Roman World," *Past & Present* 135 (1992): 3–29.

[12] On the basis of the dictum, *dina de-malkhuta dina*, "the law of the empire is law" (see below). See also M. Beer, *The Babylonian Exilarchate in the Arsacid and Sassanian Periods* (Tel Aviv: Dvir, 1970), 88–91; J. Neusner, *A History of the Jews in Babylonia*, (Brill: Leiden, 1966), 2:111–19; I. Gafni, *The Jews of Babylonia in the Talmudic Era: A Social and Cultural History* (Jerusalem: Merkaz Shazar, 1990), 42–43; and in greatest detail and most authoritatively, S. Shilo, *Dina De-Malkhuta Dina: The Law of the Land Is the Law* (Jerusalem: Jerusalem Academic Press, 1974), 1–43. See in detail below.

beasts to pagans for fear they would be used in such entertainments (M AZ 1.7). Jews were not permitted to help build amphitheaters, gallows, or even basilicas to be used in the judgment of criminals (M AZ 1.8). Unlike some Church fathers, the rabbis never considered the ethical and legal problems raised by legionary service or municipal honors, because they never seem to have considered the possibility that a Jew might be a Roman soldier.[13] Jews indubitably did serve in the legions, though, and rabbinic silence must imply that the rabbis simply did not consider this a remotely legitimate career option for a Jewish man.[14] Jewish legionaries were ipso facto blatant sinners, and the rabbis wasted no energy providing them with religious rationalizations or palliatives for their misbehavior. The rabbis did not recognize the right of the government to expropriate land from convicted criminals under the *lex cornelia de sicariis et veneficis* (Digest 48.8), or the proprietary rights of the purchasers of such land from the state (the rabbis called this *siqariqon* or *siqariqin*: M Gittin 5.6; T Gittin 3[4].10; see below).[15] The rabbis neither required nor

---

[13] Contrast Tertullian, *De idololatria* 17.2–18.9 (edited and translated by J. H. Waszink and J. C. M. van Winden [Leiden: Brill, 1987]). Tertullian unambiguously prohibited military and municipal service. The Yerushalmi does occasionally mention *bouleutai* (see M. Kosovsky, *Concordance to the Talmud Yerushalmi* [Jerusalem: Israel Academy of Sciences and Humanities / Jewish Theological Seminary, 1982], 2:373), some of whom clearly Jewish, but the only apparent rule—though in fact it sounds more like advice—is the statement of Rabbi Yohanan that "if they mention you [probably meaning "appoint you"] to the *boule* [city council], let the Jordan be your border" (Y Sanhedrin 26b). Did curial service in Tiberias and Sepphoris involve pagan religion? For discussion, see *IJS* 129–61.

[14] On Jews in the Roman army, see A. Oppenheimer, "Jewish Conscripts in the Roman Army?" in *Between Rome and Babylon: Studies in Jewish Leadership and Society*, ed. A. Oppenheimer and N. Oppenheimer (Tübingen: Mohr Siebeck, 2005), 183–91. The rabbis occasionally told stories about Roman soldiers and other officials who converted to Judaism, but these stories had no impact on rabbinic law—they never imagined a figure like the biblical Na'aman (see 2 Kgs 5).

[15] I follow the interpretation of G. Alon, *Toldot Hayehudim Be'eretz Yisrael Bitequfat Hamishnah Vehatalmud* (Tel Aviv: Hakibbutz Hame'uhad, 1961), 2:122–23 (this discussion is compressed in the English translation); S. Safrai, "Sikarikon," *Zion* 17 (1952): 56–64. The rules about such land in the Mishnah and Tosefta are complex and contradictory, but both texts take it for granted that after the war (probably the Great Revolt), the state's seizure of land had no impact de jure on its status—it continued to be owned by its original Jewish owner—though practical concessions had to be made. By contrast, S. Lieberman, *Tosefta Ki-fshutah*, part 8 (New York: JTS Press, 1995), 841–45, reasserted the older view that *siqariqon* denotes any previously Jewish-owned land seized at the time of the Great Revolt, whether by the state or by squatters exploiting the chaos. If this were so, the laws of *siqariqon* would be a far weaker expression of rabbinic resistance to Roman authority. But the Mishnah and Tosefta clearly imagine that *siqariqin* occupied expropriated land both long before and long after the revolt, which thus constituted only one episode in a long history of the Roman state's expropriation of land, and Lieberman's linguistic argument, that *siqariqon* has nothing to do with the *lex cornelia* but is simply equivalent to *leistrikon* and so means more or less "stolen stuff," "brigand's loot," is far-fetched, since in Latin the word *sicarius* means assassin or murderer, not brigand, and its only attested use in Greek is in Josephus, where *sikarios* is the name of the familiar rebel organization, and manifestly has its

(suicidally) prohibited the payment of taxes to the state.[16] They seem to have regarded taxes and other obligations imposed by the government as they would a natural disaster, to be evaded when possible but generally accepted with resignation.[17]

But there is a paradoxical aspect to this account. Not only is such thoroughly elaborated and extensively theorized hostility to a state quite unprecedented in ancient Jewish literature but for all their ostensible resistance, the rabbis lived and worked at a time when the Jews were at peace with their rulers, when after two disastrous centuries or more (starting from Pompey's conquest in 63 BCE), Jewish Palestine was at last successfully integrated in the Roman Empire. Indeed, the world we get a glimpse of—to be sure, a partial and very hazy glimpse—between the lines of the rabbinic texts (especially the Talmud and midrashim) seems to have been calmer, stabler, more orderly, and much less violent than Jerusalem or Tiberias or Caesarea as those towns were described by the integrationist Josephus. Indeed, the cities and large villages that constituted the rabbis' world were demonstrably much more typically Roman places than they, or Jerusalem, had been in the first century.[18] It is a correct truism that the rabbis were not apocalyptists: for all their show of resistance to Rome, there is an important accommodationist strain in their writings.

It is necessary, then, to produce a more nuanced and tension-filled account of the rabbis and their laws and narratives than I have provided in the last pages. Rabbinic resistance is only part of the story, though one that requires emphasis to counterbalance the simplistically integrationist account accepted, especially in the past, by so many American rabbinists.[19] We must also pay careful attention to the rabbis' embrace and even internalization of some Roman values: while they claimed, not totally incorrectly, to live outside the Roman system, and recommended such alienation to their constituents, their actual position was far more complex and interesting.

---

standard Latin meaning. The interpretation of Alon and Safrai, characteristically not addressed by Lieberman, is preferable.

[16] In T. Nedarim 2.2 and Y. Nedarim 3.4 they seem to permit lying to toll collectors (see S. Lieberman, *Tosefta Kifshutah*, part 7, Order Nashim [New York: Jewish Theological Seminary, 1967], 418–19). Elsewhere they seem troubled by the possibility that the shirking of the well-to-do may increase the tax burden on the poor; see D. Sperber, *Roman Palestine: 200–400, The Land* (Ramat Gan, Israel: Bar Ilan University Press, 1978), 125–26.

[17] There were limits to the rabbis' rejectionism. For example there is no hint that they rejected the government's right to coin silver, though they admired a rabbi who refused to look at the images on coins (though presumably he used them; Y Avodah Zarah 3.1, 42c).

[18] See Schwartz, *IJS* 129–61.

[19] See Schwartz, "Historiography on the Jews."

In what follows I examine the Yerushalmi's views on the by now familiar topics of honor, deference, and, of special importance for Roman subjects and citizens such as the rabbis, euergetism. I will not try here to provide a full account of the rabbis' compromises with institutionalized reciprocity, or still more with Mediterranean culture, or for that matter of their attitude to patronage, because these topics are simply much too large, and turn up in some form in almost every tractate. Be this as it may, I begin with a more detailed discussion of the rabbis' view of the legitimacy of Roman law and the Roman state. Predictably, no single view of honor and so forth can be extracted from the Talmud, though I would argue that the text manifests a certain coherence nonetheless. Rather surprisingly, the rabbis to some extent internalized the value of honor, and not only in the relatively weak sense of basic public dignity or, especially for women, something like Roman *pudicitia—tzeni'ut*, seemly modesty—but also in the stronger senses in which honor served as an important commodity for exchange in Roman political and social life—in other words, honor in the sense of social clout or dominance. Nevertheless, they constantly remind their audience that an economy of honor is not ideal, and (in a way that reminds us of Ben Sira) that in the best case, honor inheres especially in piety and in possession of Torah.

A word about method. Though some of the basic textual and philological work on the passages I comment on below has been done by others, in general, older scholarship for the most part took this material at face value as historical and used it to construct positivistic accounts of the social and economic history of the Jews in the Talmud period. Daniel Sperber, especially in his early attempts to write the economic and social history of Roman Palestine, is exemplary here.[20] What is striking about Sperber's work (and I mention him only because he is in some ways the best of the positivists and wrote some of the most responsible and well-informed work on the social and economic history of the ancient Jews), and what makes it now seem to belong to a different era, is that he mined texts rather than reading them. Confronted with the cycle of anecdotes and homilies on patronage in Y Berakhot 9.1, for example, he tried to date the material in the collection, and then (assuming that it provides reliable sociohistorical information, and that, even more problematically, there is no need to be worried about the *typicality* of the information the Talmud allegedly provides) to incorporate it into a historical narrative

---

[20] See D. Sperber, "Patronage in Amoraic Palestine (c.220–400): Causes and Effects," *JESHO* 14 (1971): 227–52, and idem, *Roman Palestine*, 119–35.

drawn from the standard scholarship on the effects of the "crisis of the third century."[21]

I am much less positivistic. I do think rabbinic texts provide us with information, but what they primarily tell us is what the rabbis thought worth committing to writing (or at any rate to fixed oral form), what they were concerned about. So, for example, Y Berakhot 9.1 may or may not accurately report the fascinating fact that the early to mid-third century Babylonian rabbinic immigrant to Palestine, Rav, had a powerful gentile patron, and it may or may not be correct to conclude that such relationships were common for Jews. I would argue that any such conclusions would be inherently shaky. We can be sure, though, that the rabbis thought the story worth telling and writing down, and that they even discovered in it a religious message. To make real, and reliable, sense of the issues, we must begin by treating rabbinic texts as what we know them to be: texts. In other words, we must *read* them—a requirement made all the more urgent by the texts' difficulty and complexity.

Roman Law and the Roman State: Values and Legitimacy

To recapitulate briefly, three of the most prominent characteristics of the rabbis' attitude toward the Roman state are generally merged in the sources but may be worth distinguishing for heuristic purposes. First, the rabbis had a vested interest, and one that was also heavily ideologized, in viewing their version of the law of the Torah as the only legal system under which Jews could legitimately live. This meant they regarded Roman law as basically invalid, at least for Jews. This was a view the Palestinian rabbis shared, *mutatis mutandis*, with their Babylonian colleagues, with all later rabbis, and indeed with all prerabbinic priestly and scribal mediators of the Torah. Yet almost all of these are thought to have regarded some elements of the laws of the countries in which they lived as valid, whereas the Palestinian rabbis theoretically utterly rejected the validity of Roman law, or at any rate the authority of the Roman state to intervene in the lives of its (Jewish?) subjects. So the rabbis had not simply a professional interest in limiting the jurisdiction of Roman law over their constituents and extending the jurisdiction of Jewish law, they—and here is the second point—denied in theory the legitimacy of the Roman state

---

[21] By contrast, B. Visotzky tries to read rather than mine this text, but the result is unconvincing: "Goys 'Я'nt Us: Rabbinic Anti-Gentile Polemic in Yerushalmi Berachot 9:1," in *Heresy and Identity in Late Antiquity*, ed. E. Iricinschi and H. Zellentin (Tübingen: Mohr Siebeck, 2008), 299–313.

tout court. The third point is related to the first two: they also expressed openly and frequently their alienation from nonlegal and nonpolitical aspects of Roman (or state-authorized) culture. I discuss the first two issues in the next section of this chapter and the final one in much more detail in the sequel.

The Babylonian Talmud famously stated at least twice that "the law of the (Persian) empire is law," a principle much discussed by medieval and modern rabbis in their efforts to determine where precisely their own legal authority—that is, the legal authority of the Torah—ended and that of the rulers of the country of their residence began (B Baba Batra 55a, B Baba Qama 113b).[22] In the Bavli, though, it is clear enough from the context that the statement in effect is meant to recognize the state's right to collect taxes and dispose of land:

> Rabbah said, "These three things did 'Uqban bar Nehemiah the exilarch tell me in the name of Samuel: The law of the empire is law, the land tenure of the Persians takes effect after forty years,[23] and royal officials who seize land for (nonpayment of) the *taska* (or, *taksa*, the main Sasanian land tax), their sale of such land is valid."[24]

This was no small rabbinic concession, in part because it apparently entailed overturning the tannaitic laws, which the Babylonian rabbis in principle regarded as authoritative, according to which land seized by the (Roman) government was still in theory the property of its original owner (M Gittin 5.6; T Gittin 3[4].10; see above). Yet it is the Bavli here, and not the earlier Palestinian texts, that is following time-honored Jewish tradition. The Bible itself acknowledges that Ezra and Nehemiah served, and imposed on the Jews the laws of the Torah, at the pleasure of the Achaemenid emperors; Josephus (among other writers) tells us that the high priests of the Jerusalem temple in the period before Antiochus Epiphanes (175–164 BCE) were also the chief tax collectors of Judaea on behalf of their Persian and Macedonian overlords. The Judaean authorities obviously found

[22] On the leading medieval theorist of legal accommodation, Rabbi Solomon ben Abraham ibn Adret, see J. Ray, *The Sephardic Frontier: The Reconquista and the Jewish Community of Medieval Iberia* (Ithaca, NY: Cornell University Press, 2006), 98–130.

[23] The correct reading is *darishn* de-Parsa'ei, *darishn* being a Persian loanword meaning "possession of property." The law means that if someone (including a gentile) has occupied land for forty years, even if he has expropriated it from a Jew, he is to be regarded as its legal owner, even in the absence of a deed, in keeping with Persian law, but in violation of rabbinic law. See E. S. Rosenthal, "A Contribution to the Talmudic Lexicon," *Tarbiz* 40 (1971): 178–201, esp. 187–93, and Shilo, *Dina De-Malkhuta*, 1–43.

[24] So Beer, *The Babylonian Exilarchate*, 88–91; Shilo: "great men who buy land seized for (nonpayment of) *taska*, the sale is valid." The meaning is the same.

a satisfactory Jewish legal rationale for their behavior, which probably also entailed recognizing the kings' rights to interfere in the life and property of the Judaeans in other ways. In sum, the Jews were a vassal state and seem collectively to have regarded that status as consistent with their growing recognition of the legal authority of the Torah. Of course, the Achaemenid and Hellenistic rulers of Palestine specifically endorsed the Torah as the Jews' law code. To put it crudely, the Jews had a deal with the kings: loyalty, entailing recognition of the state's right to collect tribute, assign land and other resources to officials and garrison troops, and interfere in other ways, in return for the state's recognition of the Jews' right to conduct their lives *basically* according to the laws of the Torah. It is this "diasporic compromise" that is the most ancient and traditional mode of Jewish political life, even in Palestine.

The Palestinian rabbis quite clearly felt they had no such deal with Rome. Even in the absence of evidence it would not be hard to guess why: the repeated rebellions and their disastrous aftermaths, including the destruction of the temple and the likely abrogation by Rome of the legal authority of the Torah, brought the deal to an end. The Persians (whether Achaemenid or Sasanian), as both Talmuds repeatedly remind us, were one thing, the Romans something else. In addition, a detail in the Tosefta's rules about the status of expropriated land suggests, though it does not demonstrate, that for some rabbis, the wars had changed everything, for they may have recognized the prewar (presumably a reference to the Great Revolt) authority of the Romans to expropriate land[25]; the war cancelled this recognition not because of the rabbis' nationalism in recognizing in its aftermath that so much expropriated land had

---

[25] T. Gittin 3(4):10:

> In Judaea the laws of *siqariqon* do not apply, so as to encourage the settlement of the district [that is, the rabbis permit Jews to purchase land that has been seized by the state, thereby de facto (?) recognizing the proprietary rights of its occupants]. When is this the case? With reference to those killed *before the war* and at the time of the war, but in the case of those killed afterward, the law of *siqariqon* applies [and so any activity that implies recognition of the occupants' proprietary rights is forbidden: a Jew may not buy the land]. In Galilee the law of *siqariqon* always applies."

If the final clause is indeed authentic—and it is not found in every manuscript (Lieberman, *Tosefta Ki-fshutah* 8.842)—it may simply reflect the rabbis' recognition that there were fewer casualties there. The Mishnah's presentation is somewhat different, indicating that the law prohibiting purchase of expropriated land was relaxed only at the time of the revolt (it says nothing about the situation before the revolt), whereas the Tosefta can be understood to imply that before the war, the state was thought to have authority to seize the land, though this is not precisely the way the Tosefta explains the matter. The Mishnah also describes the successive relaxation of the law, though not its complete abolition—in the Mishnah, the authority of the Roman state to dispose of land is never fully acknowledged. The issue would benefit from discrete consideration.

belonged to Jewish rebels but because it changed the relationship between the Jews and the state.

We should not, however, posit a polar antithesis between Palestine and Babylonia. The principle of *dina de-malkhuta dina* may have originated later, in the fourth rather than the third century, and may have had narrower application and less halakhic impact than is normally supposed. It may have been a principle valid mainly in exilarchic rather than purely rabbinic courts.[26] Otherwise, Babylonian rabbinic judges appear to have engaged in ad hoc accommodation to the legal and political demands of the Persian state. And so, despite their frequently expressed opposition, did the Palestinian rabbis with the Roman state: for example, though in principle the laws of *siqariqon* rejected the legality of the state's expropriations of land, in practice, purchasers of such land did enjoy certain rights under some circumstances, just as their Babylonian counterparts did.[27] We cannot even be certain that the Babylonian principle had no currency in Palestine, notwithstanding the Yerushalmi's failure to mention it: perhaps it was adopted in the patriarchal court, just as it was in the exilarchic. If this happened in the fourth century, we would never know, because the Yerushalmi has so little (in fact, nothing) to say about the last patriarchs.

The Palestinian rabbis, then, had a more complicated legal and judicial relationship with the Roman state than they were inclined to admit. What were the contours of their legal influence, their authority? As far as criminal law is concerned, they lacked even de facto jurisdiction. Admittedly, Origen famously described a (quasi-rabbinic?) "ethnarch"—probably the Gamalielide patriarch—as executing a criminal, without government approval or interference.[28] But it is striking that the Yerushalmi contains, as

[26] See the fundamental discussion of Herman, "The Exilarchate in the Sasanian Era," superceding the brief comments of Gafni, *The Jews of Babylonia*, 42–43.

[27] Indeed, the Mishnah reports three stages in the development of the law. In the first stage initial purchase from the occupant of the land was invalid: the land had to be purchased from the original owner, though with the understanding that the expropriator or occupant would have to be paid off, too. In the second stage, if the original owner could not afford to buy his land back, another purchaser could buy it but had to pay the original owner twenty-five percent of the price of the land. Finally, Rabbi Judah Ha-nasi (ca. 200 CE) convened a court that decided that purchase of expropriated land was valid after a year after the expropriation (to allow time for the original owner to repurchase it), but the purchaser was obliged to pay twenty-five percent of the price of the land to the original owner if the owner turned up. In this way, the limited authority of the state was acknowledged de facto, the owner's heirs were given the opportunity to repurchase the land, but the basic principle that the land had never legitimately changed hands was symbolically preserved.

[28] See Origen, *Epistula ad Africanum* 20 (14); M. Jacobs, *Die Institution des jüdischen Patriarchen: Eine quellen- und traditionskritische Studie zur Geschichte der Juden in der Spätantike* (Tübingen: Mohr Siebeck, 1995), 248–51.

far as I can tell, not a single story about such activity, nor does it provide any reason to think that such behavior was commonplace either among rabbis or among those patriarchs, mainly of the third century, whom the rabbis still regarded as members of their group. Perhaps it was too dangerous. Yet the rabbis very openly regarded as murder judicial activities the state itself considered legitimate and essential (see above).

Civil law was a different story. The Roman state never yielded to rabbis or to any other Jewish authorities anything like jurisdiction over civil law, not even in 398 (probably shortly after the publication of the Yerushalmi), when Jewish clergymen, a category that probably included but was not limited to rabbis, were given jurisdiction over liturgical or religious law (*CTh* 2.1.10; discussion in *IJS* 192–94). Jews, like all other Roman citizens, as the Jews mostly were after 212 CE, were obliged to bring their cases to Roman courts. But the Roman state did not oppose the use of arbitrators to settle civil cases and technically were even prepared to uphold their decisions, in some situations. A rabbi, or anyone else, who decided a case submitted to him willingly by both litigants was potentially fulfilling a recognized and legitimate role in the Roman legal system, that of an *arbiter ex compromisso*, even if, like all arbitrators, he was a judicial authority of decidedly secondary or tertiary rank.[29] How many Jews actually appealed to rabbinic arbitrators in such cases is unknown, and certainly varied over time and by place. It also probably varied by legal category: the evidence of the Yerushalmi itself is suggestive, but not probative: for example, Talmudic laws about marriage and divorce are highly detailed, their elaboration shaped by thoroughly realistic concerns, and rich in the citation of cases. The tractates Qiddushin ("marriages"), Ketubbot ("marriage contracts"), and Gittin ("divorces") seem to reflect the practical concerns of real-life judges, scribes, and legal experts in a way that few other Talmudic tractates do. By contrast, the Talmudic discussions of laws about loans, land tenure, rentals, tenancy, and harvest contracts (not to mention the ritual agricultural laws, which are the subject of the first order of the Talmud) seem thin and cite few cases; the Talmud's discussion is formulaically dialectical and little anchored in practicalities. To be sure, this could be due to the distinctive redactional history of the relevant tractate, Neziqin ("damages"), and its consequent extreme brevity.[30] But the formulaic

---

[29] On rabbis as arbitrators, see, in addition to *IJS*, H. Lapin, "Rabbis and Cities: Some Aspects of the Rabbinic Movement in its Graeco-Roman Environment," in *TYGRC* 2:62–5 (article: 51–80), and J. Harries, "Creating Legal Space: Settling Disputes in the Roman Empire," in *Rabbinic Law in Its Roman and Near Eastern Context*, ed. C. Hezser (Tübingen: Mohr Siebeck, 2003), 63–81.

[30] See J. Sussmann, "Ve-shuv Li-yrushalmi Neziqin," *Mehkerei Talmud* 1 (1990): 55–133.

character of the Talmud's agricultural legislation is not restricted to Y Ne-ziqin. Indeed, Y Shevi'it takes it for granted that many (but how many?) Jews never even made an effort to observe the laws of the sabbatical years. This impression resonates interestingly with the contents of the somewhat earlier papyrological archives of Babatha and Salome Komaise.[31] There, all property-related transactions follow Roman provincial law exclusively, while marriage contracts are varied, following either some type of Greco-Roman law resembling that of contemporaneous Egyptian papyri or a version of Jewish law similar but not identical to that of the rabbis.

We should extrapolate from these observations only with utmost cau-tion. Some Jews in the third and fourth centuries surely brought their cases to rabbis or to other Jewish authorities. Perhaps they brought more cases related to family and personal status than to land ownership or busi-ness to Jewish judges, but probably not all marriages and divorces were performed according to Jewish law, nor were all property or business dis-putes brought to Roman courts. One certainly has the sense that Jewish judges, both rabbinic and nonrabbinic, were becoming more fully institu-tionalized in the course of the third century as their patron the patriarch became more powerful, a fact that paradoxically would have enhanced their engagement with Roman legal and judicial norms. In fact, this is the theme of a brief story discussed below.

Even though the rabbis unambiguously disapproved of Jews who brought cases of civil and personal status law to Roman courts, several passages in Y indicate a realistically conciliatory strain in the way some rabbis thought about the issue.[32] The rabbis even fantasized that Roman legal experts could be convinced of the value of Jewish law.

Y Baba Qama 4.3 (4) 4b:[33]

---

[31] See Y. Yadin, N. Lewis, J. Greenfield, et al., eds., *The Documents from the Bar Kokhba Period in the Cave of Letters*, 2 vols. (Jerusalem: Israel Exploration Society, 1989–2002); H. Cotton and A. Yardeni, *Aramaic, Hebrew and Greek Documentary Texts from Nahal Hever and Other Sites* (Oxford: Clarendon Press, 1997).

[32] And this aside from the rabbis' partial recognition of the competence of "gentile" courts to decide cases of incest and other sexual misbehavior, on the grounds that according to the rabbis, laws against incest, adultery, and so forth were given to "Noachides" (that is, humanity in gen-eral) just as they were to Israelites: Y Qidd 1.1 58b–c. One might have expected the same discus-sion in connection with murder, but to the best of my knowledge no such discussion exists.

[33] For text and commentary, including full citation of parallels, see J. Lewy, "Interpretation des IV Abschnittes des palästinensischen Talmud-Traktate Nesikin," in *Jahres-Bericht des jue-disch-theologischen Seminars Fraenckel'scher Stiftung*, (Breslau: Schatzky, 1908), 113–14. For dis-cussions, see C. Hezser, *Form, Function, and Historical Significance of the Rabbinic Story in Yerushalmi Neziqin* (Tubingen: Mohr Siebeck, 1993), 16–23; and S. Fraade, *From Tradition to Commentary: Torah and Its Interpretation in the Midrash Sifre to Deuteronomy* (Albany: SUNY Press, 1991), 49–56.

It happened that the government sent two soldiers [*istratiotot*][34] to learn Torah from Rabban Gamaliel. And they learned from him Bible and Mishnah and Talmud and laws [*halakhot*] and homilies [*aggadot*].[35] At the end they said to him, "All your Torah is fine and praiseworthy except for the following two things which you say: [M Avodah Zarah 2.1] 'An Israelite woman may not be midwife for a foreign woman . . . but a foreign woman may be midwife for an Israelite woman; an Israelite woman may not be wet nurse for a foreign woman but a foreign woman may be wet nurse for an Israelite, provided she has permission.' And, an Israelite's stolen property is forbidden and a gentile's is permitted." At that moment Rabban Gamaliel decreed that a gentile's stolen property be prohibited, lest God's name be desecrated. "[An additional objection]: 'An Israelite's ox who gores a foreigner's ox is free of penalty'—but this law we will not report to the government."[36] Nevertheless, by the time they reached the Ladder of Tyre, they had forgotten everything they had learned.

This is, first of all, one of many rabbinic stories in which presumably invented gentiles serve as safe mouthpieces for the rabbis' own anxieties about their laws.[37] The Torah itself already expressed an anxiety similar to the one implied here: the Deuteronomist, influenced as he was by a universalistic Near Eastern wisdom tradition, was concerned that the nations regard God's laws as wise and so come to admire Him and his people Israel (Dt 4.5–8).[38] Hence this story's insistence that (even?) representatives of the Roman state, whose intentions in studying with Rabban Gamaliel we are probably meant to assume were hostile, recognized the goodness of the Torah.[39] But the very fact that some Jewish laws treated gentiles unfairly was in tension with the rabbis' desire that God's name be sanctified

---

[34] So MS Leiden and Ed. Pr. Venice; the fragmentary MS Escorial, though generally regarded as reliable (but see the important reservations of Sussmann, "Ve-Shuv Li-Yrushalmi Neziqin," 124–27) preserves the reading '*strnygywtwt*, unconstruable despite attempts to read it as *strategetai* (see Hezser, *Form, Function*, 16 n. 23).

[35] In many of the parallels cited by Lewy, the soldiers convert and a new set is sent.

[36] The previous sentence, following "desecrated," is absent in the Yalqut: see P. Schäfer and H.-J. Becker, eds., *Synopse zum Talmud Yerushalmi* (Tübingen: Mohr Siebeck, 1995), 4:24. See below

[37] Cf. C. E. Hayes, "Displaced Self-Perceptions: The Deployment of 'Minim' and Romans in B. Sanhedrin 90b–91a," in *Religious and Ethnic Communities in Later Roman Palestine*, ed. H. Lapin (Bethesda: University Press of Maryland, 1998), 249–89.

[38] See M. Weinfeld, *Deuteronomy and the Deuteronomic School* (Oxford: Clarendon Press, 1972), 244–319, esp. 254–57.

[39] The hostile intentions of the officials are explicit in the parallel in Sifre Deuteronomy parashah 344, on Dt 33.3.

even outside the community of Israel. And so this is also an etiological myth about Rabban Gamaliel's decree, which eliminated a law embarrassingly disadvantageous to gentiles—a decree made, according to this story, not out of a desire to ingratiate the Jews with the Roman state but out of the impeccably Jewish wish to sanctify God's name.

Formally speaking, this seems the end of the story: the final lines do not precisely fit because they add a third Roman objection to the two introduced earlier. (Alternatively, if we follow the reading of the Yalqut, only the third objection has been inserted here, not the conclusion of the story.) Apparently a part of a second version of the story has been appended here, surely earlier than the Talmud's redactional stratum, since it is only in this final section that the story is relevant to the pericope in which it is embedded. The coda changes the tone, and creates the story's interesting ambiguity.[40] Now it can also be read as in part a dramatization of James Scott's idea of the "hidden transcript," the verbal code that the dominated use as a form of covert resistance against their rulers.[41] Admirable as the Torah is, even from the Romans' perspective, it is still a peculiarly Jewish site of resistance: the Romans are admittedly won over—their objections are so minor, and one of them so swiftly remedied, that they promise not to report them to the government—yet, apparently through divine intervention, they are made to forget everything they have learned, including the admirable parts of the Torah, as soon as they leave the land of Israel. The storyteller wavers between the Deuteronomist's mildly competitive universalism (compare Josephus's introduction to *Antiquities*, where he decides that the Torah is a treasure that should be revealed to admiring gentiles), one that tacitly acknowledges the value of the Romans' approval, and differently anxious resistance.

A brief story of decidedly friendly and unangst-ridden competition between a rabbi and someone who appears to be a Roman lawyer or official is quoted at Y Ketubbot 9.10, 33b. If we interpret this exchange in light of the context in which it is quoted, then it appears to concern a situation in which the court attempts to force a man to pay off the sum stipulated in his marriage contract (thereby divorcing his wife), though on its own the discussion could concern any contract: "Rabbi Mana [fourth century?

---

[40] In the midrashic parallel the final sentence is absent.

[41] See J. Scott, *Domination and the Arts of Resistance: Hidden Transcripts* (New Haven: Yale University Press, 1990), xii: "Every subordinate group creates, out of its own ordeal, a 'hidden transcript' that represents a critique of power spoken behind the back of the dominant. The powerful, for their part, also develop a hidden transcript representing the practices and claims of their rule that cannot be openly avowed." In this story the Torah is a hidden transcript in an unusually literal way.

Several rabbis had this name] said to Alexas [unidentified, but apparently a Roman legal expert][42]: Our practice is better than yours. We issue subpoenas,[43] and if he comes, fine, and if not we expropriate his property. Alexas responded: We do this, too! We send him three letters. If he comes, fine, if not, we expropriate his property. Rabbi Mana responded: Now imagine that the man is in a distant place. In this case, we send him three letters, thirty days apart. If he comes, fine, if not, we expropriate his property."

This brief account, which concerns not law stricto sensu but court and police procedure, has several noteworthy features. First, it insists on the separateness of Jewish and Roman court procedure (*we* do X while *you* do Y), but as a corollary on something like their political parity. By contrast, the Theodosian Code (2.1.10; cf. 16.8.13), even in recognizing the limited jurisdiction of Jewish judges, is careful to emphasize that such judges derive their authority from the patriarch, who in turn derives his authority from the emperor: Jewish courts are subordinated to the Roman state, and have just as much authority as the emperor is willing to yield. Second, it acknowledges the similarity of Jewish and Roman procedure while arguing that the Jewish courts have developed a more effective way of dealing with defendants who live far away.

Less realistic, or more puzzling, is the brief note in Y Baba Batra 8.1 16a that the "*hakhmei goyim*" (gentile sages)[44] interpreted Num 27.8 ("if a man die and he has no son, you shall transfer his inheritance to his daughter") to mean that "if a man has [both a son and a daughter], they inherit equally."[45] Despite its attribution, this view is presented *as if* it were a standard, though here rejected, rabbinic view, and in fact in the parallel in B Baba Batra 110a–b, the "gentile sages'" legal exegesis is attributed to the Babylonian *amora* Rav Papa, though only as a theoretical position meant to be rejected. Whom exactly the rabbis had in mind, and what position is being attributed to them, is hard to determine. Roman law, like Jewish law, was not primogenitural; in cases of intestacy, an estate would be divided

---

[42] This is perfectly obvious and was noted already in the eighteenth-century commentary, Qorban Ha-Edah; the contemporaneous Penei Moshe, though, thought Alexas was a Babylonian rabbi.

[43] MS Leiden and Ed. Pr. have the meaningless *dyn-mwgmryn*, which I am following Sokoloff (sub v. dyytgmh) in correcting to *diatagmin*, meaning decrees, following the Constantinople edition; see Schäfer and Becker, *Synopse*, 3:216; A. Tropper, "Roman Contexts in Jewish Texts: On *Diatagma* and *Prostagma* in Rabbinic Literature," *JQR* 95 (2005): 222–27 (article: 207–27).

[44] A body (?) never mentioned elsewhere in the Yerushalmi.

[45] The biblical and Roman laws of inheritance are among the sixteen laws compared in the Collatio; see M. Hyamson, ed., *Mosaicarum et Romanarum Legum Collatio* (Oxford: Oxford University Press, 1913), title 16, 133–49.

among descendants.[46] Daughters could thus expect to receive a share whether or not there were also surviving sons. In this sense, the gentile sages are simply reporting the basic Roman law of intestacy, which, starting with the general grant of citizenship to almost all inhabitants of the Roman Empire in 212 CE, would have applied even to the rabbis, and to the Jews in general.

But there are two problems with supposing that the "gentile sages" are simply reporting Roman law. The first is that Roman law and cultural norms in general exerted strong pressure on even middling citizens to write wills—"vehicles," as Champlin put it, "for moderated deviance from the rules of intestacy" (p. 8). Intestacy, though not uncommon, was nevertheless deemed abnormal. By contrast, in rabbinic law, wills, in the sense of documents *unilaterally* bestowing property postmortem, were illegitimate since postmortem division of property was entirely mechanical and ordained by the Torah.[47] This in itself is of interest for our purposes because it implies that at least as far as rabbinic legal theory was concerned, Jews

---

[46] See E. Champlin, *Final Judgments: Duty and Emotion in Roman Wills, 200 B. C.–A. D. 250* (Berkeley and Los Angeles: University of California Press, 1991), 111–12.

[47] So it seems legitimate to conclude—following the analysis of R. Yaron, *Gifts in Contemplation of Death in Jewish and Roman Law* (Oxford: Clarendon Press, 1960)—from the very complex Mishnah, which I cite here in my own translation:

> M. Baba Batra 8.5) He who says, 'My firstborn son, X, will not receive [a double share of my property after I die],' or 'My son, Y, will not inherit a share with his brothers,' has said nothing [so his command is legally ineffective], because his command contradicts what is written in the Torah. One who divides his property among his sons by his order, increasing the share of one, decreasing that of another, equalizing their share to that of the firstborn, his words stand [they are legally effective]. But if he said, 'This [the aforementioned arrangement] is so as *yerushah* [inheritance],' he has said nothing. If he wrote [in a document altering the laws of intestacy] ... 'as a gift,' then his words stand.... One who writes [a deed of gift] giving his property to others and not his sons, what he has done is done [legally valid], but the sages are displeased with him. Rabban Shimon ben Gamliel says, "If his sons behaved improperly, then he is remembered for good [for depriving them of their share]."
> 6) ... One who dies and a *diatheke* is found tied to his thigh, this is nothing [its contents are legally invalid].

With all due hesitation and diffidence, given the difficulty of the Mishnah, and its characteristic failure to provide the rationale for its legal decisions, I am inclined to accept the following interpretation of it, based on the work of Yaron: Unlike a will, the gift, or "*matanah*," is bilateral—the donee must take possession before the death of the donor. A document discovered after the death of its author has no legal force, and a deed of gift which the author mistitles "*yerushah*" (inheritance) is also invalid: for the rabbis, *yerushah* refers exclusively to the biblical laws of intestacy. The rabbis were willing to validate some departures from these laws but only on the condition that such departures did not have the name or the characteristics of *yerushah*. The *matanah* in contemplation of death differs from a standard gift in that the donor retains usufruct of the property until his death, and also the right of retraction (and so it exemplifies the Maussian inalienability of the gift). The rabbis disapproved of some versions of the gift in contemplation of death and tried to limit the donor's freedom to dispose of his property in this way, but apparently

were deprived of one of the chief means other Romans had at their disposal for showing honor, gratitude, and recognition to *amici*, *patroni*, and *clientes* and for advertising their own beneficence.[48] Was this what motivated the rabbis to recognize the validity of the *donatio mortis causa* (gift in contemplation of death, called in the Talmud either *matanah*, gift, or, revealingly, *diatheke*, the Greek word for disposition), an instrument partly borrowed from Hellenistic or Roman law, that allowed the future decedent more freedom in the disposition of his property?[49]

Be this as it may, the legal debate recorded in Y Baba Batra does not quite reflect a correct comparison of Jewish and Roman laws of inheritance, because Roman law regarded intestacy as undesirable, while Jewish law regarded it as normative. And the fact that the "gentile sages" frame their law as biblical exegesis is, needless to say, bizarre (unless they are meant to be Christian? But Roman lawyers in the Christian Empire did not generally frame their laws as biblical exegesis), if not uncharacteristic in rabbinic stories. What is of interest to us here, though, is the rabbis' willingness to present themselves as engaging in a rabbinic-style halakhic debate with what appear to be Roman lawyers, whose views are represented as reasonable, though mistaken. This seems to be a unique case of the "rabbinization" of what is explicitly described as Roman, or at least foreign, law.[50]

But this is a very brief and, as far as I can tell, isolated and quite enigmatic passage. Whatever precisely it means, it would be a mistake to draw sweeping conclusions from it. In fact, the search for positive rabbinic engagement with the idea that the Roman state has legitimate authority as maker or executor of laws (as opposed to having the means and will to inflict violence on disobedient subjects, and therefore occasionally to be conciliated) has yielded little. Far from identifying themselves with the aims of the empire, as well-to-do Roman citizens are normally supposed to have done, the rabbis' attitude toward the state was hostile. Or at least it was so on the surface, for the rather surprising conclusion of the story of the soldiers who studied Torah with Rabban Gamaliel, a conclusion immediately contradicted within the very same story, is that it mattered to the rabbis what the Romans thought about their laws: they wanted the state to acknowledge them, to celebrate them,

---

thought it a necessary concession to practice. I thank Jonathan Milgram for his illuminating comments on the Mishnah's laws of inheritance.

[48] See Saller, *Personal Patronage under the Early Empire*, 124.

[49] For a full discussion, see note 48.

[50] This is a separate matter from the question of whether, or to what extent, the rabbis appropriated Roman law, for a recent discussion of which see C. Hayes, "Genealogy, Illegitimacy, and Personal Status: The Yerushalmi in Comparative Perspective," in *TYGRC*, 3:73–89.

yet at the same time they wished to resist the state's intervention. This tension, a sense of competitiveness with Roman values—in a way that implies their partial acceptance—balanced by the insistence on rejecting them is a tension characteristic of many of the stories (and some laws) to be discussed below. It may be said to be one of the main characteristics of the rabbis' attitude to Roman values, one whose implications are analyzed in what follows.

Euergetism and Memorialization

The Yerushalmi provides much evidence for the ways in which the rabbis complemented their self-alienation from Roman norms with a tacit acquiescence to, even internalization of, and in any event fraught engagement with some of the most important ones. I begin, however, with a case in which the rabbinic views show an unmistakable continuity with the strongly countercultural, minimally adaptationist views of Josephus, but in which the social valence of this traditional attitude has utterly shifted. Josephus believed that the mass of the Jews rejected most of the standard forms of Roman euergetism, especially those that memorialized the benefactor in plastic form, in favor of those that approximated biblical norms of piety. Monumental buildings brought no gratitude to the builder, while famine relief or the funding of nazirites' sacrifices did bring credit to the donor. But honor and gratitude to benefaction were performed orally, perhaps in the form of stories, and not inscribed on stone and displayed publicly. In Josephus's view, one of the central political and cultural problems of the first century of Roman rule in Palestine was that the Jews' leaders were under pressure from above to adopt Roman norms (which some, like Herod, had thoroughly internalized) but under pressure from below to reject them—a tension very few could negotiate.

The rabbis for the most part carefully preserved what Josephus described as the proper Jewish norms, but in a drastically different environment, one in which the mass of the Jews had come to embrace the Roman state's ideology of benefaction and honor as their own—so the rabbis thought. The rabbis' traditionalism thus was probably intended to mark them off sharply from the more romanized members of the curial (city councilor) classes and their ilk—in other words, of well-to-do local elites. Indeed, the Yerushalmi never even bothers with open denunciation of municipal euergetism as such; it simply assumes its invalidity, or rather its complete otherness. But the Talmud is well aware of the fact that the rabbis' own cities, Tiberias, Sepphoris, Caesarea, and

Lydda, relied on euergetistic practices for their existence, and supposes that the mass of the inhabitants of such places, most of whom were Jews, had now adopted the Roman's norms as their own. In such cases the rabbis were willing to meet nonrabbinic Jews halfway, especially if the performance of a *mitzvah* was involved. But they also expressed their disapproval of those elements of euergetistic practice that were beginning to be adopted by Jewish religious communities in the third and fourth centuries. Thus, an anecdote frequently repeated in the Talmud denounces the construction by individual benefaction of monumental synagogues, or at any rate dismisses the practice as useless (Y Peah 8.9, 21b).[51] And also like Josephus, the rabbis admired forms of benefaction more easily assimilable to biblical norms of charity, or those that contributed to public welfare or the performance of *mitzvot* (Y Shevi'it 3.10, 34d; Y Yebamot 4.11, 6b; Y Nazir 5.4, 54b).[52] They were even willing to engage in a peculiarly rabbinic form of reciprocity, repaying a layperson's support of Torah study with a show of halakhic leniency (Y Pesahim 7.1, 34a, on Todos of Rome).[53]

The gulf between rabbinic and general Jewish values, the latter's approximation to Roman values and the rabbis' traditionalism, the rabbis' willingness to appeal to Roman values if necessary to persuade the Jews to approximate to Jewish ones—all these themes are beautifully illustrated

[51] "Rabbi Hama bar Hanina and Rabbi Hoshayya walked among the [ruined?] synagogues of Lydda. Said Rabbi Hama to R. Hoshayya, 'How much money did my ancestors sink here!' Rabbi Hoshayya responded, 'Rather, how many souls did they sink [that is, waste or squander] here— for there was no one here laboring in Torah'"—the point being that they should have invested in the support of Torah study, not the construction of synagogues.

[52] Cf. Y Sotah 7.4, 21d:

> Rabbi Aha said in the name of Rabbi Tanhum bar Rabbi Hiyya, "One who studied and taught and observed and did, and possessed enough to support [*lehahaziq*] but did not do so, this one is counted among the cursed. One who did not study, or teach, or observe, or do, and did not possess enough to support and yet supported, this one is counted among the blessed." And Rabbi Hannah said in the name of Rabbi Jeremiah in the name of Rabbi Hiyya, "In the future [that is, the messianic era] the Holy One will cause the doers of *mitzvot* [in the typical late antique Palestinian sense of charitable acts] to shelter in the shade of the masters of Torah. What is the proof? "For in the shadow of wisdom is the shadow of silver" [Eccl 7.12] and "It is a tree of life for those that support [*lamahaziqim*] it" [Prov 3.18].

[53] "*Teni* [a formula marking quotation of a tannaitic teaching]: Rabbi Yosi said, 'Todos of Rome instructed the people of Rome to eat roasted kids on Passover eve. The sages sent and said, 'If you were not Todos we would excommunicate you [for performing the paschal sacrifice outside the temple precinct].' And what was Todos [to merit such leniency]? Rabbi Hananiah said, 'He would send [donations to pay for] the upkeep of the rabbis.'" See B. Bokser, "Todos and Rabbinic Authority in Rome," in *New Perspectives on Ancient Judaism, Volume 1: Religion, Literature, and Society in Ancient Israel, Formative Christianity and Judaism*, ed. J. Neusner et al. (Lanham, MD: University Press of America, 1987), 117–29.

by a string of stories about charity distribution in Y Peah 8.7, 21a, which does much more than demonstrate the already familiar ways in which late antiquity Jewish charity came to acquire euergetistic features.[54]

> Rabbi Yosi went to Kifra [on the outskirts of Tiberias] in order to appoint *parnasim* [charity administrators] for the inhabitants. But they [the people appointed][55] refused to accept the appointment. Rabbi Yosi came and said to them, "'Ben Bebai was in charge of the gourd' [M. Sheqalim 5.1—a list of functionaries in the Jerusalem Temple; Ben Bebai's job was the manufacture of lamp wicks from plants]. If the man who was in charge of wicks nevertheless deserved to be counted among the great men of his generation, how much the more so will you, who are being put in charge of people's lives, be so remembered!"
>
> When Rabbi Haggai would appoint *parnasim* he would hand them a Torah scroll,[56] as a way of saying to them that all the authority of their rank [*serarah*] derives from the Torah, [as it is written] "in me do kings rule," "in me do officials exercise authority" [Prov 8.15–6]. Rabbi Hiyya bar Ba would appoint *archontes* [as *parnasim*].[57]

[54] See *IJS* 274–89.

[55] Contrast the comment ad loc. of G. Wevers, in *Übersetzung des Talmud Yerushalmi*, vol. 1/2: Pea, Ackerecke, p. 205, n. 135.

[56] Following Sokoloff, sub v. T'N (*af'el*); Pnei Moshe and the Biurei Ha-Gra read *mat'im* for *mat'in* and translate, respectively, "would teach them Torah" or "would test them in Torah," but this is forced.

[57] An alternative would be to suppose the text—which reads simply *Rabbi Hiyya bar Ba havah meqim archonin* (Rabbi H. bar B would appoint *archontes*)—defective, but there is no support for this plausible hypothesis in the manuscripts and early editions. A more commonly accepted alternative is to take the sentence at its most linguistically simple—Rabbi Hiyya bar Ba would appoint *archontes*—but in that case it is not clear what it is supposed to mean, and what, if we grant that the story is making the implausible claim that a rabbi was in the position to appoint *archontes*—members of the governing body of the city council—such a claim is doing in the middle of a string of stories about charity administration. If it does mean what I think it means, then it conforms well to the theme of the rabbis exploiting the culture of euergetism to advance their own interest in the performance of the *mitzvah* of charity. For a very different approach to this text, based on the assumption that the patriarchs (not mentioned here) and their rabbinic appointees ran a state within a state and controlled municipal politics in a direct way, see M. Avi-Yonah, *The Jews of Palestine: A Political History from the Bar Kokhba War to the Arab Conquest* (New York: Schocken, 1976; Hebrew edition, Jerusalem: Mossad Bialik, 1946) 121. Avi-Yonah associates this passage with the story of the patriarchal "commission" to appoint rural schoolmasters, which included Rabbi Hiyya bar Ba: Y Hagigah 1.7, 76c. Avi-Yonah's interpretation (which conforms with linguistically the simplest meaning of the text) fails to explain what the comment in Y Peah is doing in its context. More convincing, though in the end problematic in similar ways, is the explanation of Lieberman (as supplemented in an e-mail correspondence from Shlomo Naeh, for whose comments I am grateful): Rabbi Hiyya bar Ba is occasionally said to have been a patriarchal emissary, and is also said to have traveled around in the Roman Empire, and "*archon*" is attested in some diaspora Jewish communities as the title of an official who, according to Epiphanius and

Rabbi Liezer was a *parnas*. One time he came home and said to them [the members of his household], "What has been happening?" They said to him, "One group of paupers came and ate and drank and prayed for you." He said, "This is not a proper reward." He came home a second time and asked, "What has been happening?" They said, "Another group of paupers came and ate and drank and cursed you." He said, "Now I have a proper reward!"

They wished to appoint Rabbi Aqiba *parnas*. He said, "Let me consult with my wife." They followed him and heard him saying, "[I will be appointed] in order to be cursed and scorned."[58]

These stories thematize the rabbinic conviction that an ideological or cultural gulf existed between themselves and the Jews. They ask us to admire men whose devotion to charity was pure, unmotivated by the desire for reciprocation in the forms of gratitude or honor, who even welcomed the ingratitude of their beneficiaries because it guaranteed the purity of their own motivations. The nonrabbinic administrators, however, need to be either cajoled or lectured. Rabbi Yosi seeks to convince his interlocutors by guaranteeing them that because of the importance of charity, their memory would be even more enduring than those of the temple artisans whose names were eternalized in the Mishnah (so the basic idea is that Jewish benefactors, like Roman ones, seek memorialization, but the specific promise held out to the potential charity administrators involves adducing an already judaized example, in that as in Josephus, memorialization in this case takes the form of inscription in a text, or rather in the fixed oral form of the Mishnah—a fine cultural tangle). By contrast, Rabbi Haggai reminds his appointees—obviously because he feels they need reminding—that their charity work fulfills a commandment of the Torah. For his part, Rabbi Hiyya bar Ba (if my interpretation is correct) exploited the slight overlap in function and ideology that existed in any case between charity administration and municipal euergetism in order to further the *mitzvah* of charity. He expected the *archontes* to conduct their charity work the same way they did their other public business, in the expectation of being reciprocated with honor and loyalty. In all the cases here, though,

---

Libanius, patriarchal emissaries sometimes appointed or deposed—and it is this activity which Y Peah is describing; see S. Lieberman, "Emendations on the Jerushalmi (II)," *Tarbiz* 2 (1931): 235 (article: 235–40).

[58] This can be read either as confirmation of the previous story—*parnasut* is really a *mitzvah* only if one receives no honor or gratitude in return—or as a question: Why should I be *parnas*? Do I want to be cursed and scorned? Wevers (n. 35 above) translates, "they heard her saying" ("ihre Stimme [=seine Frau]"), which implies the negative sense. But since all texts read *qaleh* (masc.), not *qalah* (fem.), Wevers's translation is impossible.

the rabbis are represented as being fully and unambiguously devoted to the *mitzvah* and as considering euergetism basically as a practice to be exploited for their own ends—not a wicked practice, but an alien one.

Other stories, though, dramatize the *conflict* between euergetism and *mitzvah*, while recapitulating the message that rabbis were willing to exploit the former to achieve the latter. Y Nazir 5.4, 54b (=Y Berakhot 7.2, 11d):

> Teni[59]: Three hundred Nazirites came up to Jerusalem in the days of Shimon ben Shetah [early first century BCE], one hundred and fifty found [with Shimon's help] a legal way of being released from their naziriteship without having to offer the required sacrifices, and one hundred and fifty did not. Shimon went to King Yannai and said to him, "There are three hundred nazirites who need nine hundred sacrifices. You pay for half of them from your money, I'll pay for half from mine." So the king sent him four hundred and fifty sacrificial victims. An evil (though true!) rumor reached the king that Shimon had not paid for any sacrifices, and King Yannai heard this and was enraged. When Shimon learned of this, he fled. Some days later some dignitaries from the Kingdom of Persia [*sic*][60] visited and said to the king, "We remember that there used to be a certain old man here who said before us words of wisdom. Let him teach us something; please send for him." The king sent, gave Shimon his word [that he would not harm him],[61] and had him brought. When Shimon arrived, he sat between the king and the queen. The king asked him, "Why did you deceive me?" He responded, "I did not deceive you—you gave from your money, I gave from my Torah, as it is written, 'For in the shadow of wisdom, in the shadow of silver' [Eccl 7.12]." The king said, "In that case why did you flee?" He said, "I heard that my lord was angry at me, and I fulfilled the verse, 'hide for a brief moment until anger passes' [Is 26.20]." And he applied to himself [or, the king applied to him] the verse, "And the advantage of the knowledge of wisdom will give life to its possessor" [Eccl 7.12]." And the king said to him, "Why did you seat yourself between the king and the queen?" He responded, "In the book of Ben Sira it is written, 'Esteem her [wisdom] and she will exalt you, and cause

---

[59] If there is anything here tannaitic at all it is limited to the first sentence, which is in Hebrew. The point of the baraita would then be the desirability of finding halakhic ways to extricate nazirites from their vows, rabbinic ambivalence/hostility toward vows of all sorts being an important theme of several tractates. The continuation is in Aramaic.

[60] A slight anachronism: Parthians, not Persians, ruled in the days of Alexander Yannai (103–76 BCE).

[61] For this sense of the idiom *yahab leh milah*, see Sokoloff, sub v. yhb, no. 6.

you to sit among the mighty' [Ben Sira 11.1]."[62] The king said, "Take a cup and make the blessing." They gave Shimon the cup, and he said, "Let us bless God for the food that Yannai and his friends have eaten![63] Or should I rather say, 'Let us bless God for the food we did not eat'?" So the king commanded food to be brought for Shimon; he ate and said, "Let us bless God for the food we have eaten."

This story thematizes a conflict of values: Shimon represents the values of Torah, of the pure, unreciprocated gift, and the king implicitly embodies the "Mediterranean" values of honor and reciprocity. This is because Shimon bestows a favor on the nazirites—using legal ingenuity to free them from the obligation to offer sacrifices—that almost by definition resists reciprocation, and for the remainder, he benefits them by convincing the king to offer them gifts. Like the rabbis in some of the stories discussed previously, he thus fulfills the values of the Torah by manipulating others who do not share those values, and so maintains the "purity" of his gift, while also performing the *mitzvah* of supporting the poor. The nazirites he could not free from their vows will be inclined to reciprocate the king, not Shimon. For his part, the king seems happy enough to offer benefits to the nazirites, but does not understand the nature of Shimon's benefaction, and so feels cheated by him. The king understands the demands of reciprocal exchange, not those of the Torah.

Shimon's interestingly stereotypical role as a conformist, but in reality covertly resistant, dominand—which sounds like still another case study from James Scott's *Domination and the Arts of Resistance*—is accentuated in the second half of the story, which also continues the theme already encountered of the social ambiguity of the sage. The king does not regard Shimon as his equal, and when he summons him back to his court it is to serve as the dinner entertainment for his guests. Shimon's job is, and apparently has been, to say "wise things" at state dinners. He does not fail to do so when he returns to Yannai's court. But the wise things all turn out to be paradoxical actions that serve the dual function of provoking witty exegeses of biblical verses and of humiliating the king (Lucian of Samosata's philosophical dinner-party entertainers are timid by comparison: *de mercede conductis potentium familiaribus* 33). In terms of the story, I believe Yannai deserves humiliation for two reasons: the explicit reason for

---

[62] On the text here see J. Labendz, "The Book of Ben Sira in Rabbinic Literature," *AJSR* 30 (2006): 371–73 (article: 347–92). Oddly, the first hemistich is not from Ben Sira but from Proverbs 4.8.

[63] Y Berakhot adds here: "The king said to him, 'Must you be so difficult/stubborn?'" (*amar leh, 'ad kedon beqashiutak*).

his culminating humiliation (Shimon's blessings over the wine) is his failure to feed Shimon—in sum, his failure as a host, but also his failure to recognize Shimon as a proper guest, as opposed to a member of the staff. Under the surface, the point clearly seems to be that the king misprises the value system that Shimon represents: for him, a sage, an expert in Torah, is not a peer, but merely someone who is useful because he keeps the real guests entertained. Shimon, by contrast, constantly subverts the proceedings, mocking the king and belittling his generosity and the rituals of the banquet as a way of insisting, I would argue, on his true honorability as a representative of the Torah. Every one of his paradoxical actions he presents as fulfillment of a biblical verse. Shimon is thus proposing an alternative system in which honor is still the paramount attainment but in which it is achieved not through social dominance but through Torah.

The Righteous Need No Monuments

In some texts the rabbis express views about benefaction and its recompense that any reader of Paul Veyne would immediately recognize. T Megillah (2.14) assumes that donors to synagogues will have their generosity eternalized in epigraphical form, and acknowledges that as long as the inscription is legible, the community must continue to display the donated object.[64] But somewhat more prominent, in my opinion, are those rabbinic stories that express views on the subject strongly continuous with those of Josephus (in a way that confirms the suggestion made in the last chapter, incidentally, that Josephus represented at least one possible Jewish view on the matter quite accurately).
    Y Moed Qatan 3.7, 83c[65]:

---

[64] See comments of Lieberman, *Tosefta Ki-Fshutah*, part 5, 1154–55.

[65] There are partial parallels to the pericope in Y Berakhot 2.1, 4b, Y Sheqalim 2.6, 47a, and B Yebamot 96b–97a. In Sheqalim the pericope is used to illustrate the following *beraita*: Rabbi Shimon ben Gamliel says, "They do not make funerary monuments [*nefashot*] for righteous men, for their words are their memorial." Helpful as this juxtaposition is for my purposes, it is secondary, since the *sugya* is surely not original to its context in Sheqalim: it appears neither in the Leiden manuscript nor in the Genizah fragments. The Sheqalim text has furthermore been revised to bring it into line with B Yebamot. To be sure, Ginzberg appears to have argued that all versions of the pericope were influenced by, or "taken from," the Bavli, at least in part, but this is manifestly untrue of the version provided in Moed Qatan. On the problems created by this passage, see J. N. Epstein, *Prolegomena ad Litteras Amoraiticas*, ed. E. Z. Melamed (Jerusalem: Magnes, 1962), 536; L. Ginzberg, *A Commentary on the Palestinian Talmud* (New York: Jewish Theological Seminary, 1941), 1:235, with n. 7; J. Sussmann, "Mesoret Limud U-Mesoret Nusah shel Ha-Talmud Ha-Yerushalmi: Le-Verur Nusha'otehah shel Yerushalmi Masekhet Sheqalim," in *Researches in*

Rabbi Yohanan walked about while leaning on Rabbi Jacob bar Idi,[66] and Rabbi Lazar saw Rabbi Yohanan and hid. Rabbi Yohanan said, "This Babylonian committed two wrongs against me, one that he did not greet me, and another that he did not recite a teaching in my name." Rabbi Jacob bar Idi said to him, "This is the custom among them [the Babylonians], that a lesser man does not greet a greater man, since they are accustomed to observe the verse, 'Youths saw me and hid, elders arose and stood'" [Job 29.8].[67]

As they were walking they saw a study house. Rabbi Jacob bar Idi said to Rabbi Yohanan, "Here Rabbi Meir would sit and expound, and recite teachings in the name of Rabbi Ishmael, but not in the name of Rabbi Aqibah." He responded, "Everyone knew that Rabbi Meir was the student of Rabbi Aqibah [and so it would have been superfluous to cite him by name]." Rabbi Jacob responded, "And everyone knows that Rabbi Lazar is the student of Rabbi Yohanan!"

Rabbi Jacob said to Rabbi Yohanan, "Is it permitted to pass before the image of Adori?"[68] He responded, "Do you show honor to

---

Talmudic Literature: A Study Conference in Honour of the Eightieth Birthday of Sha'ul Lieberman (Jerusalem: Israel Academy of Sciences and Humanities, 1983), 48 (article: 12–76). I am most grateful to Shlomo Naeh for his comments.

[66] So also in Berakhot; in Sheqalim, Rabbi Hiyya bar Ba.

[67] Interpreting this episode in terms of the modern sociology and anthropology of deference, discussed later in this chapter, we could say that the Babylonians treated their masters with greater deference than the Palestinians did, since their rituals of avoidance took a more extreme form. Characteristically, though, the distinction is presented as one of biblical exegesis. Bar Idi's response takes it for granted that among the Palestinians, it is the younger parties, or the students, who stand, in accordance with the verse, "Before the hoary head shalt thou rise"; see below, on Y Bikkurim 3.3.

[68] Following Sokoloff sub v., who follows the reading at Y Avodah Zarah 3.8, 43b. The meaning is uncertain (Adonis [unlikely], Adados? And why is it *de-Aduri tzilma* and not *tzilma de-Aduri*?), though the statue is mentioned several times in the Talmud and seems to have been a well-known landmark, perhaps in Tiberias. The suggested explanations of the words in the standard scholarship (S. Klein: Aduri = Adrianos; S. Krauss, Ad/ruri = Arueris, allegedly an Egyptian deity) are unconvincing, but Krauss reports a reading in the Midrash Shmuel (*harodim*) that may suggest that the statue portrayed Herod (Antipas? Antipas was the founder of the city in 19 CE). See S. Klein, *Galilee: Geography and History of Galilee from the Return from Babylonia to the Conclusion of the Talmud*, 2nd ed. (Jerusalem: Mossad Harav Kook, 1967), 99–100; S. Krauss, "Ägyptische und syrische Götternamen im Talmud," in *Semitic Studies in Memory of Rev. Dr. Alexander Kohut*, ed. G. A. Kohut (Berlin: Calvary, 1897), 345 (article: 339–53); E. Friedheim, *Rabbinisme et paganisme en Paléstine romaine: Étude historique des realia talmudiques (Ier–IVème siècles)* (Leiden: Brill, 2006), 100, n. 343. I thank Emmanuel Friedheim for his learned comments to me on this subject.

Qorban Ha'edah on the Y Sheqalim parallel interprets the story as an attempt to justify Rabbi Elazar's decision to hide: Rabbi Yohanan's response to the question about the idol demonstrates that to walk by something or someone without acknowledging it is to dishonor it or him, so Rabbi Elazar had to hide at Rabbi Yohanan's approach, since if he had not done so, given his

him? Pass before him and ignore him!"[69] He responded, "Then Rabbi Lazar acted properly when he did not pass before you!"

He said to him, "Rabbi Jacob bar Idi, you truly know how to pacify!"

And why was Rabbi Yohanan so insistent that they report teachings in his name? Even David sought mercy on this point, as it is written, "I shall dwell in Your tent forever" [Ps 61.4]. Rabbi Pinhas in the name of Rabbi Yirmiyah said in the name of Rabbi Yohanan, "Did David really think that he would live forever? Rather, David said as follows, "May I merit that my words be said in synagogues and study houses."

How did it benefit him? Bar Tira [?Nazira?] said, "Someone who recites a teaching in the name of its sayer, his lips move along with it in the grave, as it is written, 'gliding over sleepers' lips' [Song 7.9]— just like a shrunken mass of grapes[70] which flows of its own accord."

Rabbi Hinena bar Papa and Rabbi Simon dispute this point. One says, "He is like one who drinks spiced wine." The other says, "He is like one who drinks old wine: even though he has already drunk it its taste remains in his mouth."

No generation lacks scoffers: in David's generation, what did the libertines do? They would walk by David's windows and say, "David, David, when will the Temple be built? When will we go to the Lord's house?" And he would say, "Although they intend to anger me, I

Babylonian aversion to greeting his elder, he would have dishonored Rabbi Yohanan. I add that the story, in implicitly comparing Rabbi Yohanan to an idol, contains a hint of a reproach at what it may see as the rabbi's self-aggrandizement.

[69] "Sami 'eynoyi"—literally, "blind his eye"; see Sokoloff sub v. smy. The idiom is not uncommon. This episode is related in a complicated way to the string of halakhic anecdotes at Y Avodah Zarah 3.8, 43b:

> Gamaliel Zuga was leaning on Rabbi Shimon ben Laqish when they arrived at the Stele [tabnita; presumably another well-known, idolatrous, monument in Tiberias, vel sim.]. He said, "What is the law about passing before it?" He responded, "Pass before it and ignore it!" Rabbi Isaac bar Matnah was leaning on Rabbi Yohanan when they arrived at the statue of [at] the Boule. He said, "What is the law about passing before it?" He responded, "Pass before it and ignore it!" Rabbi Jacob bar Idi was leaning on Rabbi Joshua ben Levi when they arrived at the statue of Adori. He said to him, "Nahum of the Holy of Holies [renowned for his aversion to images] used to pass by it and you will not? Pass before it and ignore it!"

On the relationship between the passages see especially the brief comments of L. Moskowitz, "Sugyot Muhlafot in the Talmud Yerushalmi," Tarbiz 60 (1990): 28–30 (article: 19–66).

[70] So Jastrow, sub v. kumra; Even-Shoshan translates kumar as "fruit whose ripening is completed by heating it in soil." Both translations seem speculative and approximate. The rabbinic exegete appears to understand the word dbb in the biblical prooftext not as "gliding over" but as "causing to murmur."

swear that I rejoice in my heart," as it is written, "I was glad when they said to me, Let us go to the house of the Lord" [Ps 122.1]. "And it came to pass when your days were fulfilled and you lay with your fathers" [1 Chr 17.11]: Rabbi Samuel bar Nahman said, "The Holy One said to David, 'David, I am counting out for you full days, not deficient ones; is not your son Solomon building the Temple to offer sacrifices? But more beloved to me than sacrifices are the justice and righteousness which you perform." As it is written, etc.

Like many of the Yerushalmi's stories about rabbis, this one has as one its themes honor and deference; these are explored in the next section. Rabbi Yohanan, unfamiliar as he is either with alleged Babylonian practice—and it is possible that the Talmud itself believes Rabbi Jacob bar Idi has invented it in order to pacify his master—or with the sociology of deference, is offended by a student's apparent failure to pay him appropriate respect. It is very hard to know whether the Talmudic storyteller sympathizes with Rabbi Yohanan. Certainly there is at least a hint of reproach, a sense conveyed by the tone of the story that the storytellers thought Rabbi Yohanan's behavior excessive ("Why was he was he so insistent?").[71] I return to this issue below.

However, the second half of the pericope argues that the practice of reciting teachings in the name of the teachers has nothing to do with honor per se. Rather, Rabbi Yohanan was so concerned about the correct citation of his teachings because, like David, he felt it would secure his immortality, or his eternal memorialization: just as David hoped that he would live forever through the recitation and study of his Psalms in synagogues and study houses, so too Rabbi Yohanan thought the perpetuation of his teachings would secure his immortality. The medieval scribe who copied this pericope into Y Sheqalim 2.6, 47a, there to serve as commentary on the tannaitic teaching that the righteous need no funerary monuments, since "their words are their memorial," understood its gist correctly. (The material that follows immediately seems to argue that the dead secure tangible benefit from the repetition of their teachings. This to some extent subverts the point that precedes it, in that it deemphasizes the theme of memorialization.) This is a completely perspicuous rabbinization of what Josephus presents as the traditional Jewish view about

[71] Cf. Y Sanhedrin 2.6(5), 20c: "(Rabbi Yohanan) saw Rabbi Haninah bar Sisi splitting logs. He said to him, 'Rabbi, this dishonors you [let hu mi-kevodakh].' Rabbi Haninah responded, 'What can I do? I have no one to serve me [that is, a disciple, or, less likely, a slave].' Rabbi Yohanan responded, 'If you have no one to serve you then you should not have accepted minui!'" It is difficult to say whether the storyteller agrees with Rabbi Yohanan.

memorialization; it also conforms with the implications of Yerushalmi Peah, discussed above, that inscription in a text (even in what was perhaps still a purely "oral" text like the Mishnah)[72] constitutes an appropriate type of memorialization.

These considerations may also help explain the conclusion of the pericope, which otherwise seems irrelevant (as Neusner thought it was, though it appears also in all parallels except that in B Yebamot).[73] The story of David and the scoffers first of all offers consolation to those living without a temple. But it may also be setting up an antithesis between two modes of memorialization, monumental-material and moral-cognitive. God certainly approves of the idea of a temple, which performs a public service in helping to expiate the sins of the people of Israel, but prefers David's righteous behavior. His virtues will live on in people's memories at least as long as his son's great building project—in fact, the Talmudic storyteller may expect us to see, much, much longer. I would suggest with some diffidence that there is a hint here of the Josephan contrast between honor and piety, between memorialization in plastic form and in the preferred form of repetition of stories about the decedent's righteous acts. In this sense, the episode that concludes the pericope returns to the theme of the baraita that opened it: the righteous need no monuments.

It would be worth comprehensively comparing the Talmud's metaphorization of the relation between teacher and student as euergetistic with the ample evidence about rhetorical education provided by the writings of Libanius and the *Vitae Sophistarum* of Eunapius—both contemporaries of the editorial stratum of the Yerushalmi. Here, though, I will only remark in passing that, at least in Raffaella Cribiore's account, Libanius did not understand his relationship with his students in these terms, in part, I would suggest, because, while rabbis expected their students to memorize and then further transmit the details of their halakhic teaching, sophists expected their students to imitate but certainly not to duplicate their orations.[74] The substance of rabbinic teaching was thus reified in a way that made a metaphor of benefaction more appropriate in the *bet midrash* than it would have been in the contemporaneous rhetorical school.

[72] See Y. Sussmann, "'Torah She-be'al Peh' Peshutah Ke-mashma'ah—Koho shel Qutzo shel Yod,' *Mehqerei Talmud* 3, no. 1 (2005): 209–384.

[73] *The Talmud of the Land of Israel*, vol. 15, Sheqalim (Chicago: University of Chicago Press), 1991, 54.

[74] See the detailed discussion in R. Cribiore, *The School of Libanius in Late Antique Antioch* (Princeton, NJ: Princeton University Press, 2007), 137–73.

Honor, Deference, Precedence

It has been argued that honor was one of the main ideological mechanisms of Roman rule, to the extent that its circulation through the social networks that bound the Roman Empire may help explain why the empire was able to survive so long with only a tiny bureaucracy and, relative to the size of its population, a very small army, and no police force worth mentioning at all.[75] As his critics have observed, Lendon's account is damagingly short on theoretical self-consciousness. Honor is a complicated, ramified, and ultimately mercurial topic. If one is sloppy or improvident enough, one can use the word to connote so many social, cultural, and psychic phenomena that it loses its analytical utility. Lendon's account certainly flirts with this disaster, identifying as or conflating with honor things his sources fail to, but it can be salvaged through severe pruning.

Honor per se is neither a corollary of nor a tracer for dominance: there is honor among thieves, as among slaves. This—honor as emotion, as a lens through which life is subjectively viewed, as a disposition toward one's social environment—has been a crucial, and controversial, issue in Mediterranean ethnography.[76] But an account of honor as political capital in Roman public life, as a property possessed by certain Romans as a perquisite of rank or as a reward for domination disguised as generosity, can proceed quite independently of ethnographic controversies (which remain important because they can help us sharpen our investigation). We can extract from Lendon's account more modest, precise, and conceptually aware conclusions than its author may have intended: quite apart from its ultimately unrecoverable role in daily life and from its ramified and porous definition, honor, *time*, had a highly specific function in Roman politics, which Lendon described accurately. It is honor in this sense that I am mainly concerned to explore here, but, as part of our pruning exercise, it is necessary to provide a brief survey of talmudic honor in general, to give some indication of what it is necessary to skip.

Honor is a surprisingly important concept in the Yerushalmi, figuring in both legal and nonlegal contexts. Rabbinic law, starting with the Mish-

---

[75] See Lendon, *Empire of Honor*; terror played a role, too: see Hopkins, *Death and Renewal*, 1–30. For a criticism of Lendon, see Harris, "The Mediterranean and Ancient History," 27–29. C. Barton, *Roman Honor: The Fire in the Bones* (Berkeley and Los Angeles: University of California Press, 2001), is unreliable.

[76] See M. Herzfeld, "Honour and Shame: Problems in the Comparative Analysis of Moral Systems," *Man* 15 (1980): 339–51; F. H. Stewart, *Honor* (Chicago: University of Chicago Press, 1994); and de Pina-Cabral, cited above.

nah, assigns to honor and shame a much more significant role than bibli-cal law does[77]: it is a sensitive issue in the laws of charity, which mandate preserving the honor of the recipient as far as possible, even to the extent of providing extra support to an impoverished person of refined taste (that is, former wealth, Y Peah 8.8/9, 21b)—a concern that is in some ten-sion with the implicit egalitarianism of biblical poor-relief laws. Wounded honor is subjected to formal evaluation in the assessment of damages for seduction, rape (Y Ketubbot 3.7/8, 27d),[78] and assault (Y Baba Qamma 8.3–6). The Mishnah, and the Yerushalmi following it, which tend to op-pose the practice of taking vows and to encourage rabbis to find technical ways of releasing people from their vows, advise trying to convince vow-ers that their vow has brought dishonor on themselves or their families; if they then express regret for having undertaken the vow, it can be legally nullified (M and Y Nedarim 9). In this last case, the rabbis imagined that ideas about personal or family honor were broadly popular without them-selves necessarily endorsing them.

Honor and disgrace (*kavod, bizayon*) also appear frequently in rab-binic literature in the sense of basic public dignity. As such they are closely akin to the entwined Roman ideas of *pudor* ("a sense of shame and socio-ethical discomfort stemming from an awareness of oneself as the constant focus of the moralizing gaze of the community") and *pudicitia* (the nar-rowly sexual application of the same concept).[79] People are expected to behave with restraint. The burden on women here is certainly heavier than that on men: their *kavod* is exceedingly fragile, in constant danger of injury, and if injured especially prone to bring their husbands and other relations into disrepute, and so it is preferable for them to live outside public scrutiny altogether, as far as possible, though even in private any

[77] For detailed discussion, see David Hoffman's forthcoming PhD dissertation, "'All is in Ac-cord with Honor': Kavod and the Emergence of Rabbinic Judaism," Jewish Theological Seminary, 2009 (?).

[78] The Yerushalmi may prescribe in this case an inverse relationship between the honor of the injured party and the damage assessed ("the shame of the great person is great, but his damage is little"). The difficulty, though, is the meaning of the word *nezeq* (damage) here. Does it refer to the penalty assessed for shame, or to something else? The commentators, and later legal decisors (for example, *Shulhan Arukh Hoshen Mishpat*, chap. 420, title 24), all agree on the latter, but there their agreement ends. Penei Moshe argued (the more plausibly, in my view) that it referred to the *pegam* (injury) payment (not explained in Y but in B said to be the impact of the rape or seduction on the victim's "market value"): "a great person is not so easily injured." Qorban Ha-Edah, though, reads the text to say not that the damage assessed for the humiliation of the gran-dee is little but that the damage the grandee *causes* is little, since it is hardly a dishonor to be hu-miliated by a great man.

[79] On *pudor*, see R. Kaster, *Emotion, Restraint, and the Community in Ancient Rome* (Oxford: Oxford University Press, 2005); on *pudicitia*, see R. Langlands, *Sexual Morality in Ancient Rome* (Cambridge: Cambridge University Press, 2006). The quotation is from Langlands, 18.

interaction with another individual can injure a woman's modesty and bring her and her family into disgrace. The rabbis believed that Jewish women themselves were extremely sensitive to honor in this sense of modesty or restraint. The rabbis seem to have been more committed to this central trope of ethnographic mediterraneanism (one regarded with skepticism by many; see chapter 2) than their Roman contemporaries. This impression is surely created in part by class and geographic difference. All the famously licentious Roman women came from a tiny segment of the metropolitan aristocracy, and even in such circles much attention was paid to the ideal of *pudicitia*, while the rabbis were part of a provincial "middle class."[80] Some of the rabbis' concern, at least for feminine *kavod*, was also due to their legal rigor, which made them exaggeratedly anxious about sexual misbehavior. It is nevertheless striking that the rabbis conceptualized the danger inherent in female sexuality, and the fragility of all attempts to constrain it, in terms not only of sin or purity or sanctity, but of honor. This constitutes a significant departure from Pentateuchal (though not necessarily general scriptural) conceptions and shows that there were other factors besides halakhic scrupulosity in the rabbis' "Mediterranean" sensitivity to this issue.[81]

For its part, male *kavod* in general did not intersect so much with halakhic scruples. Though the rabbis certainly expected Jewish men to behave in a dignified way—and the rabbis held themselves to higher standards than they held others—[82] on the whole, their anxiety about the issue was less intense. Indeed, they even thought that *kavod* in this sense was sometimes best sacrificed to higher causes. They repeatedly told the story of Rabbi Samuel bar Rav Isaac, who made a fool of himself in the performance of *mitzvot* in a way that his fellows mocked but God Himself endorsed (Y Peah 1.1, 15d)[83]:

---

[80] On the existence of which see W. Scheidel, "Stratification, Deprivation and the Quality of Life," in *Poverty in the Roman World*, ed. M. Atkins and R. Osborne (Cambridge: Cambridge University Press, 2006), 40–59.

[81] See J. Romney Wegner, *Chattel or Person: The Status of Women in the Mishnah*, (Oxford: Oxford University Press, 1988), 18–19; M. Peskowitz, *Spinning Fantasies: Rabbis, Gender, and History* (Berkeley and Los Angeles: University of California Press, 1997), 49–76; in general, L. Grushcow, *Writing the Wayward Wife: Rabbinic Interpretations of Sotah* (Leiden: Brill, 2006); and C. Fonrobert, *Menstrual Purity: Rabbinic and Christian Reconstructions of Biblical Gender* (Stanford: Stanford University Press, 2000), 276 n. 47, on the absence of an adequate study of rabbinic shame.

[82] See note 72 above on manual labor; Y Maaserot 3.4, 50d: eating in public.

[83] Parallels (the *sugya* begins with the second sentence quoted here: "Rabbi Samuel . . .") appear at Y Avodah Zarah 3.1, 42c; Gen Rabbah 59.4; B. Ketubbot 17a. On the relationships between the parallels, see H.-J. Becker, *Die grossen rabbinischen Sammelwerke Palaestinas zur literarischen Genese von Talmud Yerushalmi und Midrash Bereshit Rabba* (Tübingen: Mohr Siebeck, 1999), 134–48; C. Milikowsky, "The Formation and Transmission of Bereshit Rabba and the Yerushalmi:

"And *gemilut hasadim*" [the bestowal of deeds of lovingkindness]:[84] As it is written, "He who seeks righteousness and lovingkindness will find life, righteousness and honor" [Prov 21.21]—"honor" in this world, and "life" in the world to come. Rabbi Samuel bar Rav Isaac would take branches and dance joyfully before brides. Rabbi Zeira would see him and hide, saying, "See how this old man embarrasses us!" And when Rabbi Samuel died, there were three hours of thunder and lightning in the world, and a divine echo [*berat qala*] was heard to say, "Rabbi Samuel bar Rav Isaac has died, the bestower of deeds of loving kindness!"[85] When they went out to bury him [*lemigmol leh hesed*!], fire descended from heaven and formed a kind of hedge of flaming branches between his bier and the congregation, and the people said, "Look at this old man who has received his recompense for his branches."

So Rabbi Samuel customarily humiliated himself to perform the *mitzvah* of helping brides rejoice, in rabbinic terms an act of *gemilut hasadim*—an act of kindness conferred on any human, regardless of their poverty.[86]

Questions of Redaction, Text-Criticism and Literary Relationships," *JQR* 92 (2002): 550–60 (article: 521–67); L. Moskowitz, "*Sugyot Muhlafot* in the Talmud Yerushalmi," *Tarbiz* 60 (1990): 56–59.

[84] Quoting M Peah 1.1: "These are the things that have no measure [that is, legal limits] . . . and *gemilut hasadim*; and these are the things whose fruits a man eats in this world but whose principle exists to sustain him in the world to come . . . and *gemilut hasadim*."

[85] In the parallels in Genesis Rabbah and Y Avodah Zarah, Rabbi Samuel's death is accompanied by the uprooting of cedars in the land of Israel.

[86] Suggestively, another story of rabbinic self-humiliation also involves marriage (Y Sotah 1.4, 16d):

> Rabbi Meir was accustomed to preach in the synagogue of Hamatha (near Tiberias) every Sabbath eve, and there was a woman there who was accustomed to listen to his voice. One time he ran late, and the woman went home to find that the candle had gone out. Her husband asked her, "Where were you?" She responded, "Listening to the voice of the preacher." He said, "I swear that this woman shall not return to this house until she spits in the face of the preacher." Rabbi Meir divined this through the Holy Spirit, and pretended to develop an eye ailment. He said, "Any woman who knows the correct incantation to recite over my eye, let her come and do it." The woman's neighbors said to her, "Here is your answer: Go to his house, pretend to recite an incantation, and spit in his eye!" She went, and he asked her if she knew the incantation for eye ailments; owing to her fear of him, she responded, "No." He said, "In that case, it also helps if you spit in the eye seven times." When she had done so he said, "Go and tell your husband, You told me to spit once and I spat seven times." His students said to the rabbi, "Is this how you disgrace [*mevazin*] the Torah? If you had asked would we not have brought him here and beat him until he took his wife back?" He responded to them, "Let not Meir's honor be greater than the honor of his Creator! For if Scripture says that the Holy Name, written in holiness, must nevertheless be erased in the waters [of the ritual of the bitter waters] in order to restore peace between a man and his wife, does the same not apply to Meir's honor a fortiori?"

In contrast to the *derash* that introduces the anecdote here (though not in the parallels), Rabbi Samuel was never honored for this in his lifetime but only after his death, which was commemorated by signs and miracles. Thus, those who once had mocked him learned that God rewards *gemilut hasadim* with public acclamation, with the *bat qol* (divine echo) playing the role of the honorary inscription in the euergetistic economy of the Roman city.

The rabbis also preserved a series of stories set in the time of the Second Temple about an aristocratic Ascalonite pagan who had so respected his parents that he allowed himself to be publicly humiliated by them; he too achieved divine reward, not to mention the rare status of being one of the very few pagans the rabbis remembered for their piety and moral excellence. (Y Qiddushin 1.7, 61b, the story of Dama b. Netina, head of the *patrobouloi*—ancestral city councillors—of Ascalon) As usual, such stories have a certain ambiguity. On the one hand, they implicitly prescribe ideals, and it is by no means insignificant that the rabbis sometimes idealized strongly countercultural behavior: the rabbis admired "holy fools" like Rabbi Samuel bar Rav Isaac, extremists who utterly rejected standard behavioral norms in the pursuit of higher ideals, in the rabbis' case, Torah and *mitzvot*. But the same stories tend to marginalize these ideals; they are not even really prescriptions but rather admiring accounts of types of behavior even the rabbis themselves were not expected to emulate day to day; their moral frisson is intentionally vicarious, achieved through the telling of the story itself, not through the mimetic enactment of its values. Such stories are the rabbinic equivalent of the Christian martyr act or saint's life, glorifying forms of behavior not meant to be generally imitated. Indeed, normally, rabbis are meant to act in a dignified way, not disgrace themselves publicly (for example, Y Maaserot 3.4, 50d; less severe than the parallel at B Qiddushin 40b). Furthermore, though the rabbis admired extremist renouncers, unlike their Christian contemporaries they never developed an institutional setting in which such behavior might be considered normative. The rabbis had no monasteries, where honor was simply irrelevant. In the highly social setting of the rabbinic study house or disciple circle,[87] not to mention the

---

[87] The following story illustrates the rabbis' preference for *havruta* (fellowship; collegiality) while acknowledging the attractions of solitary contemplation (Y Shevi'it 8.5, 38b):

> "Judah of Hutzai hid in a cave for three days because he wished to understand the reason for [a certain *halakhah*, omitted here for the sake of brevity; in the Yerushalmi, "*ta'ama*," reason, usually refers to a law's scriptural foundation]. Afterward, he visited Rabbi Yosi bar Halafta who said to him, "Where have you been?" Judah responded, "I was hiding in a cave for three days because I wished to understand the reason for [this *halakhah*]." Rabbi Yosi summoned his son, Rabbi Eurydemos, and said to him, "Tell this man the reason for [the *halakhah*]." [And he told him.] Rabbi

towns where students of the sages sometimes acted as religious functionaries, honor in the sense of basic public dignity was an important value.

In these environments, honor as public dignity shaded off into another major sense of honor: honor as political or social currency, as a tracer for dominance. This is the type of honor that is supposed to have been an important element of the Roman imperial system, and honor in this sense is surprisingly important in Palestinian rabbinic texts, too. There are two subforms: standard public *kavod*, not specifically rabbinic, and *kavod* as social currency within the rabbinic subculture. Both seem relevant to the question of the rabbis' integration into and conformity with the Roman system, and so I discuss both in some detail. I would only add that it is impossible to analyze here every rabbinic account of public honor; rather surprisingly, it is far too common a theme, especially in its inner-rabbinic form. Instead I have selected two pericopae, the first because it seems to me quite typical, the second because it is the most extended and penetrating Palestinian rabbinic discussion of the issue.

The Rabbis and Roman Honor (Y Berakhot 5.1, 9a)

The stories and laws I am analyzing here concern acts of deference. The main theoretical problem this raises is the relationship between deference and honor. In fact, as the sociologist Erving Goffman long ago demonstrated, deference exists in societies where a strong sense of honor is absent. Indeed, it has recently been argued that deference, unlike honor, is, as it were, hardwired into primate behavior.[88] For our purposes, though, this concern seems minor. The large corpus of rabbinic stories about deference are simultaneously in every case explicitly stories about honor as well. Though the second passage I am discussing here is an analysis precisely of the relationship among deference, honor, and the formal requirements of a *mitzvah*, on the whole it seems legitimate to suppose that Palestinian rabbinic texts regard deference and honor as closely related: to act deferentially toward someone routinely, but not invariably, means to acknowledge that he possesses honor.

Y Berakhot 5.1 preserves a small collection of anecdotes about rabbis' encounters with Roman officials and the competition over honor and deference that such encounters entailed, at least in the imaginations of

---

Yosi said to Judah, "Who caused you [to be unable to answer such a simple question]? It happened because you did not investigate it with your friends." [Cf. B Ta'anit 23a, the well-known *mot, o havruta o mituta*—give me *havruta* or give me death.]

[88] A. Mazur, *Biosociology of Dominance and Deference* (Lanham, MD: Rowman and Littlefield, 2005).

the storytellers, if not in real life.[89] This collection is part of the Talmud's commentary on the Mishnah's rule that if one is in the process of reciting the *Tefillah* (the main canonical daily prayer), one may not interrupt: "Even if a king greets him, he may not respond; even if a snake has wound itself around his leg, he may not stop." (This is in contrast to the *shema'*, which one is permitted to interrupt under some limited circumstances; M. Berakhot 2.1.) Now, none of the Talmud's anecdotes here concern the interruption of the *Tefillah*, but they seem collectively to constitute a paradoxical consideration of the limitations on the deference due to the powerful, an underlying concern of the Mishnah, too[90]:

> Rabbi Yohanan was sitting and reading [the *shema'*, or perhaps "studying" other biblical texts] in front of the "Babylonian synagogue" of Sepphoris. An archon passed by and the rabbi did not rise for him. [The archon's attendants] sought to strike him, but the archon said to them, "Leave him alone, since he is studying the Law of his Creator [*namosa de-baryeh*]."
>
> Rabbi Hanina and Rabbi Joshua ben Levi went to visit the proconsul of Caesarea [*anthupata de-Qisrin*]. When he saw them, he stood before them. [His attendants] said to him, "Are you rising before these Jews [*yehuda'ei*]?" He responded, "I saw [in them] the visages of angels."
>
> Rabbi Jonah and Rabbi Yosi visited Ursicinus [a historical figure: the *magister equitum per orientem* (commander-in-chief of the eastern cavalry) under Constantius II, 349–59; in the Yerushalmi often the embodiment of Roman might][91] in Antioch. When he saw them

[89] On the importance of deference in Roman political and social life, see the cautious account of Lendon, *Empire of Honor*, esp. (for the present purposes), 58–63; J. Hall, "The Deference-Greeting in Roman Society," *Maia* 50 (1998): 413–26. Almost all the stories discussed here concern rising and not more intimate gestures of deference, such as kissing (the hand, for inferiors, the lips for notional equals), or perhaps baring the head (cf. B Qiddushin 33b, where, in an anecdote set in Babylonia, a commoner is expected to *cover* his head in the presence of a rabbi). This is reminiscent of Georg Simmel's notion of the "ideal sphere": in Goffman's elaboration, the greater the social distance between the two actors, the greater the "ceremonial distance" between them tends to be, and the less physically intimate rituals of deference are likely to be: see the seminal E. Goffman, "The Nature of Deference and Demeanor," *American Anthropologist* 58 (1956): 473–502, esp. 481–82.

[90] Indeed, the Mishnah's comment here is certainly intended homiletically and not as actual law, since there is nothing else in the Mishnah that would justify martyring oneself in order to recite a prayer (this objection is raised in B. Berakhot 32b–33a). The Palestinian Talmud ad loc. accepts the legal force of the Mishnah's statement but limits its applicability nearly out of existence.

[91] See W. Portmann, "Ursicinus," *Der Neue Pauly* 12/1, 1054–55; in much greater detail, A. Lippold, in the old *Pauly-Wissowa*, sub v. For a positivistic treatment of the numerous Talmudic stories about Ursicinus, see G. Stemberger, *Jews and Christians in the Holy Land: Palestine in the Fourth Century* (Edinburgh: Clark, 1999), 161–84.

he rose before them. [His attendants] said to him, "Are you rising before these Jews?" He responded, "I saw [or, had a vision of] the faces of these men in battle and was victorious."

Rabbi Abun visited the emperor [*malkhuta*], and when he left he turned his back [*qadla*, literally, the nape of his neck]. [The emperor's attendants] sought to kill him, but they saw two bolts of lightning issuing from his neck and left him alone, in fulfillment of the verse, "And all the peoples of the land will see that the name of the Lord is called over you [applied to you], and they will be afraid of you."

The obvious if rather fantastic point of this pericope is that in the competition between rabbis and powerful outsiders over honor and deference, the rabbis, as embodiments of Torah and representatives of the God of Israel, always win. It thus resembles a great many stories told about encounters between Christians, or philosophers, or magicians like Apollonius of Tyana, and emperors or other powerful Romans, all illustrating the profound impact that Roman might had even, or especially, on some of the more marginal inhabitants of the Empire, but the rabbinic stories focus unusually tightly on issues of deference. The pericope has two complementary principles of organization: it is organized chiastically, in that the first and fourth episodes both concern a rabbi who fails to offer proper deference to an official in a way that arouses the anger of the official's slaves and the second and third episodes both concern officials who unexpectedly pay honor to rabbis, over the protests of their attendants.[92] The pericope is also organized as a crescendo of terror and implausibility: each story features a more frightening official than the previous one and a more supernatural punchline. The first anecdote is realistic: a rabbi engaged in Torah study fails to rise to greet an *archon*, a member of the governing board of the Sepphorite city council, and so a rather minor local grandee who is unable to do more to avenge the rabbi's insult than have his slaves beat him up. The *archon*, who is probably meant to be Jewish (see below), notwithstanding his reference to "*his* (not "our" or "the") Creator,"[93] but who could conceivably be Christian or pagan, restrains his slaves by acknowledging the superiority of the rabbi's pursuit, in fact by basically repeating the mishnaic law about interrupting study to pay one's respects to a passing dignitary, but translated from rabbinic Hebrew into

[92] I thank Beth Berkowitz for pointing this out to me.
[93] I owe this observation to the fellows of the Center for Advanced Judaic Studies of the University of Pennsylvania, September 2007.

quasi-philosophical pidgin Greek (a possibly not unrealistic imitation of the rhetorical style of small-town eastern *curiales*)—*be-namosa de-baryeh hu ʿasiq.*

The second anecdote raises the stakes: the Roman official is now governor of Palestine, a figure massively more powerful than a city councillor.[94] His attendants' response to his paradoxical display of deference to the rabbis expresses the rabbinic storytellers' sense of alienation (their own, and the Jews' collectively)[95] from the Roman system, a perhaps carefully cultivated sense that they had no place in the empire-wide economy of honor. The idea that the Jews are inherently contemptible is one the rabbis or editors of the Talmud frequently put into the mouths of their gentile characters (and the absence of such a comment in the first anecdote may argue that the storyteller imagined the *archon* as a Jew, though a rather compromised one). But despite this alienation, they still fantasized not about crushing the Romans but about forcing the Roman authorities to recognize their true quality, as living exemplars of the divine Law and mediators of God's power, and so to defer to them (in such stories, then, honor is moralized—detached from its association with power and presented as an ethical category).[96] In other words, in dreaming about beating the Romans at their own game, they tacitly accepted the rules of that game.

[94] The anecdote's terminology ("the *anthypatos* of [=in] Caesarea") may reflect the period before the early fifth-century split of central and northern Palestine into two provinces governed respectively by a *consularis* based in Caesarea and a *praeses* based in Scythopolis: anthypatos or proconsul is firmly attested as the title of the governor of Palaestina in the 380s. The governor at the time of Rabbi Joshua ben Levi, conventionally dated in the early to mid-third century, was still a *legatus Augusti pro praetore*. See E. M. Smallwood, *The Jews under Roman Rule from Pompey to Diocletian: A Study in Political Relations* (Leiden: Brill, 1981), 478–86; on the evidence for the 380s, confirmed by Novella 103 of Justinian, see L. di Segni, "Dated Inscriptions from Palestine from the Roman and Byzantine Periods," PhD dissertation, Hebrew University, 1997, 1:95. This would have some bearing on the date of the publication of the Yerushalmi were it not for the fact that the governors' titulature in the 360s, 370s, and 390s is so poorly attested.

[95] In the Yerushalmi the word *yehudaʾei* frequently expresses contempt; "Jew" is not necessarily a sufficiently strong translation.

[96] On the moralization of honor by the weak or the marginal, see Davis, *People of the Mediterranean*, 89–100. It may be worth observing that at least in the stories discussed here, the rabbis do not represent themselves as tricksters vis-à-vis the Romans, as people who assume and shed cultural identities, as practitioners of James Scott's "hidden transcript"—that is, people who pretend to conform but secretly engage in usually symbolic resistance (*Domination and the Arts of Resistance*). In their Talmudic self-representation, rabbis are truly who they are, and *know* they are better than the Romans. We may contrast aspects of Josephus's self-representation: see M. Gleason, "Mutilated Messengers: Body Language in Josephus," in *Being Greek Under Rome: Cultural Identity, The Second Sophistic and the Development of Empire*, ed. S. Goldhill (Cambridge: Cambridge University Press, 2001), 50–85, and the representation of Shimon ben Shetah, discussed above; cf. Shaw 1993.

That the rabbis' fantasies about the Romans contained this conservative or integrationist impulse is perhaps expressed most clearly in the third anecdote, which raises the stakes yet again. In this anecdote the rabbis visit the ferocious general Ursicinus, the subject of a large number of anecdotes in the Yerushalmi, most of which concern his power and arrogance. His capitulation to the rabbis, his acknowledgment of their numinosity, their status as divine messengers, is thus all the more striking, yet the rabbinic storytellers appear to acquiesce in the general's military glory. Given the story's obvious resonances with Constantine's widely publicized vision at the Milvian Bridge,[97] it is hard not to detect here at very least a trace of competition with Christianity, in which the (presumably, though far from definitely) Christian general, or at least a general understandably seen as promoting the cause of Christianity, is nevertheless forced to acknowledge the superiority of the rabbis.[98]

The final story is obviously meant as a climax; it involves an encounter with the emperor himself, and the miracle now occurs onstage, as it were. In other ways it breaks the pattern, or perhaps reverts to the theme of the first anecdote, in which a rabbi fails to show appropriate respect to an official. But no one shows any deference to Rabbi Abun; the response of the emperor's slaves is not deference but fear—a hint at a more subversive type of rabbinic fantasy about Rome—and here for the first time in the pericope a biblical verse is quoted, which concludes the pericope by declaring that the nations automatically fear anyone called by God's name (any Jew? A pious Jew? A rabbi?), a sentiment that would have been far less poignant if it had been any truer.

Honor Among Rabbis (Y Bikkurim 3.3)

Honor was important as currency in intrarabbinic exchange. This issue has been adumbrated in the discussion above of Rabbi Yohanan's zeal to be quoted by name: in this way, the Talmud claims, he sought to secure eternal memorialization. Indeed, there are many passages in the Yerushalmi that indicate that the rabbinic group cultivated a moral or cognitive or cultural economy that appropriated and judaized the euergetistic economy of the Roman city. There is a little evidence that leading rabbis

[97] On which see H. Drake, *Constantine and the Bishops: The Politics of Intolerance* (Baltimore, MD: Johns Hopkins University Press, 2000), 10–11.

[98] The sources collected in A. H. M. Jones, J. R. Martindale and J. Morris, *Prosopography of the Later Roman Empire* (Cambridge: Cambridge University Press, 1971), 1:985–86, appear to give no indication one way or another whether Ursicinus was Christian. To the rabbis this detail can scarcely have mattered.

patronized their junior colleagues in conventional ways, by providing them with judicial and other appointments, by helping them financially, and perhaps especially by organizing with some frequency one of the most important ritual manifestations of precedence and hierarchy in a small society or subculture, the dinner party.[99] There is also some evidence that rabbis and "disciples of sages" sometimes had nonrabbinic patrons, which reminds us that the image of complete rabbinic social and cultural cohesion they produced in their texts is partial and selective. But in the quotidian economy of the rabbinic study house such exchange was far less significant than the exchange of knowledge, which the senior *hakhamim* bestowed on their students as a group and the latter reciprocated with honor and with deference.[100] As we have seen, one of the standard forms such honor took was the practice of attributing a teaching to the person from whom it was received. Another rule, whose articulation in the Talmud is far more vehement, forbids a student to teach in the presence of his teacher. Students were expected to engage in *shimush hakhamim*, service of sages, though this expectation was not invariably met.[101]

Though all rabbinic texts valorize the rabbi-disciple relationship, and none ever suggests that students should *not* respect their teachers, the Yerushalmi does not present the broader exchange of knowledge for honor and memorialization in a consistently approving way. Sometimes it is presented simply as a matter of course, at other times with profound ambivalence. Even the story of Rabbi Yohanan already discussed seems to imply that the rabbi's concern to be quoted and deferred to by his students was somehow unseemly, though probably very mildly so. As we will see, Y Bikkurim 3.3 subjects the idea that rabbis ipso facto merit deference to a profound critique, while not discarding the value of honor.

[99] On which see Schwartz, "No Dialogue at the Symposium?"

[100] Jeffrey Rubenstein's view that honor-shame was important in the Babylonian study house but not in the Palestinian ("what we do not find in the Yerushalmi is the theme of shame *in an academic setting*") needs to be refined. Honor and shame are pervasively important in the Yerushalmi's stories of intrarabbinic relations; what is less important, though still not wholly absent (see, for example, the prayer of Rabbi Nehuniah ben Haqanah at Y Berakhot 4.2, 7d), is the theme of dishonor resulting from defeat in argument. This is perhaps because there are far fewer anecdotes about rabbinic arguments in the Yerushalmi than in the Bavli. The Bavli and Yerushalmi are not polar opposites on this point but feature slightly different inflections of a shared set of themes. The real distinction between them is not in their attitude toward honor or shame but in their attitude toward dialectical argumentation. See J. Rubenstein, *The Culture of the Babylonian Talmud* (Baltimore, MD: Johns Hopkins University Press, 2003), 67–79. The quotation appears on p. 79.

[101] On the rabbinic master-student relationship, see Hezser, *The Social Structure of the Rabbinic Movement*, 332–52.

Y Bikkurim 3.3 focuses on the rabbis' own embrace of deference and honor as inner Jewish cultural values.[102] But the embrace was ambivalent and the focus is loose. Unlike the previous passage, which is brief and well organized, the *sugya* about rabbinic deference here occupies most of a very long *halakhah* and appears to be little more than a random aggregation of sayings, both tannaitic and amoraic, and anecdotes about the issue. On the surface it proposes no very clearly defined point of view, and, as is often the case in long *sugyot* in the Yerushalmi, it is very difficult for the reader to know whether the juxtaposed elements are meant to be read together, with the reader drawing out logical connections presumably implicit in the juxtaposition, or whether the editor is simply providing the reader with raw material to treat as he sees fit.[103]

All this having been said, though, I would argue for the following as a broadly valid approach to the *sugya*. In the background of the discussion is the biblical verse, "Before the hoary head shalt thou rise, and thou shalt honor the face of the elder" (Lev 19.32). A rigorous interpretation of this

---

[102] See too the conclusion of M Horayot: there, the mishnah begins by laying out practical rules of precedence (M Horayot 3.7: "The man precedes the woman in being saved from death and for the return of lost property; the woman precedes the man for charitable gifts of clothing and redemption from captivity" (this resonates with both Mediterranean and Jewish-biblical cultural biases) and then generalizes, but in a very schematic way (M Horayot 3.8: "A priest precedes a levite [the commentators add, "for all matters of honor"], a levite an Israelite, an Israelite a bastard, a bastard a *natin*, a *natin* a proselyte and a proselyte a freedman. When does this apply? When all are equal. But if the bastard was a disciple of the sages and the high priest an ignoramus, a bastard disciple takes precedence over an ignorant high priest"). The Tosefta (T. Horayot 2.8–11) greatly extends the Mishnah's list of general precedence, but significantly, it is fleshed out with ranks that had existed only before the destruction of the Jerusalem Temple in 70, if not earlier (prophet, anointed priest, captain of the temple, temple treasurer, and so forth). If such figures are removed from the Tosefta's list, it is identical to the Mishnah's. There may be a nostalgic implication here that truly complex and substantial rules of precedence applied only when the temple still stood, and no longer matter in our disenchanted age.

[103] Further complications are generated by the existence of two partial parallels in the Babylonian Talmud, at Qiddushin 32b–33b, and Sanhedrin 7b (the latter parallels only the *sugya* on "those appointed for money"), especially since the former preserves some ostensibly tannaitic material (in particular, the Bavli's discussion takes off from a *baraita* that also appears, though without the final clause, in Sifra parashat Qedoshim, chap. 7). In general, it seems clear though that the Babylonian versions of the Palestinian traditions are secondary, normally constituting expansions and clarifications in ways that are in one or two cases quite helpful, but otherwise should be treated with utmost caution, since they manifestly reflect the very different concerns of their Babylonian tradents. A thorough study of the parallels would be an interesting exercise but will not be undertaken here. One immediately obvious difference, though, should be noted: the Bavli conveys or implies absolutely no doubt that technical *zeqenim*—that is, recipients of *semikhah* (the Babylonian equivalent of *minui*)—deserve deference, not simply the formalistic fulfillment of the Pentateuchal obligation. Even the Sanhedrin passage has transformed the Yerushalmi's *class* of inappropriate judicial appointments into *individuals* who turn out to be incompetent or corrupt, but whose existence by no means calls into question the legitimacy of the institution of judicial appointment.

verse, which underlies the tannaitic teachings scattered through the *sugya* about the obligation to rise for holders of certain ranks (*zaqen* = *hakham* = *memuneh*, patriarch, Father of the Court, and high priest), and apparently some of the amoraic anecdotes as well, is constantly subverted by the other components of the *sugya*, which are strongly critical of the notion that the biblical obligation to rise for people of a certain rank implies that rank confers honor.[104] Rising not only fulfills a legal obligation, it also constitutes a true act of deference, which technical *zeqenim* do not always merit, while non-*zeqenim* sometimes do. Thus, story after story concerns *zeqenim* who rise for mere *talmidei hakhamim* (non-*memunim*), and for commoners[105]; the obligation to rise for the high priest is criticized on the grounds that its biblical foundation is insufficient—in the best case, the Israelites rose for Moses because of his personal righteousness, not because of his rank or office; and anyway, according to this passage, rising does not always indicate deference, or rather, sometimes acts of deference are meant ironically. The Israelites may have risen for Moses to get a better look at his corruption and exploitativeness (and perhaps we are meant to understand that one might rise for the patriarch or high priest for the same reason). And finally, along similar lines, *minui* itself is no guarantee of honorability: some *memunim* are completely undeserving: their judicial gowns and high titles and expectations of deference are all meaningless. These components of the *sugya* seem, then, to constitute a penetrating if unsystematic critique of the view of some of the teachings quoted in the *sugya* that rank deserves deference, and argues as a kind of corollary that acts of deference themselves are not always what they seem to be: sometimes they signal not honor but disgrace. Y Bikkurim 3.3 embraces deference ambivalently, then, with one strand arguing formalistically that the Torah requires Jews to honor *zeqenim* but the other strand responding that inasmuch as the act of rising is thought to have content and meaning, it should be performed only for the Torah, whatever the formal rank, position, or age of the human vessel that contains it. The law may require one to rise when confronting a person of a certain rank, but this act does not constitute deference and conveys no honor.

[104] Compare the rule in Y Berakhot 2.1, 4b that one is obligated "to greet one's master or someone greater than one in Torah"—a rule that precisely does not tie deference to rank but to relationship.

[105] The Yerushalmi, unlike its Bavli parallel, does not treat the two clauses of the verse ("before the hoary head . . . and thou shalt honor") as separate commandments. Thus the Bavli can restrict the second clause to *zeqenim* sensu stricto, and can interpret the first clause as an obligation to show some tokens of respect to all elderly people, even gentiles ("Aramaeans"); in Y, by contrast, Rabbi Meir's practice of rising for elderly "*ammei ha'aretz*" (literally, people of the land; the term's precise meaning is controversial, but at the very least it implies nonrabbis) is presented as supererogatory observance of the obligation to show honor to the Torah (see below).

I would argue that this rabbinic debate has a real though oblique connection to what has recently been characterized as the standard Roman view (though I suspect that things were quite different in the late empire, with its professional bureaucracy, formally hierarchical senatorial classes, and numinously remote emperor, than in the high empire) that honor resides not in rank but in the qualities of the individual—his birth, liberality, and so forth.[106] The rabbis struggled with the same issue and reached no definite conclusion. But those who agreed with the view of Roman aristocrats in formal terms nevertheless disagreed in substance. For these rabbis, the only honor that mattered was the honor of the Torah, and this spilled over to the humans who possessed it or embodied it; as Rabbi Yannai said of his son-in-law, who never attained the rank of *zaqen*, it is forbidden to remain seated in the presence of Mount Sinai.

Why Rise?

What I described above as the subversive view is set out with tolerable clarity at the very beginning of the *sugya*. It begins with a brief discussion of the limitations on the obligation to stand before a *zaqen*, a term almost certainly used here in the technical sense: not an old man but a *memuneh* (a *hakham*, or sage, who has received judicial appointment). It quotes a tosefta that declares that the Pentateuchal obligation to rise for a *zaqen* does not apply if the one rising will incur thereby a monetary loss, and extrapolates from this to the case of the Mishnah's Jerusalemite artisans, who apparently are expected to interrupt their work to show honor to the pilgrims bearing first fruits[107]; it resolves this tension by observing that the arrival of pilgrims is a special, rare occurrence, and so the artisans of Jerusalem are not released from their obligation to greet them.

[106] See Lendon, *Empire of Honor*, 16–17. In the Berakhot passage discussed above, the rabbis seem to assume that among Romans deference is owed to rank—probably the view of many provincials of relatively modest social background, for whom it was reasonable to fear and wise to placate anyone with an official title. This does not tell us anything about how the elites themselves thought about the issue.

[107] M Bikkurim 3:3:

Those who live near [the Jerusalem temple] bring [as their] first fruits grapes (or, in other versions, bring as their first fruits figs and grapes), and those who live far away bring dried figs and raisins. And the ox walks before them, its horns gilt and an olive wreath on its head, and the flute plays before them until they arrive near Jerusalem; when they did so they sent ahead to Jerusalem and decorated their first fruits with wreaths. And "the satraps, officers" [*pahot u-seganim*, a biblical cliché: cf. Jer 51.23; Ezek 23.6, 12, 23] and treasurers come out to greet them—according to the honor of those entering did they come out; all the craftsmen of Jerusalem would stand before them and greet them [presumably, when they arrived in the city] and say, "Our brothers from X, welcome!"

But the Talmud then veers away from Pentateuchal law in a way that suggests that more is at stake in the Mishnah's displays of deference than observance of biblical prescription. In fact, no biblical text declares that pilgrims bearing first fruits to Jerusalem must be greeted by the citizen body, as the Mishnah requires. Clearly, the Mishnah has something else in mind.

> R. Yosi bar Rabbi Bun in the name of R. Huna bar Hiyya: come and see how great is the power of performers of *mitzvot*, in that one does not stand for elders [if this will cause monetary loss], but one does stand for the performers of *mitzvot*. R. Yosi bar Rabbi Bun said [furthermore], those who rise for the dead are rising not for the dead but for those who perform for them deeds of lovingkindness [that is, those participating in the funeral procession].[108]

In this view, the practice of greeting the pilgrims and their ilk is unconnected with the biblical commandment of rising "before the hoary head"; it is rather a ritual of deference, directed at the performers of *mitzvot* in a way that suggests, as the Mishnah itself seems to do by describing the reception at Jerusalem of villagers bearing their first fruits as an *adventus* ceremony (which accompanies the reception of an emperor or other grandee in a city),[109] that the pilgrims, however modest, are comparable to emperors and so receive similar treatment. Implicit here is the notion that it is the pious who are truly honorable, an idea very hard indeed to find in the Hebrew Bible but one that is given repeated emphasis in the Wisdom of Ben Sira.

Standing for Rabbis[110]

Rabbi Hizqiya in the name of Rabbi Hanina son of Rabbi Abbahu in the name of Rabbi Avduma [some texts add: of Haifa]: [One

---

[108] The Bavli parallel is subtly but significantly different (B Qidd 33a): "Rabbi Yosi bar Abin said, Come and see how beloved a commandment is *at its proper time*, for they stand before them [the pilgrims bearing first fruits] but not before *talmidei hakhamim*." This appears to merge the view attributed to R. Yosi Bar Rabbi Bun (=Abin) in the Yerushalmi and the view cited immediately preceding it—opinions presented in the Y as being in conflict.

[109] The closest parallel to the Mishnah in tone and content is the contemporaneous Menander Rhetor, *peri epideiktikon* 281 (advising the orator what to say on the occasion of an *adventus*); on the *adventus* see S. MacCormack, *Art and Ceremony in Late Antiquity* (Berkeley and Los Angeles: University of California Press, 1981), 17–89.

[110] I omit the brief *sugya* that intervenes between the two quoted here since I have failed to make complete sense of it; its gist, though, seems to be, more or less, that *zeqenim* should not abuse their right to be deferred to, either inside the lecture hall or outside it (following the interpretation of Rabbi Hayim Kanievski, *Masekhet Bikkurim min Talmud Yerushalmi 'im bi'ur mesudar mi-pi ha-shemu'ah mi-shi'urei Moreinu Rabbi Hayim Kanievski Shlit'a* [Benei Berak (no publisher), 1990], 43, following, legitimately in this case, the implications of the Bavli parallel, Qiddushin 33b, top of the page).

stands] for an elder [when he is at a distance of] four cubits; when [the elder] passes, he sits. The high priest: [one stands] from the time he comes into view until the time he is no longer visible. Why? [that is, what is the Pentateuchal source for this rule?] "And it came to pass when Moses went out to the Tent [of Meeting] all the nation stood" [Ex 33.8, slightly misquoted in all MSS and early printed editions].

Two amora'im interpreted this verse, one [that the nation stood in] praise [of Moses], the other [that they stood in order to] shame [him]. For the first, [the nation was saying,] "Behold the righteous man and acquire merit." For the second, [the nation was saying,] "Look at his thighs and his belly, see how he grows fat exploiting the Jews, how everything he owns he took from the Jews [yehuda'ei]!"

This section begins with a teaching that strongly resembles the text from Tosefta Sanhedrin that the Talmud quotes a few lines down; this text, like the Sanhedrin text, has no explicit connection to any biblical prescription; both seem interested in presenting schematic hierarchies of deference in ways that almost seem drawn from the classical sociological literature on social hierarchies and rituals of avoidance. The contribution of Rabbi Hizqiya et al. seems to be to provide the scriptural foundation for the requirement to stand for the high priest, in a way that would sub-ordinate tannaitic teachings about deference to Torah-derived legal for-malism. The biblical verses describe how Moses, having built the Tent of Meeting on the outskirts of the Israelite camp, would from time to time go out to consult God there. When he left the camp, all the Israelites would stand at the entrances to their tents and watch him until he entered the Tent of Meeting. The rabbis identified the Tent of Meeting with the Tabernacle, a kind of mobile proto-Temple, and so thought that Moses, who frequented the former, performed a quasi-priestly role: hence the force of the biblical prooftext.[111]

I believe that the second paragraph is meant as a refutation of the first, or at least partly so. Certainly the second amoraic interpretation mani-festly deprives the law about the high priest of its scriptural foundation. But arguably the friendly first interpretation does, too, by attaching "the nation's" behavior strictly to the personal qualities of Moses, the tzadiq. In this view, deference is due not to office alone but to a person.

[111] In the Bavli parallel, Qidd 33b, by contrast, the verses are used as a prooftext for a teaching derived from a source very similar to T Sanhedrin, quoted in the Yerushalmi a few lines down, about the obligation to stand for the nasi for the entire time he is visible, until he is seated in his place.

The ark faces the nation, and the priests [at the time of the priestly blessing] face the nation, but Israel [stands and?] faces the Holy Place. Rabbi L'azar said, "The Torah does not stand before its son." Samuel said, "One does not stand before a *haver* [lit., an associate, which in this context probably means, following Pnei Moshe, *talmidei hakhamim* who have not received *minui*]."

Rabbi Hila and Rabbi Jacob bar Idi were seated, Samuel bar Ba[112] [whose lack of the title "rabbi" indicates he had not received judicial appointment] passed by, and they rose for him. Samuel said to them, "You have made two mistakes, first, I am not an elder, second, 'The Torah does not stand before its son.'"

The first sentence describes the arrangement of priests and laypeople during the priestly blessing, in which priests and people stand facing each other while the Torah scroll sits in its ark, which may be intended simply as a literal account of how the priestly blessing is performed, or it may be meant somehow metaphorically, for example to convey the idea that the Torah alone deserves deference, or that the Torah, the priesthood, and lay Israelites are bound in some relationship of mutual dependency (Israel depends on the Torah and the priests, but the Torah and the priests depend on Israel). The next two statements may be meant either as contradictory or as complementary. In the first case, Rabbi L'azar means that only the Torah (and its human possessor) must be deferred to (and rank is irrelevant), while the second one means (following the explanation of Pnei Moshe) that one is required to rise only for people who are technical *zeqenim*—recipients of judicial appointments—but not for scholars who have not yet been appointed. In other words, one rises for rank, not personal achievement. Of course, Samuel's view may assume that Torah truly belongs to the *memuneh*, and not yet to his student, and if a similar assumption underlies Rabbi L'azar's view, it too can be reconciled with a hierarchical approach. The anecdote cited to illustrate these rules both clarifies and complicates our interpretation: two *memunim* rise for a non-*memuneh*, who rebukes them by citing the gemara's two rules—apparently they are understood as having separate but complementary force: Samuel bar Ba seems to be saying that not only is he not a *zaqen* but he is also inferior in Torah, a view paradoxically refuted by his citation of laws apparently unknown to the two rabbis.[113]

---

[112] In B Qidd 33b the protagonists are named Rabbi Ila'i, Rabbi Jacob bar Zabdi, and Rabbi (sic) Shimon bar Abba.

[113] H. W. Guggenheimer, following Rashi on the Bavli parallel (Qiddushin 33b), explains the episode differently: the two seated rabbis were studying when Samuel bar Ba approached, and

The *Mitzvah* of Rising for a *Zaqen*

Rabbi Ze'ira said, "Rabbi Aha used to interrupt [his studies] and rise [for an elder],[114] because he was scrupulous about the following tannaitic teaching: 'Scribes writing Torah scrolls, phylacteries and *mezuzot* interrupt for the recitation of the *shema*', but not for the *tefillah*'; Rabbi Hananiah ben 'Akavyah said, 'Just as they interrupt for the reading of the *shema*', so they interrupt for the *tefillah*, for the donning of phylacteries, and for all the commandments of the Torah (including "For the hoary head," etc.)."'

When Hizqiya Beribbi had worn himself out studying Torah he would go and sit in front of the study house, in order to see elders [*sabin*, clearly here in the sense of technical *zeqenim*] and rise before them.

These two anecdotes clearly belong together in that both present rabbis engaged in supererogatory (and in the second case conceivably slightly absurd) observance of the formal biblical commandment to rise for a *zaqen*, unambiguously understood in the second case as a *memuneh*. The first anecdote relies on an analogy, here untheorized, of the *hakham* studying Torah and the scribe copying holy books. The analogy is manifestly imperfect, which is why Rabbi Aha's practice is characterized as supererogatory.

The *Mitzvah* of Rising for the Torah

Judah bar Hiyya was accustomed to go and pay his respects [*she'il bi-shelameh*] to his father-in-law Rabbi Yannai every Friday. He [Rabbi Yannai] would sit in a high place [*atar teli*, following Sokoloff; contrast Pnei Moshe] in order to see him coming, and rise before him.[115] His students said, "[Even] for an elder [which Judah is not] one is required to stand only when they are within four cubits." [Rabbi Yannai] responded, "It is forbidden to remain seated before Mount Sinai." One time [Judah] was late in arriving and [Rabbi

the latter's quotation of the law of Rabbi L'azar means that it was unnecessary to interrupt study of the Torah to greet a scholar (a son of the Torah).

[114] Even though this was not strictly required, or may even be forbidden, if this is how the rule that "the Torah does not stand before its son" is meant to be understood, following the commentators on the Bavli Qiddushin parallel.

[115] In my opinion the story only makes sense if the riser is Rabbi Yannai; this is also the view of Penei Moshe and of Z. W. Rabinovitz, *Sha'arei Torath Eretz Israel* [Jerusalem: Weiss, 1940], 144. But the latter cites with disapproval the view of two commentators that Judah is the riser, and this is how Neusner translates the passage.

Yannai] said, "It is impossible that Judah has changed his practice, nor is it possible that infirmities have attacked that righteous body; the only possible conclusion is that Judah is no more."

This story concerns—to subordinate it crudely to my theme here—the way personal qualities trump rank: Judah is Mount Sinai—meaning either that he is a great scholar or that he is filled with *mitzvot*—and a *tzadiq* (righteous man), not least because of his deference to his father-in-law, in the form of weekly visits so regular that only death could interrupt them. We may indeed be supposed to imagine here an exchange: deference for deference, and not far in the background affection for affection. But this would not in my view change the larger point of the story, which is, at very least, that there are things more important and more honorable than rank and age:

> Rabbi Meir would see even an old *'am ha'aretz* [nonrabbi; common Jew, unlearned or not scrupulous in his observance of Jewish law] and rise before him; he would say, "It is no accident that this man has lived so long [he must have engaged in some righteous acts]."

This anecdote provides the clearest indication that the normal rabbinic understanding of the biblical law restricts it to *zeqenim* in the technical sense, to the extent that a rabbi's literal observance of the law is thought to require justification, and the justification offered is not exegetical, that is, it does not challenge the rabbinic consensus about the legal sense of the biblical verse. Rather, it ignores the legal formalities and resorts directly to the notion that the Torah, or observers of *mitzvot*, require deference.[116]

More on the *Mitzvah* of Rising for an Elder

> Rabbi Hanina would strike one who did not rise before him, and would say, "Are you trying abrogate a commandment of the Torah?"

> Rabbi Simon said, "The Holy One, Blessed be He, said, 'Before the hoary head shalt thou rise, and thou shalt honor the face of the

---

[116] In the partial parallel in B Qidd 33b the point is different. There, Rabbi Yohanan's practice of rising even for aged "Aramaeans" ("He said, 'How many vicissitudes [*harpatqei*; Sokoloff: "events"] have these people experienced'") is used to illustrate the (pseudo-?) tannaitic view that the first clause of Lev 19.32 applies to all old people, and only the second clause applies to technical *zeqenim*. The Bavli then explains why this display of deference to non-Jews or nonscholars *dishonors* the rabbi who performs it, in order to justify Rav Nahman's practice of asking his eunuch attendants to fulfill this chore on his behalf.

elder, and thou shalt fear thy God, I am the Lord'—I was the first to observe the commandment of rising before the elder'" [Gen 18.2].

The *sugya* returns to considering the obligation to rise for a *zaqen*: Rabbi Hanina's looks as if he were someone who was exceedingly sensitive about his honor, but, the little anecdote concludes (ironically? seriously?), he was only being strict about the observance of a *mitzvah*: the rules of deference are themselves Torah.[117] As to the second statement: though God is obviously under no obligation to observe commandments, Rabbi Simon's comment here conforms with a common homiletical trope. The reference may be to one rabbinic understanding of Gen 18.2 (cf. Genesis Rabbah *parashah* 48, 7—Theodor-Albeck 2:482), where the three divine messengers are said to "stand over" Abraham (*nitzavim 'alav*, probably meaning, "they approached"; the rabbinic interpretation reverses the sense of the verse, which describes Abraham's deference to the men, not vice versa).

More on the Mitzvah of Rising for the Torah

[T. Sanhedrin 7.8:] When the patriarch enters the whole nation [assembled body] rises before him and none has the right to sit until he says to them, "Be seated." When the Father of the Court [the patriarch's deputy] enters they form rows for him, and he enters whichever one he pleases [and they remain standing while the others may sit]. When a sage enters, each one he passes rises in turn and then sits, until the sage reaches his seat.

Rabbi Meir was accustomed to go to the study house and everyone there would see him and rise for him as a group. When they learned the baraita quoted above, they wished to alter their practice in accordance with it [and rise individually as he passed]. Rabbi Meir grew angry and left, saying, "I have learned that one raises in sanctity, and does not lower!" [and so the students were obligated by Jewish law to retain their more respectful practice even though it was not strictly speaking required by the law].

The baraita quoted here prescribes a well-defined hierarchy of deference based on rank, which the anecdote reported immediately following once again subverts, in that the nonpatriarchal but very great Rabbi Meir is at first given the wrong type of deference; as in the story of Rabbi Hanina above, it is impossible to tell how seriously we are meant to take

---

[117] A formulation I owe to Beth Berkowitz.

Rabbi Meir's response, since as in the earlier case it seems so blatantly self-interested, behind the legalistic sanctimony:

> They wished to appoint Rabbi Zeira to a judgeship, but he declined. Then he learned the following baraita: "For a sage [a recipient of *minui*], a bridegroom, and a patriarch, their rank atones for their sins"—and he accepted the appointment. Why a sage? Because it is written, "Thou shalt rise before the hoary head and honor the elder," and then, "If a stranger [*ger*—according to conventional rabbinic intepretation, a convert] dwells among you, thou shalt not oppress him." Just as a convert is forgiven for all his sins when he converts, so also a sage is forgiven for all his sins when he is appointed. . . .

This story, like the material below, appears in a way to be part of the Talmud's critique of *minui*: a prominent scholar (one of the most frequently quoted in the Yerushalmi) refuses *minui* until he learns that, like marriage and appointment to the patriarchate, it automatically confers the benefit of atonement for sins.

> Rabbi Mana spoke slightingly of those who were appointed for money. Rabbi Imi applied to them the verse, "You shall not make for yourselves gods of silver and gold." Rabbi Yoshiah said, "and his judicial gown is like an ass's saddle blanket." Rabbi Shian said, "One does not rise before one of those appointed for money, nor does one call him 'Rabbi,' and his judicial gown is like as ass's saddle blanket." Rabbi Zeira and one of the rabbis [sic!] were sitting and one of those appointed for money passed by. The rabbi said to Rabbi Zeira, "Let us pretend to be studying and not rise before him!"[118]

> Jacob of Kefar Neborayya recited the following paraphrastic homily [*tirgem*—applying Habakkuk 2.19–20 to judicial appointees]:[119] "Woe to the one who says to wood, 'Awake', 'Arise', to the silent stone; should this one teach?"[120] Does he know what to teach? "Lo, this one is caught up [or dressed up, referring to an idol] in gold and silver [*kesef*]." Has he not been appointed for money [*kaspayya*]? "And he has no breath [*ruah*, breath, spirit, soul] in him": he knows nothing;

---

[118] Contrast the bizarrely labored translation of Guggenheimer.

[119] See O. Ir-Shai, "Ya'akov of Kefar Niburaia—A Sage Turned Apostate," *Jerusalem Studies in Jewish Thought* 2 (1982/3): 153–68. In contrast to some other teachings attributed to and stories about Jacob, this homily seems conventional.

[120] The translation of this last phrase (*hu yoreh*)—a *crux interpretum* and most likely corrupt—reflects the rabbinic understanding of the verse.

"Woe to the one who says" I wish to be appointed. "And the Lord is in the chamber of His sanctuary," this refers to Rabbi Yitzhak bar L'azar in the Synagogue of Madartha in Caesarea.

Gedalyah Alon was clearly right to regard this as a historical source of fundamental importance.[121] For our purposes, its importance is to continue the critique of *minui*, and of the signs of rank and expectations of deference that were understood to accompany it. "Those appointed for money [and not for knowledge of the Torah; that is, because they were wealthy or paid off the patriarch for the appointment]" were nevertheless appointed and so wear a gown, are addressed as rabbi and deferred to, but were widely disrespected by "our" rabbis (who included both *memunim* and *talmidei hakhamim*). In the last episode but one, Rabbi Zeira—just encountered as a reluctant *memuneh*—plots with a fellow rabbi to deny the "*mitmeni biksaf*" the deference obviously due him even from other *memunim*. Ironically, the *mitmeni biksaf* is apparently sufficiently knowledgeable and respectful of rabbinic *halakhah* (which allows those studying to forgo rising) not to take offense (then again, in the rabbinic imagination, even a Sepphorite *archon* knew this much). It is of some interest that the rabbis feel they need to conceal their disrespect. Jacob's homily continues the critique, though in fact there is no way of knowing whether in its original context it was meant as a critique of all *memunim*, not just a limited group. The point of the final clause seems to be that if other *memunim* are analogous to idols, Rabbi Yitzhak bar L'azar is akin to God—a reference that resists explication.

Honor among Rabbis: Conclusion

Not all rabbinic discussions of deference or honor as item of exchange are so fraught. A brief but difficult *sugya* at Y Ta'anit 4.2, 68a, for example, seems to report without criticism the rabbis' acceptance of and participation in the highly developed system of precedence in the court or entourage of Rabbi Judah the Patriarch, as does a brief passage concerning a much later patriarch, at Y Shabbat 12.3, 13c, which may furthermore constitute a claim for a rabbinic role in rank-ordering access to the person of the patriarch—a concern with a markedly late imperial feel to it.[122] Conversely,

---

[121] "Ilen De-mitmenin Bi-ksaf: Le-toldot Reshuyot-Ha-dinim Be-eretz-Yisrael Bi-tequfat Ha-talmud", in *Mehkarim Betoldot Yisrael* (Tel Aviv: Hakibbutz Hameuhad, 1958),2: 15–57; English translation in *Jews, Judaism and the Classical World* (Jerusalem: Magnes, 1977).

[122] Each day Rabbi Hoshayya and his associates [*ilen de-Rabbi Hoshayya*, which I am taking as a calque of the Greek expression *hoi peri tou deina*] and Bar Pazzi and his

other stories praise rabbis who modestly declined to receive the honor or acknowledgment they merited.[123] But these stories probably do not constitute a serious critique of the value of honor or deference. Like other stories of supererogatory piety, they express a set of ideals that are extreme even within the rabbinic system; in their transgression of the standard rabbinic behavioral norms—which valorize the exchange of honor and deference, the importance of precedence and hierarchy—they serve to highlight those norms and so paradoxically to strengthen them. Indeed, an interesting set of stories purports to praise the modesty of Rabbi Judah the Prince but actually describes his manipulation of rituals of deference to enhance his own honor.[124] Such stories thus bear a family resemblance to Y Bikkurim 3.3 while being less subversive.

In sum, the rabbis acknowledged the importance of honor in their worlds—the narrowly rabbinic, the broadly Jewish, and the generally Roman—and for the most part accepted it as a positive value. They regarded it as a desirable feature in all human interchange, and they especially valued, encouraged, and strove to legislate honor or a sense of modesty or shame in women. They thought of themselves, of their God and their Torah, as being in competition with the Roman state for honor (demonstrating in this way their awareness of its importance for the Romans) and knew that, whatever happened in real life, they were the truly honorable, not Rome. To the typically Roman euergetistic cultural-political complex of benefaction-honor-memorialization the rabbis expressed neither commitment nor opposition. They clearly disapproved of most of its products—the monumental public buildings found in every public city, the basilicae and amphitheaters in which murder was committed, the idolatrous temples of the municipal cults—but about the exchange itself they said nothing. Such silence should not be misinterpreted as unawareness: they can hardly have been unaware of an institution so pervasively important in

---

associates would greet [sha'alin bi-shelameh de-] the patriarch, and Rabbi Hoshayya et al. would enter before Bar Pazzi et al. The latter then married into the patriarchal family, and requested to enter first. Rabbi Imi was asked, and he responded to them, "'And thou shalt erect the Tabernacle according to its law.' Does wood have laws? Rather, the beam which is supposed to be put in the north shall be put in the north, the one supposed to be put in the south will be put in the south (so the order of access to the patriarch may not be changed)."

[123] Y Sotah 1.4, 16d; Y Sotah 9.12, 24b.

[124] Y Ketubot 12.3, 35a:

Rabbi [Judah the Patriarch] was very modest; he would say, "I will do anything anyone tells me to do except for what the Elders of Batirah did for my ancestor [Hillel], in that they stepped down [some texts add: and appointed him (head of the court)]. If Rav Huna the Exilarch were to visit I would seat him above me, since he is of the tribe of Judah and I am of the tribe of Benjamin, and he is [descended from King David] through the male line, and I through the female."

their immediate environment, and they evinced intimate familiarity with euergetism's cousin, patronage. It is, rather, obliviousness, or even what literary theorists call abjection: they regarded it as so alien to their values that they rarely deigned to address it directly, however conspicuous it was as a feature of their quotidian lives. Instead, they treated it indirectly, by attacking its judaized forms.

What I mean by this is that in the third and fourth centuries the characteristic behavior and language of euergetism was in the process of being naturalized by the Jews. It was in this period that (as I have argued elsewhere)[125] the local religious community began to become an important mode of social organization for the Jews, and the ideology of the *qahal* as of the Christian parish combined biblical ideas about corporate solidarity and fellowship, mutual support, and poor relief, with the Greco-Roman values of public-spirited benefaction and its reciprocation with honor and memorialization. The rabbis regarded the local religious community with marked ambivalence: they embraced its care for the poor, and eventually tried to exert some control over *parnasut*, but manifestly regarded the euergetistic aspects of *parnasut* with discomfort. However much they were willing to exploit the nonrabbinic Jews' internalization of Roman values in order to perpetuate institutionalized poor relief, the rabbis themselves claimed to eschew the characteristic euergetistic exchange that motivated others to participate. Similarly, several stories indicate that they regarded the construction of massive synagogues by individuals with disdain: far from demonstrating the piety or securing the memorialization of the donors, they were a waste of money that might otherwise have been used to support Torah study.

But in one important respect they embraced euergetism, though not unhesitatingly. The core, formative social relationship of rabbinism, that between the master and his students, was understood and enacted in terms adapted from euergetism: the sage bestowed on his students Torah, and the students responded with honor, deference, and memorialization in the form of citation of their masters' teachings. They were also expected to reciprocate with personal service of their master. What the rabbis were less certain about was the relationship between formally appointed sages as an institutionalized group and the general (Jewish) public, including the class of *talmidei hakhamim* (disciples of the sages). On the one hand, they understood Leviticus 19.32 as prescribing the duty to rise for a *zaqen*, an appointed sage. On the other hand, there was a tendency to regard this as a purely formal obligation without emotional or social content; it was not a show of honor or respect, even though that is what the act of rising

[125] *IJS* 275–89.

normally conveys. You can fulfill the commandment even in the presence of a totally merit-free *zaqen*. The only thing, in this view, that truly merits the deference or honor implicit in the act of rising is the Torah: humans who possess it, whether in the form of learning or in the form of *mitzvot*, are the ones who truly merit honor, regardless of their formal rank.

In historical terms, this ambivalence is almost self-explanatory. The rabbis of the Talmud were trying to make sense of their own status, which was, in the third and fourth centuries, in the process of institutionaliza- tion. That is, the rabbis were changing from an unauthorized, loosely knit group of arbitrators and legal consultants whose claim to distinction was that they used the laws of the Torah, to which they were utterly commit- ted, into an organized class of formally appointed religious and judicial officials operating in a regime that, in the course of the fourth century es- pecially, was beginning to acquire some trappings of autonomy. Torah was the core ideological commitment of this group in the throes of insti- tutionalization, too, but the rabbis grasped that institutions have their own social and political dynamics, and some of them clearly felt the need to introduce distinctions in the broad class of Jewish scholars, judges and legal experts, between those they regarded as genuine vessels of Torah and those they did not. (By contrast, Babylonian rabbis expressed no de- tectable ambivalence about the value of rabbinic ordination as a tracer for possession of Torah: they internalized their institutional values far more than the Palestinian rabbis did.)

Roman aristocrats of a somewhat earlier period had wondered whether honor inheres in rank or in modes of behavior: do senators or knights ipso facto deserve honor, or do the liberal, public-spirited, and high- minded, whatever their census valuation? I would argue that the resem- blance between this debate and its rabbinic counterpart is structural, not genetic. Early and high imperial Roman aristocrats were experiencing the same type of ambiguous and partial political institutionalization as the slightly later Palestinian rabbis, though on a much larger scale. What is of interest to us, though, is that, like the Romans, the rabbis framed their de- bate in terms of honor. Just as the rabbi in his own study house was struc- turally equivalent to the *euergetes* in his city, so too the rabbis as institu- tionalizing bureaucracy were structurally equivalent to senators and knights in the process of transformation into a civil service—equivalen- cies that extend to the very terms in which internal group relations were understood and described. At the moment, then, that the rabbis were striving to extricate themselves from the Roman system, to provide for the Jews a coherent and apparently radical alternative, they were also demonstrating their commitment to some its core values. It would to be sure be legitimate to view this as a case of what postcolonial theorists might call mimicry-as-resistance.[126] But the rabbis were also striving to carve out for themselves and for the Jews a comfortable and tenable space *inside* the system: they had no real alternative. Even deep inside the developing rabbinic group, then, the groundwork for the restoration of the diasporic compromise between the Jews and the state was being laid.

---

[126] Most influentially, H. Bhabha, *The Location of Culture* (London: Routledge, 1994), 121–31

CHAPTER SIX

Conclusion

Were the Ancient Jews a Mediterranean Society?

The Historical Argument

My argument in this book has proceeded along two intertwined but distinguishable lines, historical (or sociological-anthropological) and hermeneutical. First, I have been making the historical argument that one of the crucial problems of ancient Jewish social history was how to come to terms, Jewishly, with the practical inevitability of social institutions founded on reciprocal exchange. I would speculate that this issue was important not only in antiquity but also in the different circumstances, and locations, of Jewish life in the Middle Ages and the early modern period. The tension between egalitarian solidarity and competitive reciprocity was a structural feature of the local Jewish religious community, wherever and whenever it appeared. This, among other factors, explains why I have sometimes enclosed the word Mediterranean, as applied to a cultural complex that validates institutionalized reciprocity, in "scare quotes": the crucial issue is not a hypothetically normative culture of a particular zone, a culture whose existence must be so hedged about with qualifications and exceptions that little of its integrity survives, but a sort of cultural model or ideal type that may or may not in fact have been common in the Mediterranean basin in various periods but has provided a useful way of conceptualizing the connections between practices such as gift exchange and honor, deference and memorialization.

The reason the issue of institutionalized reciprocity was so pressing was that in premodern economic conditions, however sentimentalized certain sorts of relationships of social dependency may have been, they derived a special power from the fact that they normally also served redistributive purposes: they constituted a network of access to resources that in the most basic possible way could save one from death by starvation or exposure. Even when hunger and homelessness were not immediate dangers, conditions of life were sufficiently fragile and middle- or long-term accumulation of surplus was sufficiently difficult and rare that institutionalized social relations often were, as Ben Sira put it, more valuable than gold. In such circumstances, the tendency of reciprocal relationships toward institutionalization was hard to suppress: even in the very specific conditions created by the massive state expenditure of democratic Athens at the peak of its imperialism-generated prosperity, such institutions could be limited but not eradicated.

I would also guess, given the basic identity of the social visions of the Hebrew Bible and the New Testament, that the tension between reciprocity-based and egalitarian political and social ideologies had a formative impact not only on Jews but also on the Christianizing Roman Empire of late antiquity and on its medieval successor states in informing debates about the political role of the Church, for example, or in providing escape routes into lives of piety and institutionalized religious devotion for those who feared they might fall foul of a secular society founded on rigid norms of social dependency and honor.

With the rise of capitalism and the modern nation-state, this urgency has dissipated, though even now the tension between the ideals of competitive reciprocity and egalitarian solidarity has not completely disappeared, as anyone who participates in Jewish communal life knows. However, the contemporary stakes are very low in that few or no competent middle-class adults in the contemporary First World (a small minority of the world's population, to be sure) rely for their most basic well-being on the support of patrons, friends, or extended family. In the contemporary world in which most Jews live, such relations have been altered. To the extent that patronage exists, its purpose is to provide access rather than sustenance, and it is in any case infrequently an enduring—and almost never a heavily institutionalized—relationship: friends are there for fellowship, whereas family is ideally for sentimental attachment and for support, which tends more often to be psychological than necessary for the practicalities of life. Essential redistributive functions are performed by the marketplace or the state, or both.

Exchange

My model's broad utility for historical analysis can be illustrated by consideration of reciprocal exchange and the formalized relationships based on it as these are reflected in ancient Jewish texts. The Torah tends to ignore or disapprove of such relationships, as it does, for example, of the *'avdut*—servitude or vassalage—of one Israelite to another. Friendship—

ahabah—is ignored, and even though the family clearly enjoys legitimacy as a legal category, its authority is severely limited, and in narratives its value is constantly questioned. (The social dependency of Israelites on gentiles is described simply as a curse.) Instead, the Torah advocates that all Israelites be bound together by unconditional *ahabah*, which is presented as the foundation of Israelite society and law. It is also in the background of legislation mandating systematic relief for the poor and the weak in a way manifestly meant to restrain the proliferation of relationships of dependency between individual Israelites. The Torah does embrace reciprocity and reciprocity-based relationships of dependency as it embraces honor but regards all these as characteristic of the relations not among Israelites but between God and Israel alone.

By contrast, all the texts examined in the previous chapters acknowledge the importance of reciprocity among humans, though they never precisely embrace it as an ideal. I have not found any passage in either Ben Sira, the Josephan corpus, or the Talmud that, in Peripatetic or Stoic style, celebrates reciprocity—as distinct from love or *ahabah* or *philia*, on the social and political importance of which all ancient texts agreed—as the glue that holds society together, and which idealizes it to the extent of ignoring the oppression, exploitation, and injustice into which reciprocity-based relationships inexorably lapse. The sense that, ideally, Jewish society should be bound together by unconditional solidarity, that all Israelites are required to love and be loyal to one another, that, in the words of the liturgy, all Israel are friends, constituted an important piece of ideological continuity with the Hebrew Bible, even if such solidarity has often been more symbolic than substantive.

In fact, the texts examined here all have highly complex things to say about the gift, friendship, the patronage network, and euergetism. It is not surprising that all of them agree in conflating—though only to some extent—the gift and the charitable donation, while retaining as an ideal the view that true charity needs no reciprocation. The rabbis could even suggest that ideally charity should be reciprocated with hostility; in this way the donor can be sure that he has performed a pure *mitzvah*. In sum, all the texts remain conscious of the tension between *mitzvah* and reciprocity, while sometimes merging the two.

Ben Sira probably comes closest of all to truly embracing reciprocity, in terms vaguely reminiscent of stoicism or other tendencies in Greek social thought. He sometimes assigns religious value to the presentation of benefits to friends, not, as in the rabbinic conception of *gemilut hasadim* (which of course is not restricted to friends), as a subspecies of charity but as a way of celebrating God-given bounty. Ben Sira strongly approved of the acquisition of social dominance, especially by sages or the righteous and wise. But in general, his view of human society was very dark: sometimes the righteous are not the dominant but the dominated, patrons can be assumed to exploit their dependents, friends to betray, guests to show ingratitude, and relatives to hatch plots. Though Ben Sira, like Seneca and Cicero, provided rules for the management of such relationships, he was very remote from their tendency to idealize them.

Josephus for his part admits the value of relationships based on exchange, but only in very limited ways, and provides much evidence for the social and political importance of friendship or patronage networks among the Jews from the Hasmonean period at the latest. Josephus adapts and reconciles, though in a slightly different and certainly less enthusiastic way than Ben Sira. One is obliged to show gratitude to proper benefactors, but proper benefactors in Josephus's view are those who honestly care for the well-being of their beneficiaries. Benefactors may be enlightened legislators, like Moses, or providers of grain to the hungry, like Queen Helena of Adiabene, or donors to the temple of Jerusalem, but not providers of entertainments or lavish public buildings. In Josephus's account the Jews conflated euergetism with biblical charity. Neither donations nor communal acknowledgment of them take monumental form: the Jews do not erect honorary or dedicatory inscriptions or statues portraying their benefactors but express their gratitude by inscription in texts or, more often, orally. Josephus leaves it unclear what the political consequences of such benefaction might be. It may at least be suggested that in Josephus's view, euergetism, even in the heavily judaized form of which Josephus in his later work manifestly approves, did not "work" on the Jews, generating little or no political loyalty and social cohesion, while patronage did. Perhaps this is why at least for a time in the first century, rebel groups—tight patronage networks—had more political impact than municipal communities. This is an issue that would benefit from further investigation.

The rabbis, too, promoted a heavily judaized and rabbinized version of euergetism. In fact, they imagined the central rabbinic act, the teaching of Torah by a rabbi to a group of students, in terms pretty clearly adapted from municipal euergetism: the master bestows Torah on his students, and they reciprocate by honoring him and perpetuating his memory in oral form, as in Josephus. About Roman euergetism per se the rabbis had little, certainly little good, to say; they had little affection even for the adaptation of euergetism characteristic of the local Jewish religious community, just beginning to emerge in the rabbinic period, which encouraged the construction of monumental synagogues. Unlike Josephus, though, the rabbis took it for granted that the Jews in general had internalized the values of Roman-style municipal benefaction and that there was little they could do to stamp it out. They did, however, advocate exploiting the euergetistic culture to convince nonrabbinic Jews to perform *mitzvot*, especially those connected with poor relief.

About other relationships of personal dependency, especially outside rabbinic and patriarchal circles, the Yerushalmi provides little information. Certainly there were rabbinic laws that, if taken seriously, would have inhibited their development: rabbinic disapproval of wills, and failure even to acknowledge the practice of testamentary adoption, would have deprived wealthy Jews of a favorite mechanism of metropolitan Roman elites for accumulating friends and clients.[1] Competitive gift exchange had an excellent chance of falling foul of the rabbinic prohibition of *ʿavaq ribit* ("the dust of interest"), which delegitimized most forms of exchange involving added value. Commensality, the reciprocal entertainment of guests, was rendered difficult even among Jews by the rabbis' insistence that "*haverim*" or "*neʾemanim*"—probably meaning Jews who observed laws of tithing and ritual purity—not eat with the *ʿam haʾaretz*, the mass of Jews who did not observe such laws.

But the rabbis were well acquainted with such relationships (which have not been explored in any detail in the last chapter) and at any rate did not express invariable and unambiguous disapproval of them. In one remarkable passage in rabbinic marriage legislation they even imagined the Jewish town or community in (presumably unconscious) Aristotelian terms, as bound together by the regular and reciprocal pulsation of services and benefits through a social network. The well-known long *sugya* on patronage in Y Berakhot 9.1, which would benefit from discrete consideration, does not absolutely reject the value of patronage, but in arguing that God performs the role much better than men do, and that men are normally unreliable patrons, the text certainly expresses skepticism about it. On the other hand, the same pericope reports an episode of successful patronage, that saved the early third-century rabbi Rav from hostile Roman troops, and uses the story to argue a fortiori about the impact of divine patronage.

---

[1] The presence of a *threptos* in the *familia* of a fourth-century patriarch, attested to in a synagogue dedication from Hamat Tiberias, may imply that at least some of the very wealthiest Jews followed Roman rather than rabbinic practice—if, that is, *threptos* here means "adopted son" and not something else. The inscription is published in M. Dothan, *Hammath Tiberias: Early Synagogues and Hellenistic and Roman Remains* (Jerusalem: Israel Exploration Society, 1983).

Honor

In the modern Western world in which most Jews now live, certain durably significant mediterraneanist practices and conceptions have lost much of their relevance. Except in the most traditionalist Jewish environments, *kavod* (honor), once the perquisite of *talmidei hakhamim*, rabbis, and communal benefactors, is no longer significant, and even those for whom it still matters tend to live in larger environments where it does not. Thus, even for them, honor no longer functions as the primary prism through which all public or communal life is refracted; rather, it has been compartmentalized, useful only in quite restricted categories of life.

The importance of *kavod* in traditional Jewish life up until the very recent past is paradoxical in light of the fact that the Torah itself largely rejects the possibility that honor might belong to humans. It probably reflects in part the significance of honor in the Talmud, where it serves not only as an important legal category but also as a natural adjunct of Torah, and so as a piece of cultural capital rabbis claimed belonged especially to them, though secondarily to all pious Jews. In this scheme, honor retained its association with domination, but the rabbis were trying to perpetuate a hierarchical social value system meant to replace, not merely to supplement, the conventional one based on wealth, land ownership, military success, political office, and so on. The ascription of political, social, and cultural value to Torah, the conviction or hope that it might serve as a key to control and domination and therefore that it confers honor on its possessor—these are all ideas first worked out in detail in the Wisdom of Ben Sira. It was Ben Sira who first argued at length for the honorability of the God-fearing man, of the wise possessor of Torah, who first tried to find a place for Torah in the workaday world of hierarchical and often oppressive social relations based on honor in the conventional sense. Ben Sira imagined that the fearer of God or the sage would take his place in the town council, at the dinner party, in the network of friends or clients, side by side with the landowner and the merchant, and he even hoped that the pious sage might come to prevail, because only he would truly understand the rules of social interaction and exchange.

Rabbinic ideas are clearly ultimately indebted to those of Ben Sira: the rabbis, too, posited the honorability of Torah and the social and political fungibility of Torah-derived honor. The history of the interaction of the "Mediterranean" value of honor and the anti-Mediterranean value of Torah is therefore a history of long-term continuities, beginning in the early second century BCE, crucially mediated through the rabbinic texts of the third century CE and following, and extending down to modern times.

But it also illustrates that our historical story is one of constant change and adaptation. The rabbinic texts' continuities with Ben Sira are striking but also imprecise, for though the rabbis imagined the sage qua vessel of Torah as honorable, they did not imagine him taking his seat among men whose honor derived from different sources (though this is of course precisely what happened in the classical—medieval and early modern—local Jewish community, which ideally worked through an alliance between the rabbis and the wealthier laypeople). In fact, the rabbis were ostensibly more extreme, caring nothing for the honor of anything *except* Torah. One could say that they synthesized Ben Sira's embrace of honor and Josephus's rejection of it, for Josephus had claimed, especially in his later work, that the Jews had little concern for honor, regarding only piety as a worthy value. Like Josephus, the rabbis entertained the possibility that under some circumstances honor might be rejected altogether. They told admiring stories about rabbis and holy men who made themselves into fools for the sake of the mitzvot, thereby idealizing a radically countercultural position, without precisely advocating it or explaining how it could be universalized into a nonsupererogatory ethical value.

On the other hand, the rabbis preserved many stories that registered their hope or wish or desire that the honorability of the Torah, and by extension of themselves, be recognized by their Roman rulers. In this way they revealed that for all their self-alienation from Rome and self-conscious rejection of its values, at some level they wished to be part of the system, if primarily, and at least before the fourth century very unrealistically, on their own terms. Strikingly, few or no rabbinic stories express the same sort of desires about secular Jewish grandees, I would argue because to have told such stories would have been to acknowledge the partial validity for Jews of a value system other than that based on Torah. This finally explains the distinction between Ben Sira and the rabbis: Ben Sira thought Torah the *most* honorable thing for Jews, the rabbis considered it the *only* honorable thing. Yet, unlike the Torah itself, both embraced the idea that honor might be a human possession.

The rabbis' ambivalence to honor was probably crucial to the future social development of Judaism, because it eventually helped enable the participation of rabbi types in the (Ben Sira-like) honor-oriented social economy of the local Jewish community, thereby shaping the culture of rabbinic education and the yeshivah, but it also provided ideological fuel for those conventicles of radical renouncers and ascetics who did not play as crucial a role in Judaism as monastics did in pre-Protestant Christianity but who nevertheless were frequently historically important, sometimes, as perhaps in twelfth-century Rhineland and definitely in early eighteenth-century Poland-Ukraine, critically so. In other words, there were important continuities not only in systemic pressures affecting Jews in all sorts of different historical periods but also in the ideological tools they used to resolve those pressures. I am arguing, then, for the general utility of my model for Jewish historians, especially of premodernity.

Integration

The ancient Jews' peculiar cultural anxieties about reciprocity and honor had at some periods important political aspects. Indeed, these anxieties may help explain something about the unusual difficulties the Jews initially had in adapting to Roman rule, as they indubitably did, and also about the Palestinian rabbis' odd and mercurial balance of accommodation and resistance. This is not to deny that other factors played a role. The Jews' religious exclusivism was easily adapted to imperial systems that worked by fostering local particularisms while partly co-opting provincial grandees. Judaism may even be regarded as to some extent an artifact of such a political system, if it was true that the compilation and promulgation of the Torah were initiated or supported by the Achaemenids. But it was much harder to adapt to a more centralizing statelike imperial system like that of Rome at its height. While not identical to the problems created much later for European Jewish communities by the rise of the nation-state, there is a certain distant family resemblance. The truism that the Jews' monotheism made it hard for them to submit to Rome is too crude when so baldly stated, but it contains a hard kernel of truth. Darius II or Antiochus III might have been happy to let the Jews submit to their superstitions provided they had a cooperative and culturally malleable high priest in Jerusalem (cultural malleability would enable his interaction with imperial officials) who was an efficient remitter of silver to the royal treasury, but the Romans wanted more, because they ruled differently.

While the Achaemenids tried to work through, and co-opt politically rather than culturally, temple establishments, and the Seleucids exploited individual local rulers, who were expected to be acculturated to the manners of a Greek court, the Romans tried to co-opt entire aristocracies, the cultural pressure on which was intense because they were intended not merely to be intermediaries between subjects and state but to become Romans. It was taken for granted—never explicitly stated—that this entailed the adoption of a set of cultural norms, a way of being in the world, that was not easily reconcilable with the exclusivistic demands of Judaism. An analysis of Josephus's writing allows us to be more specific about this: the Jews, especially in Judaea proper, had native redistributive systems and associated cultural norms that predisposed them to reject those on which the Romans founded their empire. The Jews' rejection of the cultural complex of benefaction-honor-memorialization was demonstrably not as complete as Josephus claimed, but the archaeological remains of first-century Judaea show that in this case, Josephus exaggerated, but did not invent: piety, to the exclusion of honor, really did drive Jerusalem's culture of benefaction. Wealthy Jews invested in famine relief and temple provisions, not in monumental construction and entertainments. Herod's attempt to romanize Jerusalem's culture of benefaction—though Josephus admitted that even Herod sometimes followed the native norms of pious donation—was not, contrary to Josephus's claim, a complete failure, but it had little lasting impact.

The rabbinic literature presents a picture of a Jewish culture of benefaction and honor that was utterly transformed. The Talmud Yerushalmi takes it for granted that Jews outside rabbinic circles had thoroughly internalized Roman norms. Palestinian Jews in the third and fourth centuries mostly lived in towns that had become full participants in the Roman provincial system and that had the normal complement of monumental public buildings, funded by the liberality of the wealthier citizens and commemorated in the form of inscriptions (and in some places perhaps statues) that expressed the gratitude of the municipal community. These norms were so pervasive that they structured the public life of the Jewish religious community just beginning to emerge: these too relied on the liberality of the well-to-do, expressed in the form of the monumental synagogue, reciprocated by the communities' posting of honorary inscriptions.

As suggested above, the rabbis did not entirely reject this complex of practices; indeed, they replicated it in nonplastic form in their study houses (just as the first-century Jews practiced a verbal form of euergetism, according to Josephus). But to the extent that they expressed an interest in public life, it tended to involve rejection of the culture of euergetism in favor of the culture of charity or *mitzvot*. In their own account, the rabbis played the role of the Jews in Josephus's: bearers of a potent and compelling counterculture. But the rabbis' ambivalent embrace of honor as a Jewish value and their conviction that it was in competition with Roman domination-based honor used as political currency indicate that the rabbis' true cultural situation was more complex and nuanced. Their "mimicry" of Roman values in part expressed resistance, but it also implied a hint of accommodation. Not a single word in rabbinic literature suggests that the rabbis ever saw themselves as part of the system of Roman rule (which does not mean that individual rabbis did not do so), but their adoption of some key Roman political values points to a certain willingness to compromise that is in tension with the countercultural surface of the text.

Hermeneutics

One of my fundamental assumptions has been that ancient texts are not windows into the past but artifacts of it. As such, they are never transparent and cannot speak for themselves. To be sure, they may provide gross information, and so it is not completely illegitimate to mine texts positivistically, provided only that one does so cautiously and skeptically. Such positivism has served as the foundation of all we know about antiquity, and though every inch of this foundation merits scrutiny and debate, sometimes these issue in affirmations of historicity. That having been said, though, the project of producing detailed social or cultural histories of Judaea in the Achaemenid and Hellenistic periods or of the "world of the New Testament" or that of the Mishnah and Talmud has rarely yielded convincing results. The authors of such works, unless they adopt criticism or skeptical aporia as their goals, always underestimate the amount of information required to produce a convincing history. The scraps we have at our disposal are simply not enough.

But since they are artifacts, texts can still be used; they just have to be treated differently. Some historians, including myself, may be slightly uncomfortable with the idea, but we have to figure out ways of reading them, with minute attention to detail, as expressions of sets of concerns or interests, because that is what they are. When we encounter a story in the Yerushalmi about rabbis' meetings with Roman officials, we may or may not believe that such meetings actually occurred, but even if we do, we must still admit that the storyteller has shaped the account, has decided what details to include and what to omit, what language to tell the story in, and what lessons the story teaches. The historicity of the tale is debatable, the fact that someone told it, fixed its form, and eventually wrote it down is not: it is true by definition, and so constitutes a much firmer foundation for the production of a historical account than either positivistic investment in the story's truth or blanket skepticism about it.

One of the points of this book, then, was to construct a model that would serve as a useful way of beginning to understand some features of the history of ancient Jewish social relations and cultural praxis, and their impact on the political situation of the Jews. But I have spent many of the foregoing pages exemplifying my model's utility as an exegetical tool as well. It has constituted an effective way of resisting the "Hallmark card" school of Ben Sira interpretation, whose point is precisely to deprive the sage's apophthegms of all their social and cultural specificity and transform them into bland religious-ethical sentences (even if some of the ethics are problematic). It has also allowed me to provide an alternative to the highly learned but often ahistorical philological approach, exemplified most recently by the work of Menahem Kister. It has made sense of the central hermeneutical difficulty of the text—the constant, incoherent juxtaposition of "wisdom" (hardheaded advice for coping in a dark, amoral social world) and "piety" (expressions of the Deuteronomist-derived conviction that God rewards the righteous and punishes the wicked): this juxtaposition is in a sense the whole point of the book, since it constitutes an attempt to provide a biblical or Jewish foundation for participation in, not rejection of, a reciprocity-based social economy.

Josephus was a historian, not a sage, so there has never been any tendency to interpret his works as collections of wise truisms (as opposed to historiographical topoi and lies), but every reader of any text reads past sections he or she is conditioned to regard as boilerplate, as meaning-starved space filler, or as narrative that is incomprehensible because its cultural assumptions are opaque. But here too my model has allowed me to detect important themes that have hitherto been largely ignored, and to understand the importance of passages and episodes that have never attracted much attention. Benefaction, honor, and memory have turned out to be pervasively important themes in all of Josephus's writing. When Josephus writes in the introductions to both of his major works that he intends them to memorialize people and events, he is not simply paying homage to Herodotus and Thucydides. He also means to be taken seriously. Some features of his works show that he really intended them to serve as memorials. Furthermore, Josephus, like Ben Sira before him, understood the historical sections of the Bible as memorials of the benefactions offered to Israel not only by God but by human heroes as well. Those sections of Josephus's works that most resemble wisdom texts—his moralistic evaluations of people and events—also prove to have surprisingly specific social and cultural content: the differences between the euergetistic praxeis of Herod and Agrippa I were real and consequential, though of course this does not mean Josephus reported them honestly.

For its part, the Talmud Yerushalmi is so underexploited by social and cultural historians, and so little read with such concerns (as opposed to intertextuality, Hellenism, to some extent postcolonialism) in mind by literary scholars, that my attempt to read rabbinic stories and to some ex-tent laws with issues like gift exchange and honor—after having been rig-orously refined—in mind is not extensively paralleled. Inasmuch as sto-ries tend to be about human interaction, and all human interaction features almost by definition elements of reciprocity, at some level the theme is found in almost every story. But it is striking how many stories concern these and related issues in a very blatant and pronounced way— indeed, far too many for me to have treated responsibly in the previous chapter. But here too I would like to think that my hypothesis has served successfully as a hermeneutical model, helping to make sense of previ-ously ignored or obscure elements of stories.

Ben Sira on the Social Hierarchy

A. Ben Sira 4.1–10

4.1. My son, do not mock the life of a poor man
and do not cause pain to the soul of man who is poor
and bitter-souled.

4.2. The unfortunate, hungry, soul, do not tantalize
and do not ignore those downtrodden in soul.
[2c and 3a are perhaps to be omitted; see Smend and
Segal

4.3b. Do not withhold a gift from your/an unfortunate one[1]

4.4. and do not scorn the requests of the poor man
so that you not give him place [=reason] to curse you.

4.6. The bitter-spirited man cries out in the pain of his soul
and his Rock hears the sound of his cry.

4.7. Make yourself beloved to the ʿedah[2]
and to the ruler likewise[3] bend your head.

4.8. Incline your ear to the poor man
and respond to his salute modestly.

4.9. Save the oppressed from his oppression
and do not despise a fair trial [for him].

4.10. Be like a father to orphans
and in place of a husband to widows
and God will call you son
and will bestow favor on you and save you from the Pit.

---

[1] Geniza MS A reads *mimiskenekha* (from *your* unfortunate one)—the possessive perhaps implying a state of dependency, though perhaps not much should be read into it. But both the Greek and the Syriac lack the possessive pronoun.

[2] Smend (followed by the Anchor Bible) believes this refers to the local Jewish community, Segal to judges. The Anchor Bible translates verses 7–10 as if they refer to judgment, though this is not reflected in their commentary.

[3] In the Hebrew, *ʿod*, possibly a mistake for *ʿir*, as in the Syriac, as the commentators note.

B. Ben Sira 7.18–36

7.18. Do not exchange a friend [*oheb*] for money [*mehir*]
or a dependent [?][4] brother for the gold of Ophir.

7.19. Do not loathe a wise woman
and one of good grace is better than pearls.

7.20.[5] Do not wrong a slave who works faithfully
nor a hired laborer who gives his soul.

7.21. A wise slave love [MS A: *habeb*; MS C *'ehob*] as your soul
and do not withhold from him his freedom.[6]

7.22. If you have an animal, watch over it with your own eyes
and if it is well-trained, keep it.[7]

7.23. If you have sons, discipline them,
and marry them off in their youth.

7.24. If you have daughters, guard their bodies
and do not be cheerful to them.

7.25. Remove a daughter [from your house] and concern will depart
provided you have joined her to a wise man.

7.26. If you have a wife, do not loathe her
but if she is hated do not trust her.

7.27–8 are added from Greek: With all your heart honor your father
and the mother who labored for you do not forget.
Remember that through them you came to be
and what benefit will you return to them equal to what they have bestowed on you?

7.29. With all your heart fear God
and sanctify His priests.

7.30. With all your might love [*'ehab*] your Maker
and His servants do not abandon.

7.31. Honor God and adorn the priest
and give their lot as you have been commanded [the next stich specifies the offerings but the text is difficult].

---

[4] *Talui*—literally, dependent, although, as the commentators observe, this makes little sense here; Greek has *gnesion*, either "genuine" (in the emotional sense) or "legitimate" (in the legal sense). The hemistich is difficult.

[5] Following Geniza MS C and Greek against MS A, which is corrupt, or at any rate incomprehensible.

[6] Smend (followed by the Anchor Bible) observes that this refers to all slaves, "Hebrew" and "Canaanite"; Segal observes that it refers only to "Hebrew" and not to "Canaanite" slaves.

[7] Smend: and do not sell it; Segal: and do not slaughter it.

7.32. And likewise to the pauper extend your hand
       that your blessing may be complete.

7.33. Give a gift to every living thing
       and from the dead withhold not kindness.

7.34. Do not tarry in joining the weeping
       and with mourners mourn.

7.35. Refuse not to visit the sick
       in this way you will be beloved [te' aheb] of him.

7.36. In all your deeds remember your end and you will
       never fall into the pit.

C. Ben Sira 10.19–11.1

10.19. What is the honored seed? The seed of mankind.
        What is the honored seed? The fearer of God.
        What is the dishonored seed? The seed of mankind.
        What is the dishonored seed? The violator of the
        commandment.

10.20. Among brothers their head is honored,
        and the fearer of God in His eyes.

10.21. The resident alien, the foreigner, the gentile, and the
        pauper
        their glory is the fear of God.

10.23.   One should not despise a wise pauper
        and one should not honor every intelligent man.

10.24. The great man and the ruler and the judge are honored
        but none is greater than the fearer of God.

10.25. A wise slave will free men serve
        and an intelligent man will not complain.[8]

10.26. Do not deem yourself too much of a sage[9] to do your
        work
        and do not deem yourself too honorable in the time of
        your need.

10.27. Better is the one who works and has more wealth
        than the one who deems himself honorable but lacks a
        gift [that is, enough wealth to give a gift, or, perhaps
        better, "food"].[10]

[8] Following the Greek, as the editors and commentators all advise; the second hemistich seems to mean, notwithstanding Segal, that the intelligent observer will not be displeased at the subversion of the social order represented by the wise slave.

[9] Al tithakam, with hitpaèl often having this force in later biblical Hebrew.

[10] In Greek: "Better is one who works and has abundance [or excess] in all things / than the one who wanders about honoring himself and lacks [even] bread." The commentators prefer the

10.28. My son, in modesty honor yourself
and He will give you political power [Gk: honor/rank]
as you deserve.

10.29. One who makes himself wicked, who will justify him?
And who will honor one who makes light of himself.

10.30. There is a pauper who is honored because of his mind
and there is one who is honored because of his wealth.

10.31. The one honored [in his poverty], in his wealth how
much the more so!
And the one dishonored [lit., made light of] in his
wealth, in his poverty how much the more so!

10.31c–d: an explanatory expansion

11.1. The wisdom of a pauper will lift his head
and will cause him to be seated among the great men
[nedibim].

D. Ben Sira 13

13.1. He who touches pitch, his hand will stick,
he who attaches himself to [hober el] a scoffer will learn
his way.

13.2. That which is heavier than you, will you carry?
And to one who is richer than you, will you attach
yourself [mah tithabar]?

13.3. Will an earthen pot be joined to a cauldron
so that one hits and the other is broken?
Will then a rich man be joined to a pauper?

13.3. If a rich man has committed an injustice, he threatens
his victim besides [so Gk; Heb: he takes pleasure (in his
injustice)];
if the poor man has been treated unjustly, he beseeches
his injurer in addition.

13.4. If you are amenable to him, he will enslave you,
and if you succumb, he will abandon you.[11]

13.5. If you have [reading yesh lekha instead of shelkha, following the commentators] he will speak kindly to you,
but then he will crush you [or, impoverish you] and it
will cause him no pain.

Greek for hemistich b, which presupposes a Hebrew text reading mazon instead of matan, words
that appear almost identical.

[11] The Hebrew of 4b ("if you succumb / stumble under the load, he will take pity on you")
makes little sense. The commentators try to salvage it but end by preferring the Greek and the
Syriac, followed here.

13.6. If he needs you he will enjoy himself with you
and laugh with you and make promises to you.

13.7. [Repeats 6; text is very problematic][12]

13.8. [But] take care not to act very arrogantly [toward the
rich man]
and be not like those who lack knowledge.

13.9. If a great man [*nadib*] approaches, keep your distance
and in the same measure he will draw you near to him.[13]

13.10. Do not draw close to him lest he drive you away
and do not distance yourself from him lest you be
hated.

13.11. Do not have trust in him to behave freely with him,
and do not have faith in him because of his many words.
For by the multiplicity of his words he is testing you
and he is investigating you as one mocking (?)

13.12. [Incomprehensible]

13.13. Beware and be careful
that you not walk about with men of violence.

13.15. All flesh loves [enters into friendship with] its own kind
and every man the one who resembles him.

13.16. The kind of every flesh is found with it,
and to his kind is man attached.

13.17. How will a wolf be attached to a lamb?
So too an evil man to a righteous one
and likewise a rich man to one of straitened
circumstance.

13.18. Whence is the friendship [lit., *shelom*, "peace"] of a
hyena with a dog?
Whence is the friendship of a rich man with a pauper?

13.19. The food of the lion are the wild asses of the desert,
so are the poor the pasturage of the rich.

13.20. The disgust of pride is humility,
and the disgust of a rich man is a poor man

13.21–23. The rich man has friends and influence, the poor man
has neither

13.24. Wealth is good if there is no sin,

[12] For an attempted interpretation, see Kister, "A Contribution," 325.

[13] Kister, "A Contribution," 325–26, prefers here the Greek, *proskalesamenou se dynastou*, implying a Hebrew original that reads not *qarab nadib* but *qara' nadib*. In this case the sentence means, if a great man issues you an invitation to a banquet, sit far away and he will ask you to sit closer. Kister notes the parallel to a saying of Jesus reported in Luke 14.10, but I wonder whether he has not allowed the parallel to determine the meaning of the older text.

and poverty is bad inasmuch as it is based on
wickedness.

E. Ben Sira 30(33).28–40 (20–33)

30.28. Son and wife, brother and friend[14]
do not give them dominance in your life.

30.29. As long as you live and spirit is in you
do not allow any flesh to rule over you.
Do not give what is yours to another
so that you have to return and entreat his favor.

30.30. Better that your sons entreat your favor
than that you look to your sons' hands [to support you].

30.31. In all your deeds be supreme
and give no blemish to your honor.

30.32. When the number of your days is drawing to an end[15]
on the day of your death, leave a legacy.

33.33. Fodder and the staff and a burden for the ass,
discipline and labor for the slave.[16]

33.34. Work your slave so that he not find rest,
and if he lifts up his head he will betray you.

33.36. Work your slave so that he not rebel

33.37. For much evil does idleness cause.

33.35. Yoke and ropes, rod and blows [following Segal],
for the evil slave the stocks[17] and chastisement.

33.38. Entrust to him work that is appropriate for him,
and if he does not obey multiply his shackles;
but do not lord it over any man,
and without justice do not do anything.

33.39. If you have only one slave let him be like yourself,
because your soul will be the price of his loss.[18]
If you have only one slave, think of him as a brother,
and do not avenge your soul in blood [?].

33.40. For if you torture him he will leave and be lost;
on which road will you seek him?

[14] Following the Greek. The Geniza MS E reads, "*oheb ve-reʾa*," synonymous terms for "friend."

[15] Following Greek and Syriac against the incomprehensible Hebrew.

[16] Or, the discipline of labor; Greek, perhaps apologetically, "bread and education and work."

[17] For the meaning of the unusual word *mahapekhet*, see F. Brown, S. Driver, and C. Briggs *A Hebrew and English Lexicon of the Old Testament* (Oxford: Clarendon Press, 1972), 246.

[18] That is, it is impossible to live without a slave (Segal).

Josephus on Memory and Benefaction

A. Josephus, *AJ* 6.343–49

6.343. But now I shall touch on a subject profitable to cities, peoples and nations, and of interest to all good men— one whereby all should be induced to pursue virtue and to aspire to those things that may procure them glory and eternal remembrance [*mnemen aionion*], one, more- over, that should instill in the hearts of kings of nations and rulers of cities a great desire and zeal for noble deeds, should stimulate them to face dangers and death for their country's sake, and teach them to despise all terrors.

6.344. The occasion for this discourse I find in the person of Saul, king of the Hebrews. For he, although he knew of what was to come and his impending death, which the prophet had foretold, yet determined not to flee from it or, by clinging to life, to betray his people to the enemy and outrage the dignity of the kingship;

6.345. Instead, he thought it noble to expose himself, his house and his children to these perils and, along with them, to fall fighting for his subjects. He preferred to have his sons meet death as brave men rather than leave them behind, while still uncertain what kind of men they might prove to be; for thus, he would have praise and ageless remembrance [rather than descendants] as his successors and posterity.

6.346. Such a man alone, in my opinion, is just, valiant and wise, and he, if any has been or shall be such, deserves to have all men testify to his virtue. . . .

6.348. To harbor in one's heart no hope of success, but to know beforehand that one must die and die fighting, and then not to fear nor to be appalled at this terrible

All translations in this section are adapted from the Loeb Classical Library.

fate, but to meet it with full knowledge of what is coming—that, in my judgment, is true proof of valor.

6.349. And this Saul did, thereby showing that it behoves all men who aspire to good reputation after death so to act as to leave such a name after them.

B. Josephus, *BJ* 6.104–5.

6.104. He [Jehoiachin], when his conduct had brought the Babylonian's army upon him, of his own free will left the city before it was taken, and with his family endured voluntary captivity, rather than deliver up these holy places to the enemy and see the house of God in flames.

6.105. On account of this a holy story [*logos*] hymns him among all the Jews and memory flowing ever new transmits him immortal to those coming after him.

C. Josephus, *AJ* 15.267–76

15.267. For this reason Herod went still farther in departing from the ancestral customs, and through foreign practices he gradually corrupted the ancient way of life, which had hitherto been inviolable. As a result of this we suffered considerable harm at a later time as well, because those things were neglected which had formerly induced piety in the masses.

15.268. For in the first place he established quinquennial athletic competitions in honor of Caesar, and he built a theater in Jerusalem, and after that a very large amphitheater on the plain, both being spectacularly lavish but foreign to Jewish custom, for the use of such buildings and the exhibition of such spectacles have not been transmitted [as part of Jewish tradition] . . .

(15.269–271: invitations issued to competitive athletes, artists, charioteers). And whatever costly or magnificent efforts had been made by others, all these did Herod imitate in his ambition to see his spectacle become famous.

15.272. All round the theater were inscriptions concerning Caesar and trophies of the nations which he had won in war, all of them made for Herod of pure gold and silver . . .

15.273. There was also a supply of wild beasts, a great many lions and other animals having been brought together for him, such as were of extraordinary strength or of very rare kinds.

15.274.   When the practice began of involving them in combat
with one another or setting condemned men to fight
against them, the foreigners were astonished at the expense and at the same time entertained by the dangers
of the spectacle, but for the natives it was a manifest
abrogation of the custome honored by them.

15.275.   For it seemed glaring impiety to throw men to wild
beasts for the pleasure of other men as spectators, and
impious too to exchange [their native] customs for foreign practices.

15.276.   But the trophies pained them worst of all, for thinking
that these were images surrounded by weapons, which
it was against their ancestral custom to worship, they
were exceedingly angry.

15.277.   That the Jews were highly disturbed did not escape
Herod's notice, and since he thought it inopportune to
use force against them, he spoke to some of them reas-
suringly in an attempt to remove their religious scruple
[or superstition: *deisidaimonia*]. He did not, however,
succeed, for in their displeasure at the offenses of which
they thought him guilty, they cried out with one voice
that although everything else might be endured, they
would not endure images of men being brought into the
city—meaning the trophies—for this was against their
ancestral custom.

15.278.   Herod, therefore ... summoned the most eminent
among them and leading them to the theater, showed
them the trophies and asked just what they thought
these things were.

15.279.   When they cried out "Images of men," he gave orders
for the removal of the ornaments that covered them
and showed the people the bare wood. So, as soon as
the trophies were stripped, they became the cause of
laughter, and what contributed most to the confound-
ment of these men was the fact that up to this point
they had themselves regarded the arrangement as a dis-
guise for images [? meaning unclear].

D. Josephus, *AJ* 16.150–59.

16.150.   Now it has occurred to others to marvel at the inconsis-
tency of Herod's natural tendencies. For when, on the
one hand, we consider his munificence [*philotimias*]

and the benefactions [*euergesias*] which he bestowed on all men, it is impossible for anyone, even for those who have very little respect for him, to refuse to agree that he had a most beneficent nature.

16.151. But when, on the other hand, one looks at the punishments and the wrongs which he inflicted upon his subjects and those closest to him, and when one notes how harsh and inexorable his character was, one is forced to regard him as bestial and alien to all moderation.

16.152. For this reason they think there were divergent and warring tendencies within him. But I myself have a different view and believe that both these tendencies had the same cause.

16.153. For Herod was a lover of honor [*philotimos*] and, being powerfully dominated by this passion, he was led to display generosity [*megalopsychia*] whenever there was reason to hope for future remembrance [*mneme*] or present reputation,

16.154. But since he was involved in expenses greater than his means, he was compelled to be harsh toward his subjects, for the great number of things on which he spent money as gifts to some caused him to be the provider of harm to those from whom he took this money.

16.155. And though he was aware of being hated because of the wrongs that he had done his subjects, he decided that it would not be easy to mend his sins—that would have been unprofitable in respect to revenue—and instead strove jealously against them by making their ill-will an opportunity for enhancing his own prosperity.

16.156. In fact, among his own people, if anyone did not pay court to him in speech by confessing himself his slave or was thought to be raising questions about his rule, Herod was unable to control himself and prosecuted his kin and his friends alike, and punished them as severely as enemies. These sins he committed because of his wish to be uniquely honored.

16.157. As evidence that this was the greatest of his passions, I can cite what was done by him in honor of Caesar and Agrippa and his other friends. For in the very same ways in which he paid court to his superiors, he expected to be courted by his subjects, and what he believed to be

the most beautiful thing that he good give to another he
showed a desire to obtain similarly for himself.

16.158. But, as it happens, the nation of the Jews is by law opposed to all such things and is accustomed to love righteousness [to dikaion] rather than glory [doxan]. For
this reason it was not favored by him, because it found it
impossible to flatter the king's ambition with statues or
temples or such tokens.

16.159. And this seems to me the reason for Herod's bad treatment of his own people and his councilors, and of his
beneficence to outsiders and those unattached to him.

E. Josephus, AJ 19.328–31

19.328. Now this king [Agrippa I] was by nature beneficent
[euergetikos] in gifts and strove zealously to be high
minded toward nations [? LCL: "the gentiles"]; and by
expending massive sums he raised himself to high
fame, taking pleasure in conferring favors and rejoicing
in living in good reputation, being in no way similar to
Herod, who was king before him.

19.329. The latter had an evil character, relentless in punish-
ment and unsparing in action against the objects of his
hatred. It was generally admitted that he was on more
friendly terms with Greeks than with Jews. For instance,
he adorned the cities of foreigners by giving them
money, building baths and theaters, erecting temples in
some and porticoes in others, whereas there was not a
single city of the Jews on which he deigned to bestow
even minor restoration or any gift worth mentioning.

19.330. Agrippa, though, had a gentle disposition and was
equally beneficent to all. He was benevolent [philan-
thropos] to foreigners and exhibited his love of bestowing gifts to them also; but to his compatriots he was
proportionately more generous and more
compassionate.

19.331. He enjoyed residing in Jerusalem and did so constantly,
and observed the ancestral traditions purely [katharos].
He neglected no rite of purification, and no day passed
for him without the prescribed sacrifice.

ABBREVIATIONS

AJ	Josephus, *Antiquitates Judaicae (Jewish Antiquities)*
AJP	*American Journal of Philology*
AJSR	*AJS Review*
ANRW	*Aufstieg und Niedergang der Römischen Welt* (Berlin: de Gruyter, 1979)
B	Talmud Bavli (Babylonian Talmud)
BJ	*Josephus, Bellum Judaicum (Jewish War)*
CA	*Classical Antiquity*
CAp	Josephus, *Contra Apionem* (*Against Apion*)
CBQ	*Catholic Biblical Quarterly*
CHJ	*Cambridge History of Judaism*
CIJ	J.-B. Frey, ed., *Corpus Inscriptionum Judaicarum*, 2 vols. (Rome: Pontificio Istituto di Archeologia Cristiana, 1936–1952)
CP	*Classical Philology*
CQ	*Classical Quarterly*
CSSH	*Comparative Studies in Society and History*
CTh	*Codex Theodosianus: Theodosiani Iibri XVI cum Constitutionibus Sirmondianis et Leges Novellae ad Theodosianum Pertinentes, Consilio et Auctoritate Academiae Litterarum Regiae Borussicae ediderunt Theodorus Mommsen et Paulus Meyer* (Berlin: Weidmann, 1954)
HTR	*Harvard Theological Review*
HUCA	*Hebrew Union College Annual*
IEJ	*Israel Exploration Journal*
IJS	S. Schwartz, *Imperialism and Jewish Society, 200 BCE to 640 CE* (Princeton, NJ: Princeton University Press, 2001)
JBL	*Journal of Biblical Literature*
JESHO	*Journal of the Economic and Social History of the Orient*
JJS	*Journal of Jewish Studies*
JQR	*Jewish Quarterly Review*
JRA	*Journal of Roman Archaeology*
JRS	*Journal of Roman Studies*
JSJ	*Journal for the Study of Judaism*
LSJ	H. G. Liddell, R. Scott and H. S. Jones, *A Greek-English Lexicon*, 9th ed. (Oxford, 1968)

M	Mishnah
PCPS	*Proceedings of the Cambridge Philological Society*
R.	Rabbi
RB	*Revue Biblique*
Schürer-Vermes	E. Schürer, *The History of the Jewish People in the Age of Jesus Christ*, rev. and ed. G. Vermes et al., in 4 vol. (Edinburgh: T. and T. Clark, 1973–1987)
SCI	*Scripta Classica Israelica*
T	Tosefta
TYGRC	P. Schäfer & Catherine Hezser, eds., *The Talmud Yerushalmi and Graeco-Roman Culture*, in 3 vol. (Tübingen: Mohr Siebeck, 1998–2002)
V	*Josephus, Vita (Autobiography)*
VT	*Vetus Testamentum*
Y	Talmud Yerushalmi (Palestinian Talmud)

BIBLIOGRAPHY

Abulafia, D. "What Is the Mediterranean?" In *The Mediterranean in History*, edited by D. Abulafia, 11–26. London: Thames and Hudson, 2003.

Ackerman, S. "The Personal Is Political: Covenantal and Affectionate Love ('aheb, 'ahaba) in the Hebrew Bible." *VT* 52 (2002): 437–58.

Ackroyd, P. R. "The Verb Love—Aheb in the David-Jonathan Narratives—A Footnote." *VT* 25 (1975): 213–14.

Aitken, J. "Biblical Interpretation as Political Manifesto: Ben Sira in His Seleucid Setting." *JJS* 51 (2000): 191–208.

Alcock, S. *Archaeologies of the Greek Past: Landscapes, Monuments, and Memories*. Cambridge: Cambridge University Press, 2002.

Alon, G. "Ilen De-mitmenin Bi-ksaf: Le-toldot Reshuyot-Ha-dinim Be-eretz-Yisrael Bi-tequfat Ha-talmud." In *Mehkarim Betoldot Yisrael*, vol. 2, 15–57. Tel Aviv: Hakibbutz Hameuhad, 1958.

Alon, G. *Toldot Hayehudim Be'eretz Yisrael Bitequfat Hamishnah Vehatalmud*, vol. 2. Tel Aviv: Hakibbutz Hame'uhad, 1961.

Anderson, B. *Imagined Communities: Reflections on the Origins and Spread of Nationalism*. London: Verso, 1991. First published 1983.

Argall, R. *I Enoch and Sirach: A Comparative Literary and Conceptual Analysis of the Themes of Revelation, Creation and Judgement*. Atlanta, GA: Scholars Press, 1995.

Aristotle. *Ethica Eudemia, recensuerunt brevique adnotatione critica instruxerunt R. R. Walzer et J. M. Mingay*. Oxford: Clarendon, 1991.

Avi-Yonah, M. *The Jews of Palestine: A Political History from the Bar Kokhba War to the Arab Conquest*. New York: Schocken, 1976. First published 1946 by Mossad Bialik, Jerusalem.

Banfield, E. C. *The Moral Basis of a Backward Society*. Glencoe, IL: Free Press, 1958.

Barag, D. "The 2000–2001 Exploration of the Tombs of Benei Hezir and Zechariah." *IEJ* 53 (2003): 78–110.

Barr, J. "Hebrew, Aramaic and Greek in the Hellenistic Age." In *Cambridge History of Judaism*, edited by L. Finkelstein and W. D. Davies, vol. 2, 79–114. Cambridge: Cambridge University Press, 1989.

Barthélemy, D. and O. Rickenbacher. *Konkordanz zum Hebräischen Sirach*. Göttingen: Vandenhoeck & Ruprecht, 1973.

Barton, C. *Roman Honor: The Fire in the Bones*. Berkeley and Los Angeles: University of California Press, 2001.

Baumgarten, A. *The Flourishing of Jewish Sects in the Maccabean Era: An Interpretation*. Leiden: Brill, 1997.

Baumgarten, A. "The Pharisaic Paradosis." *HTR* 80 (1987): 63–77.

Beard, M. "Writing and Religion: *Ancient Literacy* and the Function of the Written Word in Roman Religion." In *Literacy in the Roman World*, edited by J. Humphrey, 133–43. *JRA* Suppl. 3, 1991.

Becker, H.-J. *Die grossen rabbinischen Sammelwerke Palaestinas zur literarischen Genese von Talmud Yerushalmi und Midrash Bereshit Rabba*. Tübingen: Mohr Siebeck, 1999.

Beentjes, P. *The Book of Ben Sira in Hebrew: A Text Edition of All Extant Hebrew Manuscripts and a Synopsis of All Parallel Hebrew Ben Sira Texts*. Leiden: Brill, 1997.

Beer, M. *The Babylonian Exilarchate in the Arsacid and Sassanian Periods*. Tel Aviv: Dvir, 1970.

Bhabha, H. *The Location of Culture*. London: Routledge, 1994.

Biale, D. ed. *The Cultures of the Jews: A New History*. New York: Schocken, 2002.

Biale, D. *Power and Powerlessness in Jewish History*. New York: Schocken, 1986.

Bickerman, E. J. *The Jews in the Greek Age*. Cambridge, MA: Harvard University Press, 1988.

Bilde, P. *Flavius Josephus, Between Jerusalem and Rome*. Sheffield, UK: Sheffield Academic Press, 1988.

Bloch, M., and J. Parry, eds. *Money and the Morality of Exchange*. Cambridge: Cambridge University Press, 1989.

Boccaccini, G. "Il tema della memoria in Giuseppe Flavio." *Henoch* 6 (1984): 147–63.

Bockmuehl, M. "The Noachide Commandments and New Testament Ethics with Special Reference to Acts 15 and Pauline Halakhah." *RB* 102 (1995): 72–101.

Bohak, G. "Ethnic Continuity in the Jewish Diaspora in Antiquity." In *Jews in the Hellenistic and Roman Cities*, edited by J. Bartlett, 175–92. London: Routledge, 2002.

Bokser, B. "An Annotated Bibliographical Guide to the Study of the Palestinian Talmud." In *Aufstieg und Niedergang der römischen Welt* 2.19.2, 139–256. Berlin: de Gruyter, 1979.

Bourdieu, P. *Outline of a Theory of Practice*. Cambridge: Cambridge University Press, 1977. First published 1972.

Bourdieu, P., and L. Wacquant. *An Invitation to Reflexive Sociology*. Chicago: University of Chicago Press, 1992.

Braudel, F. *The Mediterranean and the Mediterranean World in the Age of Philip II*. New York: Harper & Row, 1972.

Brettler, M. "Memory in Ancient Israel." In *Memory and History in Christianity and Judaism*, edited by M. Signer, 1–17. Notre Dame, IN: Notre Dame University Press, 2001.

Broshi, M. "The Inhabitants of Jerusalem." In *The City of the Great King: Jerusalem from David to the Present*, edited by N. Rosovsky, 9–34. Cambridge, MA: Harvard University Press, 1996.

Broshi, M. "La population de l'ancienne Jérusalem." *RB* 82 (1975): 5–14.

Brown, P. *Poverty and Leadership in the Later Roman Empire*. Hanover, NH: University Press of New England, 2002.

Brunt, P. "Did Rome Disarm Its Subjects?" In *Roman Imperial Themes*, 255–81. Oxford: Oxford University Press, 1990.

Camp, C. "Honor and Shame in Ben Sira: Anthropological and Theological Reflections." In *The Book of Ben Sira in Modern Research: Proceedings of the First International Ben Sira Conference, 28–31 July 1996, Soesterberg, Netherlands,* edited by P. C. Beentjes, 171–87. BZAW 225. Berlin-New York: de Gruyter, 1997.

Cancik, H. "Theokratia und Priesterherrschaft." *Theokratie: Religionstheorie und Politische Theologie* 3 (1987): 65–77.

Castelli, S. "Antiquities 3–4 and Against Apion 2.145ff: Different Approaches to the Law." In *Internationales Josephus-Kolloquium Amsterdam 2000*, edited by J. Kalms, 151–69. Münster: LIT, 2001.

Champlin, E. *Final Judgments: Duty and Emotion in Roman Wills, 200 B. C.–A. D. 250*. Berkeley and Los Angeles: University of California Press, 1991.

Chance, J. K. "The Anthropology of Honor and Shame: Culture, Value, and Practice." *Semeia* 68 (1994/1996): 139–51.

Chaniotis, A. "From Communal Spirit to Individuality: The Epigraphic Habit in Hellenistic and Roman Crete." In *Creta Romana e Protobizantina: Atti del Congresso Internazionale (Iraklion, 23–30 Settembre, 2000)*, edited by M. Livadiotti and I. Simiakaki, 75–87. Padua: Bottega d'Erasmo, 2004.

Cicero. *De Officiis, recognovit brevique adnotatione critica instruxit M. Winterbottom*. Oxford: Clarendon, 1994.

Cohen, S. *Josephus in Galilee and Rome: His Vita and Development as a Historian*. Leiden: Brill, 1979.

Cohen, D. *Law, Sexuality, and Society: The Enforcement of Morals in Classical Athens*. Cambridge: Cambridge University Press, 1991.

Cohen, D. *Law, Violence, and Community in Classical Athens*. Cambridge: Cambridge University Press, 1995.

Cohen, S. "The Significance of Yavneh: Pharisees, Rabbis, and the End of Jewish Sectarianism." *HUCA* 55 (1984): 27–53.

Collins, J. J. *Jewish Wisdom in the Hellenistic Age*. Louisville, KY: Westminster John Knox Press, 1997.

Corley, J. *Ben Sira's Teaching on Friendship*. Brown Judaic Studies 316. Providence, RI: Brown Judaic Studies, 2002.

Cotton, H. "The Date of the Fall of Masada: The Evidence of the Masada Papyri." *ZPE* 78 (1989): 157–62.

Cotton, H., and A. Yardeni. *Aramaic, Hebrew and Greek Documentary Texts from Nahal Hever and Other Sites*. Oxford: Clarendon Press, 1997.

Cribiore, R. *The School of Libanius in Late Antique Antioch*. Princeton, NJ: Princeton University Press, 2007.

Dan, Y. "Seher Penim ve-Seher Hutz be-Eretz Yisrael Biyemei Bayit Sheni." In *Commerce in Palestine Throughout the Ages*, edited by B. Z. Kedar, T. Dothan, and S. Safrai, 91–107. Jerusalem: Yad Ben Zvi, 1990.

Davis, J. *Exchange*. Minneapolis: University of Minnesota Press, 1992.

Davis, J. *People of the Mediterranean: An Essay in Comparative Social Anthropology*. London: Routledge and Kegan Paul, 1977.

Davis, N. Z. *The Gift in Sixteenth Century France*. Madison: University of Wisconsin Press, 2000.

de Pina-Cabral, J. "The Mediterranean as a Category of Regional Comparison: A Critical View." *Current Anthropology* 30 (1989): 399–406.

de Silva, D. A. "The Wisdom of Ben Sira: Honor, Shame, and the Maintenance of the Values of a Minority Culture." *CBQ* 58 (1996): 433–55.

de Vaux, R. *Ancient Israel: Its Life and Institutions*. London: Darton, Longman and Todd, 1961.

di Lella, A. A. "Conservative and Progressive Theology: Sirach and Wisdom." *CBQ* 38 (1966): 139–54.

di Lella, A. A. "Use and Abuse of the Tongue: Ben Sira 5,9–6,1." In *'Jedes Ding hat seine Zeit . . .': Studien zur israelitischen und altorientalischen Weisheit. Diethelm Michel zum 65. Geburtstag*, edited by A. A. Diesel et al., 33–48. BZAW 241. Berlin: de Gruyter, 1996.

di Segni, L. "Dated Inscriptions from Palestine from the Roman and Byzantine Periods." PhD dissertation, Hebrew University, 1997, 2 vols.

Donlan, W. "Pistos Philos Hetairos." In *Theognis of Megara: Poetry and the Polis*, edited by T. Figueira and G. Nagy, 176–96. Baltimore, MD: Johns Hopkins University Press 1985.

Dothan, M. *Hammath Tiberias: Early Synagogues and Hellenistic and Roman Remains*. Jerusalem: Israel Exploration Society, 1983.

Drake, H. *Constantine and the Bishops: The Politics of Intolerance*. Baltimore, MD: Johns Hopkins University Press, 2000.

Dyson, S. "Native Revolt Patterns in the Roman Empire." *ANRW* II, 3:138–75.

Dyson, S. "Native Revolts in the Roman Empire." *Historia* 20 (1971): 239–74.

Eckstein, A. "Josephus and Polybius: A Reconsideration." *CA* 9 (1990): 175–208.

Eisenstadt, S. N., and Roniger, L. "Patron-Client Relations as a Model of Structuring Social Exchange." *CSSH* 22 (1980): 42–77.

Elsner, J. "Pausanias: A Greek Pilgrim in the Roman World." *Past & Present* 135 (1992): 3–29.

Epstein, J. N. *Prolegomena ad Litteras Amoraiticas*, edited by E. Z. Melamed. Jerusalem: Magnes, 1962.

Feldman, L. *Jew and Gentile in the Ancient World*. Princeton, NJ: Princeton University Press, 1993.

Fentress, J., and C. Wickham. *Social Memory*. Oxford: Blackwell, 1992.

Finley, M. I. *The World of Odysseus*. New York: Viking, 1954.

Fischel, H. A. ed. *Essays in Greco-Roman and Related Talmudic Literature*. New York: Ktav, 1977.

Fonrobert, C. *Menstrual Purity: Rabbinic and Christian Reconstructions of Biblical Gender*. Stanford: Stanford University Press, 2000.

Fraade, S. *From Tradition to Commentary: Torah and Its Interpretation in the Midrash Sifre to Deuteronomy*. Albany: SUNY Press, 1991.

Frey, J.-B. "La question des images chez les juifs à la lumière des récentes découvertes." *Biblica* 15 (1934): 265–300.

Friedheim, E. *Rabbinisme et paganisme en Palestine romaine: Etude historique des realia talmudiques (Ier–IVeme siecles)*. Leiden: Brill, 2006.

Fritz, V., and R. Deines. "Jewish Ossuaries in the German Protestant Institute of Archaeology." *IEJ* 49 (1999): 222–41.

Gafni, I. *The Jews of Babylonia in the Talmudic Era: A Social and Cultural History*. Jerusalem: Merkaz Shazar, 1990.

Garnsey, P. "The Generosity of Veyne." *JRS* 81 (1991): 164–68.

Garnsey, P., and R. Saller. *The Roman Empire: Economy, Society and Culture*. Cambridge: Cambridge University Press, 1987.

Gellner, E. *Nations and Nationalism*. Ithaca, NY: Cornell University Press, 1983.

Gellner, E., and J. Waterbury, eds. *Patrons and Clients in Mediterranean Societies*. London: Duckworth, 1977.

Geva, H. "Jerusalem." *NEAEHL* 2: 717–57.

Geva, H. ed. *Jewish Quarter Excavations in the Old City of Jerusalem conducted by Nahman Avigad 1968–1982*, vol. 2. Jerusalem: Israel Exploration Society, 2003.

Ginzberg, L. *A Commentary on the Palestinian Talmud*, vol. 1. New York: Jewish Theological Seminary, 1941.

Goff, M. "Hellenistic Instruction in Palestine and Egypt: Ben Sira and Papyrus Insinger." *JSJ* 36 (2005): 147–72.

Goffman, E. "The Nature of Deference and Demeanor." *American Anthropologist* 58 (1956): 473–502.

Goldhill, S., ed. *Being Greek Under Rome: Roman Cultural Identity, the Second Sophistic and the Development of Empire*. Cambridge: Cambridge University Press, 2001.

Goodblatt, D. "Agrippa I and Palestinian Judaism in the First Century." *Jewish History* 2 (1987): 7–32.

Goodman, M. "Current Scholarship on the First Revolt." In *The First Jewish Revolt: Archaeology, History and Ideology*, edited by A. Berlin and J. A. Overman, 15–25. London: Routledge, 2002.

Goodman, M. "Josephus as a Roman Citizen." In *Josephus and the History of the Greco-Roman Period: Essays in Memory of Morton Smith*, edited by F. Parente and J. Sievers, 329–38. Leiden: Brill, 1994.

Goodman, M. "A Note on Josephus, the Pharisees, and the Ancestral Tradition." *JJS* 50 (1999): 17–20.

Goodman, M. *Rome and Jerusalem: The Clash of Ancient Civilizations*. London: Penguin, 2007.

Goodman, M. *The Ruling Class of Judaea: The Origins of the Jewish Revolt Against Rome A.D. 66–70*. Cambridge: Cambridge University Press, 1987.

Gordon, R. "Religion in the Roman Empire: The Civic Compromise and its Limits." In *Pagan Priests: Religion and Power in the Ancient World*, edited by M. Beard and J. North, 235–55. Ithaca, NY: Cornell University Press, 1990.

Gouldner, A. "The Norm of Reciprocity: A Preliminary Statement." *American Sociological Review* 25 (1960): 161–78.

Griffin, M. "*De Beneficiis* and Roman Society." *JRS* 93 (2003): 92–113.

Gruen, E. *Diaspora: Jews amidst Greeks and Romans*. Cambridge, MA: Harvard University Press, 2002.

Grushcow, L. *Writing the Wayward Wife: Rabbinic Interpretations of Sotah*. Leiden: Brill, 2006.

Hakham, A. "Mishar Ve-khalkalah Ba-miqra." *Mahanaim* 2 (1991): 20–39.

Hall, J. "The Deference-Greeting in Roman Society." *Maia* 50 (1998): 413–26.

Harari, Y. *Harba De-Moshe: Mahadurah Hadashah U-Mehqar*. Jerusalem: Akademon, 1997.

Harries, J. "Creating Legal Space: Settling Disputes in the Roman Empire." In *Rabbinic Law in Its Roman and Near Eastern Context*, edited by C. Hezser, 63–81. Tübingen: Mohr Siebeck, 2003.

Harris, W. V. *Ancient Literacy*. Cambridge, MA: Harvard University Press, 1989.

Harris, W. V. "The Mediterranean and Ancient History." In *Rethinking the Mediterranean*, edited by W. V. Harris, 1–42. Oxford: Oxford University Press, 2005.

Harris, W. V. *War and Imperialism in Republican Rome 327–70 BC*. Oxford: Clarendon Press, 1979.

Hayes, C. "Displaced Self-Perceptions: The Deployment of 'Minim' and Romans in B. Sanhedrin 90b–91a." In *Religious and Ethnic Communities in Later Roman Palestine*, edited by H. Lapin, 249–89. Bethesda: University Press of Maryland, 1998.

Hayes, C. "Genealogy, Illegitimacy, and Personal Status: The Yerushalmi in Comparative Perspective," in *TYGRC*, 3:73–89.

Hendel, R. *Remembering Abraham: Culture, Memory, and History in the Hebrew Bible*. New York: Oxford University Press, 2005.

Hengel, M. *Judaism and Hellenism: Studies in Their Encounter in Palestine in the Early Hellenistic Period*. London: SCM Press, 1974.

Hengel, M. *Die Zeloten: Untersuchungen zur jüdischer Freiheitsbewegung in der Zeit von Herodes I bis 70 n. Chr*. Leiden: Brill, 1976.

Herman, Geoffrey. "The Exilarchate in the Sasanian Era". PhD dissertation, Hebrew University, 2005.

Herman, G. *Morality and Behaviour in Classical Athens: A Social History*. Cambridge: Cambridge University Press, 2006.

Herman, G. *Ritualised Friendship and the Greek City*. Cambridge: Cambridge University Press, 1987.

Herodotus. *Historiarum Libri IX, Edidit Henricus Rudolphus Dietsch, Editio Altera Curavit Curatamque Emendavit H. Kallenberg*. 2 vols. Leipzig: Teubner, 1899.

Herzfeld, M. *Anthropology Through the Looking Glass: Critical Ethnography in the Margins of Europe*. Cambridge: Cambridge University Press, 1987.

Herzfeld, M. "Honour and Shame: Problems in the Comparative Analysis of Moral Systems." *Man* 15 (1980): 339–51.

Hewitt, J. "The Terminology of 'Gratitude' in Greek." *CP* 22 (1927): 142–61.

Hezser, C. *Form, Function, and Historical Significance of the Rabbinic Story in Yerushalmi Neziqin*. Tübingen: Mohr Siebeck, 1993.

Hezser, C. "Interfaces Between Rabbinic Literature and Graeco-Roman Philosophy," in *TYGRC* vol. 2:161–87.

Hezser, C. *The Social Structure of the Rabbinic Movement in Roman Palestine*. Tübingen: Mohr Siebeck, 1997.

Hinnant, C. "The Patriarchal Narratives of *Genesis* and the Ethos of Gift Exchange." In *The Question of the Gift: Essays Across Disciplines*, edited by M. Osteen, 105–17. London: Routledge, 2002.

Hirschfeld, Y. *The Judean Desert Monasteries in the Byzantine Period*. New Haven, CT: Yale University Press, 1992.

Höffken, P. "Überlegungen zum Lesekreis der 'Antiquitates' des Josephus." *JSJ* 38 (2007): 328–41.

Hoffman, D. "'All Is in Accord with Honor': Kavod and the Emergence of Rabbinic Judaism." Ph.D. dissertation, Jewish Theological Seminary, New York, forthcoming.

Hopkins, K. "Brother-Sister Marriage in Roman Egypt." *CSSH* 22 (1980): 303–54.

Hopkins, K. *Death and Renewal: Sociological Studies in Roman History 2*. Cambridge: Cambridge University Press, 1983.

Horden, P., and N. Purcell. *The Corrupting Sea: A Study of Mediterranean History*. Oxford: Blackwell, 2000

Horsley, R., and P. Tiller. "Ben Sira and the Sociology of the Second Temple." In *Second Temple Studies III: Studies in Politics, Class and Material Culture*, edited by P. R. Davies and J. M. Halligan, 74–107. JSOT Supplement Series 340. Sheffield, UK: Sheffield Academic Press, 2002.

Howgego, C. *Ancient History from Coins*. London: Routledge, 1995.

Huebner, S. "Brother-Sister Marriage in Roman Egypt: A Curiosity of Humankind or a Widespread Family Strategy?" *JRS* 97 (2007): 21–49.

Hurvitz, A. *Wisdom Language in Biblical Psalmody*. Jerusalem: Magnes, 1991.

Hyamson, M., ed. *Mosaicarum et Romanarum Legum Collatio*. Oxford: Oxford University Press, 1913.

Immerwahr, H. "Ergon: History as a Monument in Herodotus and Thucydides." *AJP* 81 (1960): 261–90.

Inwood, B. "Politics and Paradox in Seneca's *De beneficiis*." In *Justice and Generosity: Studies in Hellenistic Social and Political Philosophy*, edited by A. Laks and M. Schofield, 241–65. Cambridge: Cambridge University Press, 1995.

Ir-Shai, O. "Ya'akov of Kefar Niburaia: A Sage Turned Apostate." *Jerusalem Studies in Jewish Thought* 2 (1982/3): 153–68.

Isaac, B. "A Donation for Herod's Temple in Jerusalem." *IEJ* 33 (1983): 86–92.

Jacobs, M. *Die Institution des jüdischen Patriarchen: Eine quellen- und traditionskritische Studie zur Geschichte der Juden in der Spätantike.* Tübingen: Mohr Siebeck, 1995.

Jones, C. P. "Towards a Chronology of Josephus." *SCI* 21 (2002): 113–21.

Justinian. *The Digest of Justinian, Latin Text edited by Theodor Mommsen with the aid of Paul Krueger, English Translation edited by Alan Watson.* Philadelphia: University of Pennsylvania Press, 1985.

Kanievski, H. *Masekhet Bikkurim min Talmud Yerushalmi 'im bi'ur mesudar mi-pi ha-shemu'ah mi-shi'urei Moreinu Rabbi Hayim Kanievski Shlit'a.* Benei Berak (no publisher), 1990.

Kaster, R. *Emotion, Restraint, and the Community in Ancient Rome.* Oxford: Oxford University Press, 2005.

Kister, M. "A Contribution to the Interpretation of Ben Sira." *Tarbiz* 59 (1990): 303–78.

Kloner, A., and Zissu, B. *The Necropolis of Jerusalem in the Second Temple Period.* Jerusalem: Yad Ben Zvi / Israel Exploration Society, 2003.

Kloppenborg-Verbin, J. "Dating Theodotos (*CIJ* II 1404)." *JJS* 51 (2000): 243–80.

Komter, A. *Social Solidarity and the Gift.* Cambridge: Cambridge University Press, 2005.

Kon, M. *The Tombs of the Kings.* Tel Aviv: Dvir, 1947.

Konstan, D. *Friendship in the Classical World.* Cambridge: Cambridge University Press, 1997.

Kosovsky, M. *Concordance to the Talmud Yerushalmi*, 5 vols. Jerusalem: Israel Academy of Sciences and Humanities / Jewish Theological Seminary, 1979–1990.

Kurke, L. *Coins, Bodies, Games, and Gold: The Politics of Meaning in Ancient Greece.* Princeton, NJ: Princeton University Press, 1999.

Labendz, J. "The Book of Ben Sira in Rabbinic Literature." *AJSR* 30 (2006): 347–92.

Laidlaw, J. "A Free Gift Makes No Friends." In *The Question of the Gift: Essays Across Disciplines*, edited by M. Osteen, 45–66. London: Routledge, 2002.

Langlands, R. *Sexual Morality in Ancient Rome.* Cambridge: Cambridge University Press, 2006.

Lapin, H. *Economy, Geography, and Provincial History in Later Roman Palestine.* Tübingen: Mohr Siebeck, 2001.

Lapin, H. "The Origins and Development of the Rabbinic Movement in the Land of Israel." in *CHJ* 4:206–29.

Lapin, H. "Rabbis and Cities: Some Aspects of the Rabbinic Movement in its Graeco-Roman Environment." In *TYGRC* 2:51–80.

Lateiner, D. *The Historical Method of Herodotus.* Toronto: University of Toronto Press, 1989.

Leach, E. *The Political System of Highland Burma: A Study of Kachin Social Structure*. LSE Monographs on Social Anthropology 44. London: Athlone Press, 1970.

Lemche, N. P. "Kings and Clients: On Loyalty Between the Ruler and the Ruled in Ancient 'Israel.'" *Semeia* 68 (1994/1996): 119–32.

Lendon, J. E. *Empire of Honor: The Art of Government in the Roman World*. Oxford: Clarendon, 1997.

Leroy Ladurie, E. "The Court Surrounds the King: Louis XIV, the Palatine Princess, and Saint-Simon." In *Honor and Grace in Anthropology*, edited by J. G. Peristiany and J. Pitt-Rivers, 51–78. Cambridge: Cambridge University Press, 1992.

Levine, L. *Jerusalem: Portrait of the City in the Second Temple Period*. Philadelphia / New York: JPS / JTS, 2002.

Levine, L. "The Patriarch (Nasi) in Third Century Palestine." *ANRW* II, 19.2 (1979): 649–88.

Levine, L. "The Status of the Patriarch in the Third and Fourth Centuries: Sources and Methodology." *JJS* 47 (1996): 1–32.

Levinson, J. "'Tragedies Natural and Performed': Fatal Charades, Parodia Sacra, and the Death of Titus." In *Jewish Culture and Society under the Christian Roman Empire*, edited by R. Kalmin and S. Schwartz, 349–82. Leuven: Peeters, 2003.

Levinson, J. "The Tragedy of Romance: A Case of Literary Exile." *HTR* 89 (1996): 227–44.

Lewy, J. "Interpretation des IV Abschnittes des palästinensischen Talmud-Traktate Nesikin." In *Jahres-Bericht des juedisch-theologischen Seminars Fraenckel'scher Stiftung*. Breslau: Schatzky, 1908.

Lichtheim, M. *Ancient Egyptian Literature*, vol. 3: *The Late Period*. Berkeley and Los Angeles: University of California Press, 1980.

Lichtheim, M. *Late Egyptian Wisdom Literature in the International Context: A Study of Demotic Instructions*. Orbis Biblicus et Orientalis 52. Freiburg: Universitätsverlag, 1983.

Lieberman, S. "Emendations on the Jerushalmi (II)." *Tarbiz* 2 (1931): 235–40.

Lieberman, S. *Greek in Jewish Palestine*. New York: JTS, 1942.

Lieberman, S. *Hellenism in Jewish Palestine*. New York: JTS, 1950.

Lieberman, S. *Tosefta Ki-fshutah: Be'ur Arokh La-Tosefta*, 10 vols. New York: Jewish Theological Seminary, 1955–1988.

Mack, B. L. *Wisdom and the Hebrew Epic: Ben Sira's Hymn in Praise of the Fathers*. Chicago: University of Chicago Press, 1985.

Malinowski, B. *Argonauts of the Western Pacific*. London: Routledge, 1922.

Mason, S. "Of Audience and Meaning: Reading Josephus' Bellum Judaicum in the Context of a Flavian Audience." In *Josephus and Jewish History in Flavian Rome and Beyond*, edited by J. Sievers and G. Lembi, 71–100. Leiden: Brill, 2005.

Mason, S. "Should Anyone Wish to Inquire Further (Ant 1.25): The Aim and Audience of Josephus's Judean Antiquities/Life." In *Understanding Josephus: Seven Approaches*, edited by S. Mason. Sheffield, UK: Sheffield Academic Press, 1998.

Matthews, V., and D. Benjamin. "Social Sciences and Biblical Studies." *Semeia* 68 (1994/1996): 7–21.

Matthews, V. H. "The Unwanted Gift: Implications of Obligatory Gift Giving in Ancient Israel." *Semeia* 87 (1999): 91–104.

Mauss, M. "Essai sur le don: Forme et raison de l'échange dans les sociétés archaiques." *L'Année sociologique*, new series, 1 (1925). (*The Gift: The Form and Reason for Exchange in Archaic Societies*, translated by W. D. Halls, New York-London: Norton, 1990.)

Mazar, B. "A Hebrew Inscription from the Temple Area in Jerusalem." *Qadmoniot* 3 (1970): 142–44.

Mazur, A. *Biosociology of Dominance and Deference*. Lanham, MD: Rowman and Littlefield, 2005.

Merkelbach, R., and J. Stauber, eds. *Steinepigrammen aus dem griechischen Osten*, vol. 5. Munich: Saur, 2004.

Miles, G. "Roman and Modern Imperialism: A Reassessment." *CSSH* 32 (1990): 629–59.

Milikowsky, C. "The Formation and Transmission of Bereshit Rabba and the Yerushalmi: Questions of Redaction, Text-Criticism and Literary Relationships." *JQR* 92 (2002): 521–67.

Millar, F. "Last Year in Jerusalem: Monuments of the Jewish War in Rome." In *Flavius Josephus and Flavian Rome*, edited by J. Edmondson, S. Mason, and J. Rives, 101–28. Oxford: Oxford University Press, 2005.

Millar, F. *A Study of Cassius Dio*. Oxford: Clarendon, 1964.

Misgav, H. "The Epigraphic Sources (Hebrew and Aramaic) in Comparison with the Tradition Reflected in Talmudic Literature." PhD Dissertation, Hebrew University, 1999.

Moran, W. L. "The Ancient Near Eastern Background of the Love of God in Deuteronomy." *CBQ* 25 (1963): 77–87.

Moskowitz, L. "*Sugyot Muhlafot* in the Talmud Yerushalmi." *Tarbiz* 60 (1990): 19–66.

Mouritsen, H. "Freedmen and Decurions: Epitaphs and Social History in Imperial Italy." *JRS* 95 (2005): 38–63.

Naveh, J. "An Aramaic Tomb Inscription Written in Paleo-Hebrew Script." *IEJ* 23 (1973): 82–91.

Neusner, J. *A History of the Jews in Babylonia*, vol. 2. Brill: Leiden, 1966.

Novak, D. *The Image of the Non-Jew in Judaism: An Historical and Constructive Study of the Noahide Laws*. New York: Edwin Mellen Press, 1983.

Okoye, J. *Speech in Ben Sira with Special Reference to 5.9–6.1*. Frankfurt am Main: Lang, 1995.

Olick, J., and J. Robbins. "Social Memory Studies: From 'Collective Memory' to the Historical Sociology of Mnemonic Practices." *Annual Review of Sociology* 24 (1998): 105–40.

Olyan, S. "Honor, Shame, and Covenant Relations in Ancient Israel and Its Environment." *JBL* 115 (1996): 201–18.

Oppenheimer, A. "Jewish Conscripts in the Roman Army?" In *Between Rome and Babylon: Studies in Jewish Leadership*, edited by A. Oppenheimer and N. Oppenheimer, 183–91. Tübingen: Mohr Siebeck, 2005.

Oppenheimer, A., and N. Oppenheimer, eds. *Between Rome and Babylon: Studies in Jewish Leadership and Society*. Tübingen: Mohr Siebeck, 2005.

Otto, W. *Herodes: Beiträge zur Geschichte des letzten jüdischen Königshauses*. Stuttgart: Metzler, 1913.

Pastor, J. *Land and Economy in Ancient Palestine*. London: Routledge, 1997.

Patrich, J. "Herod's Theatre in Jerusalem: A New Proposal." *IEJ* 52 (2002): 231–39.

Peristiany, J. G., ed. *Honor and Shame: The Values of Mediterranean Society*. Chicago: University of Chicago Press, 1966.

Peskowitz, M. *Spinning Fantasies: Rabbis, Gender, and History*. Berkeley and Los Angeles: University of California Press, 1997.

Philo. *Works in ten volumes (and Two supplementary volumes); with an English translation by F. H. Colson and G. H. Whitaker*. Cambrdige, MA: Harvard University Press, 1929–1962.

Pope, M. *Job* (Anchor Bible). New York: Doubleday, 1965.

Portmann, W. "Ursicinus." *Der Neue Pauly* 12/1, 1054–55.

Price, J. *Jerusalem Under Siege: The Collapse of the Jewish State, 66–70 C.E.* Leiden: Brill, 1992.

Price, J. "Josephus's First Sentence and the Preface to BJ." In *For Uriel: Studies in the History of Israel in Antiquity, Presented to Professor Uriel Rappaport*, edited by M. Mor, Jack Pastor, Israel Ronen, and Yaakov Ashkenazi, 131–44. Jerusalem: Merkaz Shazar, 2005.

Price, J. "The Provincial Historian in Rome." In *Josephus and Jewish History in Flavian Rome and Beyond*, edited by J. Sievers and G. Lembi, 101–18. Leiden: Brill, 2005.

Pucci Ben Zeev, M. *Diaspora Judaism in Turmoil, 116/117 CE: Ancient Sources and Modern Insights*. Leuven: Peeters, 2005.

Rabinovitz, Z. W. *Sha'arei Torath Eretz Israel*. Jerusalem: Weiss, 1940.

Rahmani, L. Y. *A Catalogue of Jewish Ossuaries in the Collections of the State of Israel*. Jerusalem: IAA, 1994.

Rajak, T. "The Against Apion and the Continuities in Josephus' Political Thought." In T. Rajak, *The Jewish Dialogue with Greece and Rome: Studies in Cultural and Social Interaction*, 195–217. Leiden: Brill, 2001.

Rajak, T. *The Jewish Dialogue with Greece and Rome: Studies in Cultural and Social Interaction*. Leiden: Brill, 2001.

Rajak, T. *Josephus: The Historian and His Society*. London: Duckworth, 1983.

Rajak, T. "Justus of Tiberias." *CQ* 23 (1973): 246–68.

Ray, J. *The Sephardic Frontier: The Reconquista and the Jewish Community of Medieval Iberia*. Ithaca, NY: Cornell University Press, 2006.

Redfield, M. P., ed. *Human Nature and the Study of Society: The Papers of Robert Redfield*, 2 vols. Chicago: University of Chicago Press, 1962.

Reed, A. Y. *Fallen Angels and the History of Judaism and Christianity: The Reception of Enochic Literature*. Cambridge: Cambridge University Press, 2005.

Reif, S. "The Discovery of the Cambridge Genizah Fragments of Ben Sira: Scholars and Texts." In *The Book of Ben Sira in Modern Research: Proceedings of the First International Ben Sira Conference, 28–31 July 1996, Soesterberg, Netherlands*, edited by P. Beentjes, 1–22. BZAW 255. Berlin: de Gruyter, 1997.

Reiterer, F. V., ed. *Freundschaft bei Ben Sira: Beiträge des ersten Symposions zu Ben Sira, Salzburg, 1995*. BZAW 244. Berlin: de Gruyter, 1996.

Richardson, P. *Herod: King of the Jews and Friend of the Romans*. Columbia: University of South Carolina Press, 1996.

Rives, J. "Christian Expansion and Christian Ideology." In *The Spread of Christianity in the First Four Centuries: Essays in Explanation*, edited by W. V. Harris, 15–41. Leiden: Brill, 2005.

Romney Wegner, J. *Chattel or Person: The Status of Women in the Mishnah*. Oxford: Oxford University Press, 1988.

Rosenthal, E. S. "A Contribution to the Talmudic Lexicon." *Tarbiz* 40 (1971): 178–201.

Rosenthal, E. S. "The Givat Ha-Mivtar Inscription." *IEJ* 23 (1973): 72–81.

Rubenstein, J. *The Culture of the Babylonian Talmud*. Baltimore, MD: Johns Hopkins University Press, 2003.

Safrai, S. "Sikarikon." *Zion* 17 (1952): 56–64.

Sahlins, M. "Poor Man, Rich Man, Big-man, Chief: Political Types in Melanesia and Polynesia." *CSSH* 5 (1963): 285–303.

Sahlins, M. *Stone Age Economics*. New York: Aldine, 1972.

Saller, R. *Personal Patronage under the Early Empire*. Cambridge: Cambridge University Press, 1982.

Sanders, E. P. *Judaism, Practice and Belief: 63 BCE–66 CE*. Philadelphia: Trinity Press International, 1992.

Sanders, J. T. *Ben Sira and Demotic Wisdom*. Chico, CA: Scholars Press, 1983.

Sanders, J. T. "Concerning Ben Sira and Demotic Wisdom: A Response to Matthew J. Goff." *JSJ* 38 (2007): 297–306.

Schäfer, P., ed. *The Bar Kokhba War Reconsidered: New Perspectives on the Second Jewish Revolt Against Rome*. Tübingen: Mohr Siebeck, 2003.

Schäfer, P. *The Hidden and Manifest God: Themes in Early Jewish Mysticism*. Albany: SUNY Press, 1992.

Schäfer, P., and H.-J. Becker, eds. *Synopse zum Talmud Yerushalmi*, 4 vols. Tübingen: Mohr Siebeck, 1991–1998.

Schäfer, P., and C. Hezser, eds. *The Talmud Yerushalmi and Graeco-Roman Culture*, 3 vols. Tübingen: Mohr Siebeck, 1998–2002.

Schalit, A. *König Herodes: Der Mann und sein Werk*. Berlin: de Gruyter, 1969.

Scheidel, W. "Stratification, Deprivation and the Quality of Life." In *Poverty in the Roman World*, edited by M. Atkins and R. Osborne, 40–59. Cambridge: Cambridge University Press, 2006.

Schökel, L. A. "The Vision of Man in Sirach 16.24–17.14." In *Israelite Wisdom: Theological and Literary Essays in Honor of Samuel Terrien*, edited by J. G. Gammie, W. Brueggemann, W. Lee, Humphreys, and J. M. Ward, 235–45. Missoula, MT: Scholars Press, 1978.

Schremer, A. "Comments Concerning King Uziahu's Burial Place." *Cathedra* 46 (1987): 188–90.

Schwartz, D. *Agrippa I: The Last King of Judaea*. Tübingen: Mohr Siebeck, 1990.

Schwartz, D. "God, Gentiles and Jewish Law: On Acts 15 and Josephus' Adiabene Narrative." In *Geschichte-Tradition-Reflexion: Festschrift für Martin Hengel zum 70. Geburtstag*, vol 1, edited by P. Schäfer, 263–282. Tübingen: Mohr Siebeck, 1996.

Schwartz, D. "Josephus on the Jewish Constitution and Community." *SCI* 7 (1983): 30–52.

Schwartz, D. "On Sacrifice by Gentiles in the Temple of Jerusalem." *Studies in the Jewish Background of Christianity*, 102–16. Tübingen: Mohr Siebeck, 1992.

Schwartz, S. "Conversion to Judaism in the Second Temple Period: A Functionalist Approach." In *Studies in Josephus and the Varieties of Ancient Judaism: Louis H. Feldman Jubilee Volume*, edited by S. Cohen and J. Schwartz, 223–36. Leiden: Brill, 2007.

Schwartz, S. "Historiography on the Jews in the 'Talmudic Period.'" In *The Oxford Handbook of Jewish Studies*, edited by M. Goodman, 79–114. Oxford: Oxford University Press, 2002.

Schwartz, S. *Imperialism and Jewish Society, 200 BCE to 640 CE*. Princeton, NJ: Princeton University Press.

Schwartz, S. *Josephus and Judaean Politics*. Leiden: Brill, 1990.

Schwartz, S. "Josephus in Galilee: Rural Patronage and Social Breakdown." In *Josephus and the History of the Greco-Roman Period: Essays in Memory of Morton Smith*, edited by F. Parente and J. Sievers, 290–308. Leiden: Brill, 1994.

Schwartz, S. "King Herod, Friend of the Jews." In *Jerusalem and Eretz Israel: Arie Kindler Volume*, edited by J. Schwartz, Z. Amar and I. Ziffer, *67–*76. Tel Aviv: Rennert Center, Bar Ilan University / Eretz Israel Museum, 2000.

Schwartz, S. "Language, Power and Identity in Ancient Palestine." *Past & Present* 148 (1995): 3–47.

Schwartz S. "No Dialogue at the Symposium? Conviviality in Ben Sira and the Palestinian Talmud." In *The End of Dialogue in Antiquity* edited by S. Goldhill. Cambridge: Cambridge University Press, in press.

Schwartz, S. "The Political Geography of Rabbinic Texts." In *The Cambridge Companion to the Talmud and Rabbinic Literature*, edited by C. Fonrobert and M. Jaffee, 75–96. Cambridge: Cambridge University Press, 2007.

Schwartz, S. "Political, Social, and Economic Life in the Land of Israel, 66–c.235." In *Cambridge History of Judaism*, edited by S. Katz, 4:23–52. Cambridge: Cambridge University Press, 2006.

Schwartz, S. "The Rabbi in Aphrodite's Bath: Palestinian Society and Jewish Identity in the High Roman Empire." In *Being Greek under Rome: Cultural Identity,* the Second Sophistic and the Development of Empire, edited by S. Goldhill, 335–61. Cambridge: Cambridge University Press, 2001.

Schwartz, S. "*Sunt Lachrymae Rerum*: Martin Goodman's *Rome and Jerusalem*. *JQR* 99(2009): 56–64.

Schwartz, S. "The Patriarchs and the Diaspora." *JJS* 50 (1999): 208–22.

Scott, J. C. *Domination and the Arts of Resistance: Hidden Transcripts*. New Haven, CT: Yale University Press, 1990.

Segal, M. Z. *Sefer Ben Sira Ha-Shalem*. Jerusalem: Mossad Bialik, 1972. First published 1953.

Seneca, *Lucii Annaei Senecae Opera quae Supersunt*. Leipzig: Teubner, 1898–1907.

Sevenster, J. N. *Do You Know Greek? How Much Greek Could the First Jewish Christians Have Known?* Leiden: Brill, 1968.

Shaw, B. "Josephus: Roman Power and Jewish Responses to It." *Athenaeum* 83 (1995): 357–90.

Shaw, B. Review of Goodman. *JRS* 79 (1989): 246–47.

Shilo, S. *Dina De-Malkhuta Dina: The Law of the Land Is the Law*. Jerusalem: Jerusalem Academic Press, 1974.

Silverman, S. "Patronage as Myth." In *Patrons and Clients in Mediterranean Societies*, edited by E. Gellner and J. Waterbury, 7–19. London: Duckworth, 1977.

Simkins, R. "Patronage and the Political Economy of Monarchic Israel." *Semeia* 87 (1999): 123–44.

Skehan, P. W., and A. A. di Lella. *The Wisdom of Ben Sira* (Anchor Bible 39). New York: Doubleday, 1987.

Smend, R. *Die Weisheit des Jesus Sirach, hebräisch und deutsch*. Berlin: Georg Reimer, 1906.

Smith, M. *Palestinian Parties and Politics That Shaped the Old Testamen*, 2nd ed. London: SCM Press, 1987. First published 1971 by Columbia University Press.

Sperber, D. "Patronage in Amoraic Palestine (c.220–400): Causes and Effects." *JESHO* 14 (1971): 227–52.

Sperber, D. *Roman Palestine: 200–400, The Land*. Ramat Gan, Israel: Bar Ilan University Press, 1978.

Spilsbury, P. "Contra Apionem and Antiquitates Judaicae: Points of Contact." In *Josephus' Contra Apionem*, edited by L. Feldman and J. Levison, 348–68. Leiden: Brill, 1996.

Stansell, G. "The Gift in Ancient Israel." *Semeia* 87 (1999): 65–90.

Stemberger, G. *Jews and Christians in the Holy Land: Palestine in the Fourth Century*. Edinburgh: Clark, 1999.

Sterling, G., ed. *The Ancestral Philosophy: Hellenistic Philosophy in Second Temple Judaism. Essays of David Winston*. Brown Judaic Studies 331, Studia Philonica Monographs 4. Providence, RI: Brown Judaic Studies, 2001.

Stern, M. "'Jerusalem, the Most Famous of the Cities of the East' (Pliny, Natural History V, 70)." In *Jerusalem in the Second Temple Period: Abraham Schalit Memorial Volume*, edited by A. Oppenheimer, U. Rappaport, and M. Stern, 257–70. Jerusalem: Yad Ben Zvi, 1980.

Stern, M. "Josephus and the Roman Empire." In *Josephus Flavius: Historian of Eretz-Israel in the Hellenistic-Roman Period*, edited by U. Rappaport, 237–45. Jerusalem: Yad Ben Zvi, 1982.

Stern, Y. [S.] "Figurative Art and Halakhah in the Mishnaic-Talmudic Period." *Zion* 61 (1996): 397–419.

Stewart, F. H. *Honor*. Chicago: University of Chicago Press, 1994.

Strack, H., G. Stemberger, and M. Bockmuehl. *Introduction to the Talmud and Midrash*. Minneapolis: Fortress, 1996.

Strobel, K. "Jüdisches Patriarchat, Rabbinentum, und Priesterdynastie von Emesa: Historische Phänomene innerhalb des Imperium Romanum der Kaiserzeit." *Ktema* 14 (1989/1994): 39–77.

Sukenik, E. L. "An Epitaph of Uzziahu King of Judah." *Tarbiz* 2 (1931): 288–92.

Sussmann, J. "Mesoret Limud U-Mesoret Nusah shel Ha-Talmud Ha-Yerushalmi: Le-Verur Nusha'otehah shel Yerushalmi Masekhet Sheqalim." In *Researches in Talmudic Literature: A Study Conference in Honour of the Eightieth Birthday of Sha'ul Lieberman*, 12–76. Jerusalem: Israel Academy of Sciences and Humanities, 1983.

Sussmann, J. *Talmud Yerushalmi According to Ms. Or. 4720 (Scal. 3) of the Leiden University Library With Restorations and Corrections*. Jerusalem: Academy of the Hebrew Language, 2005.

Sussmann, J. "'Torah She-be'al Peh' Peshutah Ke-mashma'ah—Koho shel Qutzo shel Yod.'" *Mehqerei Talmud* 3, no. 1 (2005): 209–384.

Sussmann, J. "Ve-shuv Li-yrushalmi Neziqin." *Mehkerei Talmud* 1 (1990): 55–133.

Swain, S. *Hellenism and Empire: Language, Classicism, and Power in the Greek World, AD 50–250*. Oxford: Clarendon, 1996.

Swartz, M. *Scholastic Magic: Ritual and Revelation in Early Jewish Mysticism*. Princeton, NJ: Princeton University Press, 1996.

Tcherikover, V. "Was Jerusalem a 'Polis'?" *IEJ* 14 (1964): 61–78.

Thackeray, H. St. J. *Josephus the Man and the Historian*. New York: JIR Press, 1929.

Thucydides. *De Bello Peloponnesiaco, iterum recognovit et praefatus est Godofredus Boehme*, 2 vols. Leipzig: Teubner, 1890.

Tropper, A. "Roman Contexts in Jewish Texts: On *Diatagma* and *Prostagma* in Rabbinic Literature." *JQR* 95 (2005): 207–27.

van der Horst, P. "Greek in Jewish Palestine in Light of Epigraphy." In *Hellenism in the Land of Israel*, edited by J. Collins and G. Sterling, 154–74. Notre Dame, IN: University of Notre Dame Press, 2001.

van Wees, H. "The Law of Gratitude: Reciprocity in Anthropological Theory." In *Reciprocity in Ancient Greece*, edited by C. Gill, N. Postlethwaite, and R. Seaford, 13–49. Oxford: Oxford University Press, 1998.

Veyne, P. *Bread and Circuses: Historical Sociology and Political Pluralism*. London: Penguin, 1990.

Veyne, P. *Le pain et le cirque: Sociologie historique d'un pluralisme politique*. Paris: Editions du Seuil, 1995. First edition 1976.

von Reden, S. *Exchange in Ancient Greece*. London: Duckworth, 1995.

Vriezen, T. C., and A. S. van der Woude. *Ancient Israelite and Early Jewish Literature*. Leiden: Brill, 2005.

Wallace-Hadrill, A., ed. *Patronage in Ancient Society*. London: Routledge, 1989.

Weber, M. *Economy and Society: An Outline of Interpretive Sociology*, edited by G. Roth and C. Wittich. Berkeley and Los Angeles: University of California Press, 1978.

Weinfeld, M. *Deuteronomy and the Deuteronomic School*. Oxford: Clarendon Press, 1972.

Weitzman, S. *Surviving Sacrilege: Cultural Persistence in Jewish Antiquity*. Cambridge: Harvard University Press, 2005.

Westbrook, R. "Patronage in the Ancient Near East." *JESHO* 48 (2005): 210–33.

Whybray, N. *The Book of Proverbs: A Survey of Modern Study*. Leiden: Brill, 1995.

Woolf, G. "Becoming Roman, Staying Greek: Culture, Identity and the Civilizing Process in the Roman East." *PCPS* 40 (1994): 116–43.

Woolf, G. *Becoming Roman: The Origins of Provincial Civilization in Gaul*. Cambridge: Cambridge University Press, 1998.

Woolf, G. "Monumental Writing and the Expansion of Roman Society in the Early Empire." *JRS* 86 (1996): 22–39.

Woolf, G. "A Sea of Faith?" *Mediterranean Historical Review* 18 (2003): 126–43.

Wright, B. *No Small Difference: Sirach's Relation to Its Hebrew Parent Text*. Atlanta, GA: Scholars Press, 1989.

Wright, B. G., III. " 'Fear the Lord and Honor the Priest': Ben Sira as Defender of the Jerusalem Priesthood." In *The Book of Ben Sira in Modern Research: Proceedings of the First International Ben Sira Conference, 28–31 July 1996, Soesterberg, Netherlands,* edited by P. C. Beentjes, 189–222. BZAW 255. Berlin: de Gruyter, 1997.

Wright, B. G., III. and Camp, C. "Ben Sira's Discourse of Riches and Poverty." *Henoch* 23 (2001): 153–74.

Yadin, Y., Lewis, N., Greenfield, J. et al., eds. *The Documents from the Bar Kokhba Period in the Cave of Letters*, 2 vols. Jerusalem: Israel Exploration Society, 1989–2002.

Yaron, R. *Gifts in Contemplation of Death in Jewish and Roman Law*. Oxford: Clarendon Press, 1960.

Ziegler, J. *Sapientia Iesu Filii Sirach*. Göttingen: Vandenhoeck-Ruprecht, 1965.

INDEX

Lightning Source UK Ltd.
Milton Keynes UK
UKHW022002200122
397475UK00005B/186